Hemispheric Blackface

Dissident Acts

A series edited by Macarena Gómez-Barris and Diana Taylor

DANIELLE ROPER

Hemispheric Blackface

Impersonation and Nationalist

Fictions in the Americas

DUKE UNIVERSITY PRESS   DURHAM AND LONDON   2025

Project Editor: Lisa Lawley
Designed by Matthew Tauch
Typeset in Garamond Premier Pro and ITC
Avant Garde Std by Copperline Book Services

Library of Congress Cataloging-in-Publication Data
Names: Roper, Danielle, [date] author.
Title: Hemispheric blackface : impersonation and nationalist fictions
in the Americas / Danielle Roper.
Other titles: Dissident acts.
Description: Durham : Duke University Press, 2025. | Series: Dissident
acts | Includes bibliographical references and index.
Identifiers: LCCN 2024038042 | (print) LCCN 2024038043 (ebook) |
ISBN 9781478031888 (paperback) | ISBN 9781478028642 (hardcover) |
ISBN 9781478060871 (ebook)
Subjects: LCSH: Blackface—History. | Blackface minstrel shows—History. |
Performing arts—Social aspects—America—History. | Race in the theater—
History. | Racism against Black people—America—History. | Post-racialism—
America. | Multiculturalism—Latin America.
Classification: LCC PN2071.B58 R67 2025 (print) |
LCC PN2071.B58 (ebook) | DDC 306.4/8480899607—dc23/eng/20250131
LC record available at https://lccn.loc.gov/2024038042
LC ebook record available at https://lccn.loc.gov/2024038043

Cover art: Leasho Johnson, *Banjee* #2, 2020. Charcoal,
watercolor, acrylic, oil, and gesso on paper mounted on canvas,
25½ × 33½ × 2 in. Courtesy of the artist.

For my family

This book is the result of the incredible mentorship and support that I have received from family, friends, colleagues, and acquaintances. I thank my parents Garnett Roper and Georgia Tulloch Roper for teaching me to think, to be driven, kind, thoughtful, truthful, disciplined, and to be committed to political struggle. I love you, Mommy and Daddy. Thank you, Daddy, for being my first interlocutor, for teaching me to think, and for inspiring me. I miss our intellectual conversations every day. Thank you, Mommy, for being my rock, for teaching me Spanish, and for all those childhood trips to parts of Latin America. *Cho, look ow mi naym gawn abroad!* You two are who I aspire to be. To my siblings, Shani and Steven: thanks for your constant support. Thank you to Stephanie McIntyre Groves for being that sistrin I always need.

I am grateful to all my mentors and friends from Hamilton College. Meeting my close mentor and very dear friend, Susan Sánchez-Casal, as an undergraduate student completely changed the course of my life. Susie, I can never thank you enough for everything. I also remember fondly my time on the hill where I met people who have since become lifelong friends: Wangechi Thuo, Keya Advani, Shraddha Shah, Latoya Malcolm, and Michelle LeMasurier. My conversations with the women of ICWES as well as the folks from the West Indian African Association, the Womyn's Center, and in the classes I took with Professors Shelley Haley, Chandra Mohanty, and Gita Rajan have left an indelible mark on my thinking. I remain indebted to the Thomas J. Watson Foundation for granting me the incredible opportunity to explore my interests in humor and politics in Latin America. The lessons I learned during my Watson year became the early seeds of this book.

I feel lucky to have pursued graduate study in the Departments of Performance Studies and Spanish and Portuguese at New York University where I learned from Diana Taylor, Jill Lane, Ana Dopico, José Muñoz, Gabriel Giorgi, Deb Willis, Mary Louise Pratt, and so many other exceptional scholars. I am especially grateful to Diana, who encouraged me to apply to Performance Studies and who has remained a mentor and a friend at every step of my professional career. I am also honored to have learned so much from Jill, whose thinking continues to shape my own and whose work is foundational for me. Thank you, Jill, Diana, and Ana, for every phone call, letter of recommendation, and word of advice. I would also like to thank the people who walked beside me during grad school: Cristel Jusino Díaz, Kaitlin Murphy, Leticia Robles, Eman Morsi, and so many others. I am grateful to all the folks at the Hemispheric Institute, especially Marcial Godoy and Lisandra Ramos for their friendship and for granting me the space to think about performance and politics. I appreciate Maya Berry, Brittany Meché, and Yanilda González for reading early drafts of so much of my work and for being such fabulous friends. A very special thank you to Matthew Chin, Neish McLean, Nadia Ellis, Shanya Cordis, Traci Wint Hayles, Nadia Chana, Naima Fine Isles, Nnenna Okeke, Gervais Marsh, Thandika Brown, and everyone else whose friendship, feedback, or support kept me going.

My time at the University of Chicago has been truly incredible. I am privileged to have such wonderful colleagues in the Department of Romance Languages and Literatures, the Working Group on Slavery and Visual Culture, the Committee on Theatre and Performance, the Center for the Study of Gender and Sexuality, the Department of Race, Diaspora, and Indigeneity, and the Center for the Study of Race, Politics, and Culture. I am grateful to all of you. My deepest appreciation to Agnes Lugo Ortiz for being such an amazing guide and friend. Thank you for (re)reading a draft of everything in this book, for pushing me, for asking such hard questions, for advocating for me, and for celebrating with me. *La verdad que te agradezco mucho, Agnes*. I am especially grateful to Mario Santana, Victoria Saramago, Larissa Brewer García, Miguel Martínez, David Levin, and Chris Taylor, who each read different versions of this book's manuscript over the years. To Daisy Delogu, I appreciate your having made the time to meet with me and to offer feedback on every paragraph of an earlier draft of the book's introduction. Thank you to Ally Fields, Larry Norman, and Bob Kendrick for all your help and feedback over the years. The experience of having to answer hard questions and critiques about my work throughout my time at this university has made me a better scholar.

This book would not have been possible without the support of the Neubauer Family Assistant Professorship. Many thanks to Cathy Cohen, Waldo Johnson, and Melissa Gilliam for all your support. Words cannot express the depth of my gratitude to Anitra Grisales, my developmental editor, who helped me figure out how to write this book. I would like to also acknowledge the hard work of all the research and editorial assistants whose support was essential to the completion of this manuscript: Khalila Chaar-Pérez, Evelyn Pappas, Eduardo Leão, Eva Pensis, Pedro Doreste, and Ricardo Soler Rubio. A very special thank you to Allie Scholten and the team at the Visual Resource Center at the University of Chicago for all their assistance with the images in this book. My deepest appreciation to Albert Laguna, Daphne Brooks, and Donette Francis for giving me such helpful and honest feedback in the manuscript workshop and beyond. I am indebted to Ken Wissoker, Kate Mullen, Lisa Lawley, and the team at Duke University Press.

I am blessed to have such wonderful friends here in Chicago. I am profoundly grateful to my inner circle: Jessica Swanston Baker, Eve Ewing, Adom Getachew, Ryan Jobson, and Kaneesha Parsard: you all inspire me! It is not an exaggeration to say that Jessica was either beside me or across from me as I wrote almost every word of this book. What a privilege to have you by my side, Jess. I am grateful to the amazing people on campus who make my time here so enjoyable: Thuto Thipe, Patricia Posey, Adrienne Brown, Kamala Russell, Samuel Fury Childs Daly, and so many others.

To Lemis, you remain the person whose company I enjoy the most in this world. Thank you.

Scenes of Racial Enjoyment
in the Hemispheric Fold

In 2018, Teatro Trail (Trail Theater) in South Florida released a promotional video of the Spanish-language comedy *Tres viudas en un crucero* (Three Widows on a Cruise), about three older women in Hialeah who plan to go on a cruise and then recount their stories upon their return. One of the white Cuban actresses, Martha Velasco, appears in blackface. People were outraged. In their coverage of the controversy, *NBCMiami* news and *Miami Herald* showed the same video clip. Velasco is in a living room talking to an older white woman dressed in an elegant black outfit and red floral vest and a younger white woman wearing jean overalls and a cowboy hat. They all stand beside one another on stage and face the audience, sitting in darkness below. Velasco's face is painted black, her eyebrows are thick and dark, her lips are bright red, and her large Afro wig is shaggy and unkempt. She wears a bluish jacket, bright red pants, and a white shirt and holds a folding fan in her hand. As she speaks to the women beside her, she bends her knees, almost crouching in an open stance. She turns to the audience with her eyes wide open. The video's audio only captures her saying one line: "¡Bailar, tomar, y gozar como TRES GORILAS!" (Dance, drink, and have fun like three gorillas!). Velasco punctuates each word with an exaggerated movement: she claps the fan onto her left palm, shimmies, pounds her chest, and then throws her hands in the air. The two white women laugh. The one wearing the cowboy hat also pounds her chest and softly grunts "hoo hoo!" like a gorilla. Some audience members laugh.

The backlash was swift. Afro-Latino activist groups in Miami lobbied for the removal of the blackface character. Initially, the directors and many sympathizers defended the portrayal, insisting that there is no racism in Cuba and that blackface is part of Cuba's *teatro bufo* tradition—a national theater genre for which blackface was a central feature.[1] Like many black people in Miami critiquing the play's use of blackface, Brenda Medina, an Afro-Dominican journalist for *El Nuevo Herald* who first reported on the story, was accused of being ignorant of the specificities of Cuba's cultural tradition and of projecting her own racial trauma onto a celebrated national practice. However, one Afro-Cuban, Nérida Rodríguez, a sixty-six-year-old who grew up in Cuba, insisted, "It's not that we are offended now, we were always offended. White Cubans, they tell you there was no racism in Cuba. There was and there is racism in Cuba."[2] This controversy in Miami points to the imbrication of racial impersonation and nationalist fictions in the hemispheric Americas.

Until recently, discourses of racelessness, creole nationalism, and *mestizaje* were central to state constructions of national identities in Latin America and the Caribbean.[3] These fictions are grounded in the notion that racial mixture in the populace insulated the nation from racial discord, and they were wielded to homogenize the population under a shared national identity. Yet, as Rodríguez points out and scholars show, national myths of racial democracy produced structures of denialism that sidestepped or obscured systems of racial exclusion.[4] In recent years, many states have moved away from colorblindness toward multiculturalism and Black activists have made strides toward racial equality. But controversies about the use of racial impersonation, as in *Tres viudas*, reveal both the endurance of nationalist fictions of racial democracy on the ground and the way blackness continues to operate on the margins of the category of the human, even in cultural spaces where the "race problem" has historically been conceptualized as foreign to the national polity.

Hemispheric Blackface insists upon the ongoing power of these nationalist fictions through an examination of blackface performance. Across the four chapters of this book, I show how acts of racial conjuring reinscribe, resist, and reconfigure the racial scripts of these fictions in an era defined by the presumed end of myths of racial democracy. The meaning of an individual blackface performance is always contingent. But I open with Velasco's performance in *Tres viudas* because it was a scene of racial enjoyment—a ludic imaginary in which racial fantasies are staged for public or personal viewing and which activate the conscious or unconscious assumptions and beliefs we hold about racial others. I examine the workings of blackface in scenes of racial enjoyment to show how people fix or deconstruct familiar racial scripts in moments of political change. Because I neither see forms of racial conjuring as good or bad, liberatory or oppressive, nor as an inherent expression of antiblackness, each chapter conceptualizes different domains of racial enjoyment: subjection, resistance, ambiguity, and abject pleasures. Together, I demonstrate that acts of racial conjuring serve as a recourse that allow people to levy and rework these scripts as the nationalist fictions persist and evolve.

Velasco's conjuring of blackness through simian tropes and her activation of scripts of black musicality show the role of impersonation in illuminating the ongoing racial constraints placed on black personhood and citizenship in a moment of new political articulations in the Americas. The blackface performances I analyze take place from 2001 to 2019 — after the world conference against racism in Durban, South Africa, and before the COVID-19 pandemic and the George Floyd protests — two decades characterized by political gains and reversals for black people in the Americas. After decades of organizing by Black activists, the early 2000s saw major advancements in race relations across the region, including state recognition of the rights of racial minorities, formal documentation of black populations in these countries, the election of Barack Obama to the presidency of the United States in 2008, and the emergence of Black Lives Matter and the Pink Tide in Latin America.[5] Racial impersonation allows people to make sense of the changes around them, to set new terms of belonging and citizenship, to redefine relations of power, and to activate the very racial scripts new state policies purportedly left behind.

Because nationally bounded scholarship dominates the field of blackface studies, this book insists upon thinking with and across national silos to attend to multivalent meanings of blackface performance. This controversy surrounding Velasco's blackface act, for example, reveals the limitations of the nation and its geohistorical specificities for reckoning with the meaning of racial impersonation. By this, I do not mean that the local context is unimportant. But, as Rodríguez's comment suggests, appeals to the sanctity of an autochthonous cultural tradition presume a national consensus that may not actually exist, or that the cultural specificities themselves are free of antiblackness. Furthermore, because it took place in Miami — the crossroads of the two Americas — this blackface performance exemplifies the encounter of multiple traditions of racial impersonation, different histories, and structures of racial formation. It occurred in a transitional moment of processes of racial formation when the postracial discourse surrounding Barack Obama's presidency had receded and the white revanchist fantasy of Donald Trump's reign in the United States had taken hold. Blackface on stage resonated with the racist ethos of the times and multiple histories of impersonation, even if the performers themselves sought to limit its meaning to Cuba's racial politics. Still, the history of US blackface minstrelsy in Miami, by itself, cannot fully account for the layers of meaning in Velasco's blackface act and its entanglement with nationalist fictions of racial democracy. Centering US blackface minstrelsy would simply reproduce rhetorical appeals to the nation. Thrust before a hemispheric audience composed primarily of immigrants from Latin America and the Caribbean, the figuration of blackness on stage multiplied in meaning, surpassing cultural and national differences.

Miami is an exemplar of what I call the *hemispheric fold*—an intercultural space where repeating nationalist fictions of racial democracy, geographies of antiblackness, and practices of racial conjuring collide and coincide with one another. Bounded by the hemispheric Americas— North, Central, and South, the West Indies, the Pacific, and the Andes— the hemispheric fold is forged by a set of geopolitical relationships: US empire and its histories of interventionism in the region, anti-imperialist struggle, south-south connections, the multidirectional migration of peoples, and the circulation and exchange of their practices. The fold is spawned by a set of foundational events: chattel slavery, indigenous genocide, and indentureship that, I insist, produced a set of nationalist fictions whose afterlives reverberate today. I privilege the term *hemispheric* over *transnational* to invoke the fraught histories and political tensions between the two Americas. Jill Lane rightly argues that the fold "encompasses colonial and postcolonial blackface practices."[6] The multiple registers of signification in Velasco's performance in Miami underscore the necessity of thinking with the particularities of the nation and the fact that histories and practices are shared. The hemispheric fold thus brings into view the capaciousness of the blackface sign and enables me to reorient blackface performance away from a singular performance or national tradition toward shared histories of slavery and their legacies of racial silence. Through the hemispheric fold, I imagine the Americas as linked by geographies of racial silence, and I theorize versions of postracialism and blackface performance as defining legacies of slavery in the Americas.

I argue that it is in acts of racial conjuring that slavery's logics of racial mastery, ownership, domination, and rebellion reassert themselves. While scholars in black studies have focused on how legacies of slavery are enacted through the precarity of black life, I attempt to glean how such legacies reverberate through acts of racial play. Since the ludic remains one of the few arenas in which publics can openly enact the fantasy of racial possession, I seek to map the domains of racial enjoyment where slavery's logics are articulated as nationalist fictions persist and evolve. Grounded in a hemispheric frame, this book is conceptually organized to attend to the different domains of racial enjoyment and to the tensions between nationalist fictions and the everyday actions on the ground. I traverse multiple scenes of racial enjoyment by studying blackface performances at a carnival in Peru, on a Spanish-language television show in Miami, in a visual art exhibit by a black artist in Colombia, and in popular theater in Jamaica. The heterogeneity of these scenes enables me to trace how slavery's logics are imprinted across cultural practice: in "high" and "low" art, the quotidian and the spectacular, the formal and informal, the embodied and the discursive, and the private and the public. The objects of each chapter show how slavery's logics permeate the material, the performative, the theatrical, and the visual. Analyzed together, they illustrate that slavery's logics are not limited to a singular ludic domain; rather, they remain an ever-present feature of all forms of racial enjoyment today.

Racial enjoyment refers to an affective range of gratification—pleasure, wonder, fascination, desire, endearment, nostalgia, and even admiration—that acts of racial conjuring produce for performers and spectators alike. As used in this book, racial enjoyment is a terrain of struggle and negotiation. Charting its different domains illuminates how black, indigenous, mestizo, and white people alike summon slavery's logics to mediate the persistence and the evolution of these nationalist fictions in the Americas. The heterogeneity of the objects and the multivalent nature of these scenes of racial enjoyment also invite critical engagement with what blackface looks like today.

Blackface: A Set of Multivalent Practices

Blackface is a spectrum of aesthetic practices that involve different prosthetic techniques of racial caricature. It is a mode of stylizing the body that entails "blacking up"—the literal painting of the body and face to imitate black skin—and the exaggeration of lips, hair, and phenotypical features associated with people of African descent. Blackface characters are usually marked by the deformation of black vernacular or the incorporation of malapropisms. People typically associate blackface with the US blackface minstrel theater tradition, which in its infancy in the 1830s and 1840s involved white male actors who painted their faces black, gave stump speeches, and imitated the singing and dancing of enslaved Africans.[7] But scholars have shown that long before the US blackface minstrel tradition emerged, blacking up and imitating black vernacular forms were already a feature of performance traditions across the globe. Practices of impersonating blackness were widespread across early modern Europe and the Americas.[8] Transnational in nature, blackface mediated colonial relationships between empire and colonies across Anglo-Atlantic and the Iberian worlds as well as genealogies of black performances across the African diaspora.[9] Performance theorist Catherine Cole rightly insists that we view blackface as a colonial sign that, as other scholars show, has never been limited to the Anglo-American world, has long been crucial to the articulation and configuration of power in the formation of Western modernity, and has shaped "how we understand the national in the first place."[10] Despite its hegemonic position in blackface studies, US blackface minstrelsy is only one tradition among a set of global practices.

This book therefore decenters US blackface minstrelsy and thinks across national silos to show that blackface is a set of multivalent and varied practices across all cultural forms that are not confined to a single historical period, tradition, nation, or geographical space.[11] The popularity of *negrito* figures—from teatro bufo and local blackface performance troupes along Río de la Plata in the nineteenth century, blackface characters on television and radio like "Diplo" played by Ramón Rivero in Puerto Rico, and the famous comic book character Memín Pinguín—from the 1940s onward demonstrates that blackface has been crucial to the articulation of national identity, the development of mass media, technological modernization, and representations of race across Latin America and the Caribbean.[12] Each chapter shows the multiplicity of instantiations of blackface, its many valences, and its power in negotiating the myths of racial democracy and their afterlives in the hemispheric fold. I analyze heterogeneous forms of blackface to show their ubiquity across the Americas, and I suggest that their meanings may or may not bear any relation to US blackface minstrelsy. Blackface, I insist, is a vernacular of racial power that demarcates and recodifies hierarchies and categories of racial difference amid the uncertainties and shifts in racial formation in the twenty-first century.

While blackface performance traditions that included stock figures, segregated theater audiences, actors specializing in blackface theatrical forms, and other old-school conventions are mostly gone, blackface has not disappeared. Instead, it merely evolved to keep up with the changing sensibilities of the times. Scholars and writers in popular culture alike have attended to the heterogeneity of the blackface form through the added qualifiers like "discursive blackface," or "digital blackface."[13] New cultural forms enter a preexisting racial matrix that has long codified blackness through the regimes of racial distortion—the exaggeration and deformation of black physiognomy—and racist tropes of buffoonery, hypersexuality, musicality, and servility. To account for its heterogeneity, scholars define blackface as "a racial idiom," "a lingua franca," "a transnational language of race," and "a floating signifier" that has always transcended national borders.[14] This emphasis on blackface as a diffuse practice wielded across disparate cultural forms and geographical spaces, rather than a singular formal performance tradition limited to bodily acts and established theatrical conventions, is crucial for how this book accounts for the capaciousness of the blackface sign and the realities of our contemporary moment. The heterogeneity of the objects in these chapters shows how slavery's logics refashion themselves and adapt to the complexities of today's world and to new cultural forms.

Theorist Jill Lane explains that while impersonation is at the very heart of any theatrical practice, racial impersonation leads artists to draw, traverse, or complicate lines of differential social power that produce such categories as race, gender, and ethnicity in the first place.[15] Racial impersonation, she explains, refers to the figurative crossing of racial terrains or the occupation of racialized roles. It is a form of cross-racial identification, an act of substitution and occupation, where one stands in for or takes figurative possession of the Other.[16] Blackface is one practice that belongs to the broader category of racial impersonation. Although it is the primary feature of the performances I analyze in this book, blackface, in my view, must be combined with racial distortion or the invocation of racial stereotypes to be considered blackface. It is through the trafficking of racial distortion that racial impersonation reinscribes racialized bodies into the realm of the nonnormative, demarcating blackness as the sign of the ridiculous, of the strange, and of the spectacularly different. Blackface is thus a game of artifice whereby blackness is made present as racial distortion. It summons blackness as the marker of a racial excess plastered onto the conjurer's body.

Blackface is rarely contingent on the presence of a direct "original"; it is less concerned with truthfulness than it is with pleasure and political efficaciousness.[17] Because of this, I privilege the term *racial conjuring* to connote the projection of blackness as a figuration that enacts an *idea* of blackness rather than the reflection of any *real* black person. Drawing on Glenda Carpio's usage of "racial conjuring" to refer to the projection and amplification of stereotypes by African American humorists, this book treats racial conjuring as the amplification of a set of racial fantasies of blackness.[18] The images that acts of racial conjuring produce are spectral presences that index the fungibility of blackness. These acts serve as figurative manifestations of a set of racial relationships conditioned by the history of chattel slavery in the Americas. Racial conjuring troubles the notion of the real because the figurations of blackness it produces on stage are ongoing fictions of blackness. These fictions are lodged in racial imaginaries plagued by the legacies of racial violence and dispossession. The term *racial conjuring* more accurately captures the multifaceted nature of blackface as an aesthetic practice whose logics of symbolic possession have never been limited to embodied practice and that has extended to material, digital, literary, and other cultural realms.

The blackface performances I analyze in Peru and Miami, for example, both emerge from popular and formal traditions of racial impersonation, the Bolivian Tundique dance and Cuba's teatro bufo traditions. These renditions of blackness bear the formal cosmetic techniques of their traditions: blackened skin, exaggerated lips, Afro wigs, and other markers of racial caricature that distort black physiognomy or black vernacular. I also consider how racial conjuring by black artists signify on practices of racial distortion by reworking the colors and tones of black skin. In my analysis of impersonations of black womanhood by artist Liliana Angulo's work in Colombia and then performer Andrea Wright's work in Jamaica, I pay close attention to how these artists blacken their faces to varying levels of (il)legibility by playing with the thickness of the layers of black paint. This play with different gradations of skin tone renders blackface an ambivalent reworking of bodily surface, the transformation of black skin into shine and gloss.[19] The range of skin-darkening combined with other markers of racial caricature across these performances demonstrate the multifaceted nature of blackface as a practice, its dynamism, ambiguities, and ongoing evolutions in contemporary acts of racial conjuring.

The vocabulary of racial distortion transcends renditions of blackness staged by and on the body to other cultural forms. In my analysis of Angulo's imitation of kitchen kitsch made in the likeness of black women, I explicate how the vocabulary of racial distortion extends to material culture: souvenirs, memorabilia, disposable candy wrappers, and cartoons. These are mass-produced, cheap objects that articulate, transmit, and circulate racial fantasies and meanings. Racial impersonation—and in this context I mean either the act of painting or fashioning an object into the likeness of blackness or plastering a caricature of blackness onto an object— enlivens material objects, transforming them into effigies of our racial attachments, memories, desires, and dreams. This transformation, in turn, animates a whole dynamic of racial power when we interact with them. I therefore use the heterogeneity of mediums in this book—including television, theater, popular dance at a carnival, and multimedia installation at a museum—to track the pervasiveness of the blackface form and its transmogrification across different domains of racial enjoyment. Together these mediums mark diverse temporal registers and modes of diffusion and enable different forms of identification in the hemispheric fold. They have varying implications for how blackface and the relations of racial power it articulates live in the present, past, and future.

Acts of racial conjuring not only map out dynamics of racial power but also demarcate blackness as a racial category in spaces of racial fluidity. Critical engagement with renditions of blackness in parts of Latin America and the Caribbean is particularly challenging because racial categories in individual societies are often nebulous. Only people with distinctly African features and dark skin are typically referred to as "negro." But while a person may not be phenotypically black, they may very well still identify as black. In my discussion of blackness and blackface, I both acknowledge the ocular registers of race while accepting that ocular registers are not the only ways race or blackness are defined in each context. Regimes of racial signification have marked specific features and speech as indexing blackness, even in sites where there are no stable categories of racial affiliation. While sociological and anthropological approaches survey what the individual actors believe or understand their impersonations of blackness to mean and what blackness is, performance and visual studies attend to the relations of power that are embedded in the production of racial signs and signifiers of blackness. I therefore ground definitions of blackface in these fields because they treat embodied forms and visual culture as epistemes that serve both as objects of analysis and as constitutive sites of knowledge production.[20] Their methodological approaches enable me to emphasize how gestures, actions, speech, and other tools of racial conjuring bring blackness into being and to ascertain *how* and *under what constraints* blackness comes to be produced in visual culture and in embodied practice. I therefore consider how bodily enactments and visual artifacts propose what blackness is and how such proposals, in turn, constitute and sustain racial ideology within an imaginary where racial categories are fluid and nebulous.

Because for some, the word *blackface* imposes an imperial gaze upon a local practice, where appropriate, I acknowledge the rejection of the term by the individual artist or performer.[21] Although it is a space of tension, I deploy the term because scholarly understandings of blackface as a colonial sign have rendered it capacious enough to include aesthetic forms outside the US blackface minstrel tradition.[22] In the contemporary moment, blackface acts are promiscuous in their engagement with historical conventions. Sometimes, unbeknownst to the performer, a single blackface performance may riff on a heterogeneity of historical traditions and tropes of blackness that are not limited to a singular geographical space. Since historically the movement of blackface tropes in the hemispheric Americas has always been multidirectional, I presume the reality of fusion and contact as a precondition of blackface forms in the hemispheric fold.[23] Velasco's blackface act in *Tres viudas* in Miami is a testament to the ways an individual performance may signify on multiple traditions and be totally legible to different audiences. While there is a need for historicist research that tracks the genealogies and circulation of blackface tropes in Latin America and the Caribbean, such questions are not my primary concern. Instead, this book seeks to critically engage the function of acts of racial conjuring in geographies of racial silence and the structures of antiblackness lurking beneath nationalist fictions in the Americas.

Repeating Nationalist Fictions: Myths of Racial Democracy in the Hemispheric Fold

Hemispheric blackface is a conceptual frame that I use to name a complex geographical space constituted by competing sites of racial formation, repeating nationalist fictions of racial democracy and their afterlives, and the practices of racial conjuring that mediate, trouble, or reinforce them. In the hemispheric fold, the racial taxonomy of the colonial order—the *casta* system of the plantation economy—collided with and rearticulated itself across multiple racial geographies that transcended the linguistic, historical, and geographical differences of the hemispheric Americas.[24] The casta system, plantation economies, and indentureship produced a set of "racializing assemblages" wherein race functions "as a set of sociopolitical processes that discipline humanity into full humans, not-quite-humans, and non-humans."[25] These systems relegated blackness to the margins of the category of the human and the citizen. But during independence, the leaders of the new nations in Latin America and the Caribbean sought to distance themselves from the colonial order and its systems of racial stratification. They created a set of repeating nationalist fictions that were each grounded in the notion that racial miscegenation in a population insulates a nation from racial discord.[26] Despite the linguistic and cultural differences and geographic distances between the Atlantic/Pacific or Andes/ Caribbean in each of the countries I examine in this book, these celebrations of racial mixture were deployed to sidestep the problem of racial difference and to homogenize the population under the auspices of a national identity. Articulated through local vocabularies of mestizaje, creole nationalism, and *mestiçagem*, these myths of racial democracy were a hemispheric phenomenon, foundational precepts of nationalist discourses in the region, and, despite the regional turns from colorblindness to multiculturalism, have continued to plague black people today.

In the nineteenth century, when Latin American nations gained independence, elites sought to unify societies that had previously been defined by systems of racial stratification under colonial rule.[27] Rather than adhere to colonialist paradigms and prevailing discourses of scientific racism that deemed racial miscegenation a sign of inferiority, elites across the region romanticized racial mixture and emphasized cultural homogeneity.[28] Even though scholars have long demonstrated how these celebrations of racial mixture cloaked the reality of material structures of racial exclusion in the region, according to the logic of *mestizaje*—which may be translated as miscegenation or racial mixing—racial mixture supposedly insulated the nation from racial discord.[29] As leaders of the burgeoning new nations, American-born Europeans or *criollos* who Ángel Rama calls *letrados* (lettered people) wielded nationalist discourses of mestizaje to position themselves as rightful heirs to European colonizers and continued to expropriate land and labor from black and indigenous populations.[30] Nevertheless, rosy versions of racial democracy were touted as a stark contrast to the racial divisions of the United States.

In his 1891 essay "Our America," the influential Cuban thinker José Martí issued a pan-Americanist call to reject the colonial and neocolonial impositions of Europe and the United States in favor of unifying "our America." He envisioned what he called *nuestra América mestiza* (our mixed-race America) as one that embraced its racial and cultural differences and overcame the problem of race. The quintessential emblem of Martí's America is a false originary figure he calls *el mestizo autóctono* (the native half-breed or the indigenous mestizo)—a mixed-race offspring of the colonial contact between European conquerors and indigenous women who emerges as the protagonist of Cuba's new nation as well as that of other budding Hispanic American nations.[31] While the mestizo autóctono may celebrate racial hybridity, he was also wielded to disavow and transcend the problem of race itself. In the essay's concluding remarks, Martí declares "no hay odio de razas porque no hay razas" (there is no racial hate because there are no races).[32] In his estimation, the mestizo was both a marker of a celebrated multiculturalism and a postracial future to be ushered in by the new nation. He was a fictional device wielded to overcome the racial divisions of the colonial era and to discursively erase the problem of race itself. Little wonder, then, that Martí, the father of Cuban independence, would so famously define Cuban national identity as "more than white, more than mulatto, more than black."[33] This dual paradox of racial invocation and racial disavowal, racial celebration and racial erasure, is at the heart of repeating nationalist fictions of mestizaje and racial democracy that have permeated the region.

Martí was not alone in his formulation of a Latin American nationalism that used a mixed-race protagonist to both celebrate racial miscegenation and to disavow race itself. From the 1900s onward, discourses of racial inclusion proliferated across the region. Key thinkers of the Hispanophone and Lusophone worlds like Juan Pablo Sojo from Venezuela, Fernando Ortiz from Cuba, José Vasconcelos from Mexico, Gilberto Freyre of Brazil, and many others offered their own versions of "racial democracy" replete with celebrations of racial miscegenation among the African, white, and indigenous elements of the population. Until quite recently, Latin American discourses of "racial democracy" centered around the notion that colonialism had bequeathed a rather benign form of slavery, racial miscegenation, and fluid racial categorizations.[34] White Brazilian nationalist Freyre, who popularized the term *racial democracy* in his research on race relations in Brazil, claimed that the intimate and affectionate relationships among masters and slaves during slavery served as the basis for Brazil's peaceful race relations.[35] In his estimation, social intimacy meant that every Brazilian was part-African or -mestizo. The fact of this racial mixture was a source of national pride, the foundation of a national racial fraternity, and the antidote to racial discord.[36] Freyre's position has since been heavily critiqued, but at the heart of the myth of racial democracy is the long-standing sanitization of a racial past that effaces the brutal realities of sexual and racial violence of slave societies.

Celebrations of a mixed-race polity and the veneration of the mixed-race subject did not undermine racist ideas about blackness and indigeneity as backward and undesirable; rather, in many countries, it cloaked the veneration of whiteness. Scholars contended that mestizaje required assimilation or the erasure of blackness.[37] Some Colombian thinkers in the early twentieth century, for example, believed that racial mixture would produce a "culturally and biologically homogenous people that were stronger than any of their individual roots."[38] And Mexican thinker José Vasconcelos published *The Cosmic Race* in 1925, advocating for the intermixing of diverse races and ethnic elements to form one "synthetic race," so that " blacks could be redeemed, . . . inferior races . . . would become less prolific, and better specimens would go on ascending a scale of ethnic improvement."[39] The repeating nationalist fictions not only created national stories that celebrated a mixed-race or brown protagonist, but paradoxically, also produced a set of racial scripts as instruments of differentiation that maintained racial hierarchies. While these racial scripts are articulated in culture, they are also present in state policies. Nationalist celebrations of racial democracy coexisted with varying structures of antiblackness and racial inequality. Across the region, practices of *blanqueamiento* (whitening) of the population through immigration policies geared toward Europeans, eugenics, the erasure of the black population in racial censuses, and continued discrimination in the workplace and other cultural spheres all persisted.[40] Racism also operated through customary law wherein housing officials or state employees often enacted racist social norms in their deployment of state resources, and the enactment of these social norms ultimately had the force of (unwritten) law.[41] Others have noted the centrality of antiblackness in families and bodily capital that affords more value to whiteness than blackness. But the fact that people of African descent often occupied the lowest rungs of societies in the region was seen as a sign of class and economic inequality, not racial discrimination.[42]

These celebrations of racial miscegenation are not unique to Latin America, and they certainly did not go unnoticed by West Indian thinkers seeking independence from Britain in the twentieth century. Like mestizaje in Latin America, creole nationalism in the Anglophone Caribbean was initially an anticolonial project developed by (West Indian) thinkers seeking to throw off colonial rule and unify a racially stratified society. Creole nationalism is a "Caribbean form of European liberal nationalism" that sought to account for "both the European origin of dominant institutions and the African origin of the dominated mass."[43] Trinidadian thinker Eric Williams and Jamaican prime minister Norman Manley were key leaders who sought to imagine a West Indian identity that superseded the racial divisions of the colonial era. In a speech given on August 16, 1955, at the "University of Woodford Square," Williams declared, "Man in the West Indies is more than white, more than mulatto, more than Negro, more than Indian, more than Chinese. He is West Indian."[44] Williams took cues from Cuban nationalists when he further proclaimed, "Our democratic development, like Maceo's revolution in Cuba, has no color. It has no little Negroes, no little whites, no little Indians, no little Chinese; it has only West Indians."[45] In Williams's estimation, a national or regional identity would supersede racial difference. Jamaican prime minister Norman Manley similarly proclaimed, "We are neither Africans though most of us are black, nor are we Anglo-Saxon though some of us would have others believe this. We are Jamaicans! . . . We are a mixture of races living in perfect harmony and as such provide a useful lesson to a world torn apart by race prejudice."[46] Both Manley and Williams believed that newly independent Caribbean nations would serve as beacons of racial harmony and as counterpoints to countries such as South Africa and the United States, which were plagued by racial divisions.

Creole nationalism spawned a set of national slogans across the region that imagined a multiracial and multicultural society. Jamaica's discourse of creole nationalism was consolidated between the 1940s and cemented after independence in 1962 through its national motto, "Out of Many, One People."[47] Although over 90 percent of the Jamaican population is black, the motto suggests a multicultural, multiracial society. Critics have noted that the national motto was in fact designed to stymie the black nationalist mobilizations of the time and to reorder a racial hierarchy of the new nation to ultimately privilege Jamaica's brown class.[48] The motto occludes the fact that the national elite idealizes European culture and "puts everything . . . of African origin in a lesser place."[49] Trinidad and Tobago's motto, "Every creed and race find an equal place," also articulated a version of creole nationalism that "celebrated mixture along an African-European Christian axis but subordinated overtly African or non-Christian practices."[50] Scholars argue that though this version of creole nationalism rejected colonialism, it simultaneously celebrated proximity to whiteness and left the structural position of blackness unchanged.[51] Similarly, in Guyana, creoleness historically functioned as a disciplinary technology that legitimated the colonial project, privileged the local "near white" population, and maintained a color-class continuum that ensured the subjugation of the colonized population.[52] Guyanese independence occasioned the birth of the motto "One people, one nation, one destiny," an aspirational maxim that discursively imagined a unified nation free of racial discord. But the racial divisions of the colonial era and party politics after independence fomented racial antagonism between African and Indian populations and consolidated the dispossession of Guyana's indigenous population.[53] I place creole nationalism alongside mestizaje to emphasize the varying modalities of the repeating nationalist fictions in the hemispheric Americas.

Miami shows the reach and life of the repeating nationalist fictions in the United States. The city also functions as a point of hemispheric convergence, a crucial site of encounter for these disparate racial geographies that shaped structures of antiblackness in the hemispheric fold. The interconnected history of hemispheric migration and culture has rendered Miami the site of distinct modalities of the repeating nationalist fictions and an exception to US racial politics centered around Anglo-Saxon whiteness. As I explain in chapter 2, after multiple waves of migration and an immigration policy that granted Cubans a fast path to citizenship and government assistance for resettlement in the twentieth century, the Cuban ethnic enclave emerged as one of the strongest and most politically significant groups in South Florida. Theorists have critically engaged the racial hierarchies within the Cuban ethnic enclave by highlighting the ways race organized migration and resettlement patterns and, ultimately, produced Miami as the capital of Cuban whiteness.[54] When they first arrived, the Cuban exile generation, composed of the island's white ruling class fleeing Fidel Castro's 1959 revolution, reproduced Cuba's preexisting racial order in Miami. They clung to the notion of a racially democratic or race-neutral society while enacting antiblackness against their Afro-Cuban counterparts.[55] For the Cuban diaspora, clinging to the nationalist ideal of race neutrality has served to hide the complicity of white Cubans and US Latinos in producing antiblackness against African American and Afro-Latino communities living in the city.[56] This nationalist ideal of racelessness is precisely the discourse that Rodríguez referenced in her critique of racial impersonation in *Tres viudas*.

Whether through mestizaje or creole nationalism, nationalist fictions and their celebrations of racial harmony that historically sidestepped or silenced the problem of race are a shared hemispheric phenomenon. Since many of these nations have moved away from nationalist discourses of colorblindness to multiculturalism, I treat these myths of racial democracy as a historical foundation upon which I theorize blackness in the hemispheric fold. In thinking across disciplinary silos and conventional geographic paradigms that have traditionally cordoned off discussions of race in the West Indies from Latin America, I am better able to ascertain how shared and divergent histories of slavery and colonialism not only created structures of antiblackness but also occasioned formal structures of national disavowal that, by design, denied their very existence. Black people in the hemispheric fold must not only navigate structures of antiblackness in the afterlives of slavery but also the afterlives of structures of racial silence.

I trace antiblackness as articulated in a racial landscape where national identity centers around indigeneity (Peru and Bolivia), or in relationship to creole whiteness (Miami), brownness (Jamaica), or mestizoness and whiteness (Colombia).[57] In juxtaposing disparate sites, I identify different modalities of these repeating nationalist fictions and assess the implication of their evolution for constructs of blackness today.[58] Myths of racial democracy are constructed through multiple stories, different histories, and are articulated in different ways in the hemispheric fold. The repetitions of these nationalist fictions are imperfect, partially (un)faithful to the original. No two repeating nationalist fictions are exactly alike. I critically engage their myriad modes of articulation, their individual nuances, and their ongoing power amid the turn away from colorblindness. Each of these modalities allows me to highlight "relation across differences rather than equivalence," to focus on linked but not identical genealogies that emerge from a shared history of slavery and the foundational fictions that disavowed its legacies.[59] I am also able to distill the various registers of antiblackness that they produce today.

Since these nationalist fictions are grounded in the notion that because everybody is mixed no one can be racist, I define antiblackness in this book not through a black/white binary associated with the United States, but through a skin-color axis that rearticulates itself across different configurations of racial hierarchies. Indeed, social scientists have explained that skin color is in fact a primary stratifying variable across Latin America and the Caribbean that can determine social advantages or the worth assigned to an individual.[60] The reality of racial fluidity and the fact that many people across the region may not clearly identify with a given racial category does not contradict the widespread nature of discrimination; rather, it has often worked to obscure it as an ongoing reality. That an individual who is the victim of discrimination may not self-identify as black, for example, does not change the fact that people whose features are typically identified as indigenous or of African descent often do face discrimination or social disadvantages in surprisingly common and measurable ways. These different constellations of racial hierarchies help us see how antiblackness operates as the foundational axis of racial power, even when a white majority is not necessarily present or when a nation's population (as in Jamaica) is predominantly black. Antiblackness is a registry of skin-color or phenotypical valuation that adheres to white supremacist logics that venerate proximity to whiteness without requiring the presence of actual white people. By attending to the modalities of the repeating nationalist fictions, I can better understand the nuances of how antiblackness works as a persistent structure that adapts to the racial scripts of multiple national stories. I show that slavery's logics of symbolic possession remain an organizing precept of racial power that can be consistently mapped across the diverse racial constellations of the hemispheric fold.

Racial Enjoyment: Troubling and Enforcing
Myths and Scripts

Rodríguez's response to the controversy about blackface in *Tres viudas* not only signaled how slavery's logics remain hidden, but it also emphasized that scenes of racial enjoyment operate within a larger cultural landscape of "racial innocence" that renders quotidian expressions of antiblackness harmless or mere rituals of social camaraderie and deems extreme or explicit acts of violence as the benchmark of racism. Racial innocence is the "cloak that veils" antiblackness, that insists that unique racial mixtures of Latin American and Caribbean populations render them "incapable of racist attitudes," and that wields nationalist appeals to cultural specificities as the antidote to any interrogation of the antiblackness on display.[61] This landscape of racial innocence continues to shape how acts of racial conjuring are generally interpreted or perceived, even as nations across the region have turned toward multiculturalism.

In the 1980s and 1990s, Latin American states moved away from discourses of colorblindness, and instead systematically recognized ethnoracial difference, acknowledged the need to protect racial minorities, and began to conduct racial censuses in their populations. In 1987, Nicaragua became the first country to undertake multicultural reforms as the Sandinista government granted land rights and autonomy to its indigenous populace along the Atlantic coast.[62] Honduras, Ecuador, Colombia, and Bolivia quickly followed suit, and in 2000 Brazil undertook some of the most comprehensive multicultural reforms when it implemented affirmative action policies in its education system and a slew of other legislative reforms.[63] Argentina, Cuba, Panama, and Uruguay explicitly condemned racial discrimination, and activists demanded the inclusion of ethno-racial categories on national censuses in the region to combat the invisibility of black populations. Thus, the early 2000s were a moment of new political articulation that required the evolution and reconfiguration of the repeating nationalist fictions.

It is unsurprising that the multicultural state did not dismantle anti-blackness in the region. Statistical evidence shows widespread rejection of intermarriage with black people, a correlation between social disadvantages and having darker skin tones, discrimination in the workplace, and social prejudices in parental attitudes and standards of beauty.[64] Moreover, scholars insist that the recognition of cultural and racial difference of the multicultural turn was tethered to neoliberal logics that sought to define the ideal new citizen, to "shape the terms of political contestations, to distinguish between acceptable and disruptive cultural demands," and to make "high-stakes distinctions between those cultural rights that deserve recognitions and those that do not."[65] The multicultural turn did not alter the racial scripts of mestizaje as much as they required their evolution, often leading to the creation of *el indio permitido* (the permitted Indian) or *el negro permitido* (the permitted black).[66] Furthermore, they did not necessarily rid nations of myths of racial democracy. Some of the processes even reproduced the silencing of race in new ways. Instead of treating the multicultural reforms as the end of the hemispheric phenomenon of the repeating nationalist fiction, I mark them as one of its afterlives. By tracking the endurance of the very racial scripts of mestizaje, I highlight how nationalist fictions evolved to account for global and local processes that demand the recognition of race but not the actual dismantling of racial inequality.

Because I see the contemporary moment as being defined by both the persistence and evolution of the repeating nationalist fictions in the hemispheric fold, I juxtapose sites where state policies have turned toward multiculturalism with those where nationalist fictions have remained intact. In keeping with the conceptual organization of this book, each chapter examines different evolutions of the fictions to ascertain their ongoing power. To capture the range of the multicultural shift, I dedicate one chapter to Peru, which operated on the margins of the multicultural turn, and another to Colombia, because it was home to some of the most extensive reforms. Both examples illuminate the geographical specificities of the multicultural turn, but they also demonstrate that, as a hemispheric phenomenon, the repeating nationalist fictions cannot be undone by the advancements of a singular nation-state or shifts in state policy. The chapters on Miami and Jamaica show the persistence of the repeating nationalist fictions and their racial scripts both at the level of state policy (Jamaica) and in diasporic communities from Latin America and the Caribbean (Miami). By taking a conceptual approach, I can emphasize moments of new political articulation and attend to the many valences of the afterlives of myths of racial democracy in the hemispheric fold.

Across all the chapters, I show how those who engage in acts of racial conjuring levy racial scripts to forge a sense of social belonging, to reimagine citizenship, and to make sense of changes around them. When Velasco thumped her chest as a gorilla in the scene of *Tres viudas* and one of the other white characters grunted to punctuate the construction of blackness as simian, they worked together to relegate blackness to the margins of the human and to thereby codify the terms of social belonging in that space. I use the term *scenes of racial enjoyment* to refer to the vast gamut and varied constellations of racial gratification, delight, resistance, and subjection that blackface performance facilitates in today's world. In *Tres viudas*, the invocation of black animality and black people as symbols of fun brought delight to the audience at the theater. Whether as part of the everyday or a formal event, scenes of racial enjoyment, like those in *Tres viudas*, reveal the centrality of race for setting terms of belonging and defining relations of racial power in the afterlives of myths of racial democracy.

Instead of assigning a fixed or singular meaning to blackface acts in this book, I see impersonation as a set of ludic actions through which people test and figure out the racial terms for the formation of a given collective or social belonging, as they negotiate the ongoing power of the nationalist fictions and the changes in racial formation around them. As Lauren Berlant and Sianne Ngai write about comedy and pleasure, comedy can both dispel and produce anxiety, and it can intensify and impede pleasure.[67] They explain that comedy is "epistemologically troubling" and that it "helps us test or figure out what it means to say 'us.' Always crossing lines, it helps us figure out what lines we desire or can bear."[68] Acts of racial conjuring enable conjurers to amplify and rework, reinforce and defamiliarize, consolidate and invert the dynamics of racial power that determine belonging, notions of personhood, and ideas about who is marginalized or who is venerated as the ideal citizen. They may sustain, subvert, or confront the racial scripts of the national story, or in the context of black social spaces, be levied for black enjoyment. I focus on scenes of racial enjoyment because they are meaning-making paradigms that offer up representations of race that entertain or disturb, titillate, or confront. Through racial enjoyment, black, indigenous, mestizo, creole, and white people critically rework their positionalities within or contest or reinforce hierarchies of the racial matrix in the hemispheric fold. The figurations of blackness that appear in this book cater to black, indigenous, white, and mestizo publics in different ways. Hence, I make space for the various reconfigurations of racial power that scenes of racial enjoyment produce in the hemispheric fold.

Racial enjoyment operates in a contemporary reality where black people have a level of agency that our ancestors simply did not have. To live in the wake of slavery in the hemispheric fold is to contend with the gains and limitations of black organizing, the ascension and co-optation of black subjects into positions of power. Although as black people we are not free from the political and social constraints of white supremacy, black people are cultural producers and critical actors who consume the figurations of blackness on stage for our own devices. Scenes of racial enjoyment enable me to account for the complexities of racial power and identification that racial impersonation permits, including among black people. I show enjoyment as operating along multiple axes of subjection, resistance, and even abject pleasures. Although not all scenes of racial enjoyment showcase acts of impersonation, as used in this book, they are the cultural *venues* for blackface forms. Belonging to the realm of the popular mythic, a scene is a place and a segment in a series of continuous action, the node in a plot, that offers snapshots of our psychic racial dreams, desires, and fears.[69] Scenes of racial enjoyment bring us joy, comfort, laughter, and pleasure. They reveal how logics of symbolic possession permeate the visual and the performative: a photograph, a play at a theater, a dance performance at a carnival or in media; a television show, a commercial, a cartoon, a TikTok or Facebook video, or a GIF on social media; a souvenir, kitchen kitsch, and even a candy wrapper.

Scenes of racial enjoyment like the video clip of Velasco's performance give us glimpses of how people rehearse and test the boundaries of social belonging at a particular moment in time. They are the points of entry to different domains of racial enjoyment. In this book, I track hierarchies of racial power by critiquing the racial scripts of mestizaje that appear in each scene. Grounded in racial fantasy and fiction, these racial scripts are the popular mythologies that circulate around an individual racial group in a national story. Racial scripts make themselves felt in the sayings, the aphorisms, the jokes, and the stereotypes that circulate in the realm of culture. Black people are constructed as lazy fools who cannot think beyond midday, naturally musical, delinquents, hypersexual, and natural athletes, while indigenous people are configured as backward, primitive, and dirty. Velasco's reference to dancing and having fun, for example, tapped into the racial script of black women as being natural dancers or carefree figures of enjoyment and fun. All these racial scripts emerge from the romance of racial harmony that has adjudicated values and roles to a particular racial group in the national imaginary. Each scene shows the ongoing power of the racial script.

Hemispheric Blackface: Ludic Imaginaries in the Americas

This book is organized to engage different dimensions of racial enjoyment in the hemispheric fold. I neither use each performance to make an inherent judgment about a particular nation nor suggest that one blackface performance represents the totality of the politics of racial impersonation in a given locale. The first half of this book examines renditions of blackness by indigenous, mestizo, and white performers that reinforce racial hierarchies, and the second analyzes those by black performers living in the wake of slavery to discern how they subvert, contest, and defamiliarize slavery's logics of symbolic possession.

The first two chapters focus on the politics of subjection as a domain of racial enjoyment in the hemispheric fold. I begin by analyzing a performance by the Peruvian group Sambos Illimani at the 2013 Fiesta de la Virgen de la Candelaria, in which they use racial impersonation to commemorate the history of African enslavement in the Andes. In this chapter, I argue that the blackface performance reproduces the racial script of black disappearance at a time when the nation has moved away from nationalist regimes of colorblindness toward the recognition of race. Grounded in the popular lore that the black population in the Andes died out during slavery, this script has been crucial to the nationalist fiction of mestizaje in Peru. I track slavery's logics and interrogate the entanglement of subjection and racial enjoyment by analyzing Sambos's use of racial impersonation in its slave scene and show how the racial script is grounded in popular imaginations of the slave past. Since impersonation is a central part of performance traditions that commemorate the history of slavery across the Andean highlands, I argue that traditions are neither static nor innocent; rather, they house racial fantasies about the slave past and reflect the hemispheric representations of blackness with which the performers come in contact. I trace the origin of the Danza de Caporales, a neofolkloric dance created in the 1960s, to its predecessor, the controversial Bolivian indigenous blackface dance known as the Tundique, to illuminate how the revolving fictions and fantasies about blackness circulating in the hemispheric fold are levied to construct a slave past and sustain a racial script. In doing so, I show how the zambo/sambo figure of their performance functions as a hemispheric double. Furthermore, I emphasize that subjection, as a domain of racial enjoyment, works to negotiate dynamics of gender and sexual power. I pay close attention to the invocation of queer desire and the act of gender-bending in Sambos Illimani's performance to show how staging the script of black disappearance allows antiblackness to stay intact even as normative boundaries of gender and sexuality are transgressed at the carnival. Ultimately, I not only show how Sambos's act of impersonation sustains a local racial script, bypassing sexual and gender transgression, but by highlighting its hemispheric dimensions, I also underscore how the performance surpassed its national context and resonated with an international audience.

In the second chapter, I pay further attention to the hemispheric dimensions of blackface performance by showing how subjection, as a domain of racial enjoyment, mediates the geopolitical relationships between the two Americas and works to create a sense of belonging across national differences in the hemispheric fold. In Miami, the racial script appears through the trope of the black buffoon who operates as a cultural symbol of a postracial nationalism for Cuban Americans. Conjured by and for Miami's Cuban diaspora, Yeyo Vargas is a negrito figure from the Spanish-language late-night TV program *Esta Noche Tu Night*, who was invented in 2008 just as Barack Obama rose to power as the first black president of the United States. Yeyo is the deluded leader of a fictional political party who serves as an adviser to President Obama and as a liaison to the president for Latinos and Latin Americans. As the familiar negrito of teatro bufo, he is a symbol of national identity and cultural memory for Cubans in the diaspora, but he also negotiates the postracial frenzy surrounding Barack Obama's candidacy, discourses of mestizaje circulating among Latin American immigrants in the city, and hemispheric formations of antiblackness and of whiteness in Miami and Cuba. Like the hemispheric double of chapter 1, Yeyo is a stand-in for multiple figurations of blackness circulating in the two Americas. As a domain of racial enjoyment, here subjection negotiates the geopolitical changes in the hemispheric Americas, including the emergence of a Latin American left during the Pink Tide and a new set of policies between the United States and Cuba. In this context, racial scripts are levied to negotiate new political shifts between the two Americas and the evolution and convergence of multiple repeating nationalist fictions in the hemispheric fold.

The second half of the book underscores how black performers wield impersonation to challenge or deconstruct racial scripts. Here I discuss black performers who conjure racial stereotypes to humanize, register an oppositional gaze, engage in acts of spectacular opacity, or defamiliarize racist tropes. In my examination of the multimedia exhibit *Mambo negrita* (2006) by the Colombian black artist Liliana Angulo, I show how she conjures the stereotype of the *negrita*—which translates to little black girl or woman—to subvert and confront racial scripts that define black women as either domestic servants or hypersexual objects of desire. In an act that I call *spatial drag*, Angulo uses impersonation to present the negrita as a literal fixture of the kitchen and to highlight the role of space in racializing the black female body. She critically engages the relationship between black womanhood and objecthood by imitating the negrita in advertising, kitchen kitsch, and other material objects. In doing so, she illuminates the prevalence of blackface in material culture. Because her intervention took place amid Colombia's turn away from colorblindness to multiculturalism and new celebrations of diversity in art, I theorize resistance as a domain of racial enjoyment and show how black people wield impersonation to negotiate the state's shift toward the recognition of race. She exposes the endurance of nationalist fiction of mestizaje by subverting and resisting the racial scripts that construct black women as perpetual servants. Here I show how racial scripts are critically reworked to challenge the presumed end of mestizaje and the inauguration of the multicultural nation.

In the final chapter on racial conjuring in Jamaica, I examine black enjoyment and abject pleasures as a domain of racial enjoyment. Beginning in 2008, a popular blackface character, Delcita Coldwater, appeared in several plays from a theatrical genre in Jamaica known as "roots theater." A dismissed and denigrated theatrical form consumed and produced by Jamaica's black working class, roots theater uses farce to center the experience of the black underclass. Delcita, an immensely popular roots character, plays the racial script of the country bumpkin who comes to town. But she is not just a caricature of Jamaica's black underclass. This figuration of blackness doubles as the voice of working-class resistance who both confronts social prejudices and outsmarts the brown ruling class. I argue that Delcita is conjured by and for Jamaica's black underclass to articulate a counternarrative that challenges the racial scripts of Jamaica's nationalist fiction of creole nationalism. These racial scripts persist despite the emergence of "modern blackness" in the 1990s that entailed the recasting of race in the public and cultural sphere.[70] In her performance, Delcita oscillates between resisting the racial script and pandering to debased stereotypes of blackness, thereby countering any notion that this performance is solely about resisting the stereotype. I attend to the paradoxes of black enjoyment of black tropes to underscore why subjection and resistance, by themselves, do not capture the complexities of blackface performance. I emphasize the function of abject pleasures and radical disregard and examine the presence of black diasporic ludic circuits in the hemispheric fold.

Together, these domains of racial enjoyment all underscore how blackface, as a multivalent set of material, theatrical, performative, and visual practices, negotiates distinct modalities of repeating nationalist fictions in the hemispheric fold in an era of political change. I examine racial impersonation to not only highlight the endurance of these repeating nationalist fictions, but also to illuminate the disconnect between official state shifts toward the recognition of race and the reality people still face on the ground. I track how racial enjoyment enables ordinary people to both reconfigure and consolidate dynamics of racial power in the contemporary moment, amid shifts toward multiculturalism and the recognition of race. And as I emphasize in the last two chapters, I think about how black people wield racial conjuring to demarcate spaces for themselves, to affirm their own humanity, to create spaces of black sociality, and to develop ludic strategies to negotiate life in the wake of slavery and the afterlives of myths of racial democracy.

After public backlash about her performance in *Tres viudas*, the actress Velasco, the director and writer Pedro Román, and Teatro Trail announced their collective decision to modify the character. She ceased appearing in blackface.[71] Her act of racial conjuring and the controversy that ensued in Miami had activated racial scripts, exposed the endurance of nationalist fictions, and sparked public conversation about antiblack racism in the hemispheric fold. The scene of racial enjoyment and the controversy it generated serve as an invitation to attend to the politics of racial conjuring in the Americas, to think with and across national silos, to wrestle with the ongoing power of repeating nationalist fictions, and to think critically about the figurations of blackness circulating in our midst. I take up this invitation in the pages that follow.

CHAPTER ONE

Blackface and Racial Scripts at the Andean Fiesta

Staging the Slave Past in the Andes

"Siempre se ha visto al negrito loco con su sandía"
(You've always seen the crazy little black with his watermelon)
—Performer from Sambos Illimani con Sentimiento y Devoción (2013)

The drums sound and the performers shout "*ZAMBO*!" (pronounced *Sambo*). Their voices echo through the stadium filled with thousands of international tourists and local Peruvians who have traveled to Puno, Peru, for La Fiesta de la Virgen de la Candelaria. I sit in the stands beneath the scorching sun and struggle to see beyond the media crews. Members of the press stand on the red-and-white track behind silver barriers that cordon off the stadium's large field, which has been converted into a stage. La Fiesta de la Virgen de la Candelaria is one of Peru's most important yearly media events, and the press stream performances live on national television. The stadium is so big that the patrons packed in the stands across from me look like flies. I can only see the giant Cusqueña bottles, Coca-Cola and Claro billboard signs that drape the walls of the stands. About fifty Italian, Peruvian, and American tourists are seated in my row alone; locals and patrons in the stands converse in Quechua, Aymara, French, Italian, Spanish, and English.

"Zambo!" The second shout drowns out the chatter. *Zambo* is the colonial category for the progeny of a black and indigenous or black and Asian union.[1] Nowadays, it is a term for any racial mixture that emphasizes blackness.[2]

I finally see a squadron of performers on the stage. There are hundreds of dancers; some huddle behind a man carrying a banner that reads "Sambos con Sentimiento y Devoción" (Sambos with feeling and devotion), announcing the performance troupe, Sambos Illimani from Lima.[3]

While some performers are the children of Andean migrants who traveled from the province to the capital, other group members hail from different parts of Peru. Most of them are racially ambiguous, but none are identifiably black. Today, however, they all claim to be sambos/zambos, and they ready themselves to perform a popular dance called the Danza de Caporales. At this fiesta—a carnivalesque ritual event celebrating both the Virgen de la Candelaria and the Andean Pachamama—impersonation is the order of the day.[4] These performers are therefore authorized to occupy blackness, to take hold of its remnants, and through this act of figurative possession they will enact a scene of African enslavement.

The Danza de Caporales is a neofolkloric dance that was created in 1969 by members of the Estrada family from Chijini—a working-class neighborhood in La Paz, Bolivia. The dance quickly became a hit among young people. It arrived in Peru in the early 1970s and spread rapidly across South America and the globe. As the dance grew in popularity, its origins became the subject of controversy, as Peruvians and Bolivians alike claim to have invented it. The *caporal*, protagonist of the Danza de Caporales, has always been a feature of carnivals acting as the foreman of a dance squad or performance troupe. The dance merges this figure with representations of blackness in a blackface dance known as the Tundique or Tundiki. The Tundique belongs to a tradition of dances in Latin America known as the Baile de los Negritos (Dance of the Little Blacks) and to a pantheon of satirical Andean dances that represent blackness, called *negrerías*.[5] Some versions of the Tundique satirize African enslavement and are danced in blackface by mestizo and indigenous people.[6] These versions would typically feature a *capataz* (slave driver) character who represents brutal authority. The capataz is a racially ambiguous figure who may be a black, indigenous, white, or mestizo slave driver of the slave gang. The caporal figure of the Danza de Caporales is a fusion of the capataz character and the foreman of street carnivals. While the caporal is a softer figure of racial ambiguity, like the capataz, he functions as a symbol of power, virility, and prestige.

The young performers of Sambos Illimani standing onstage have certainly dressed the part of an imposing authority figure. The men all wear large green vests, black pants, and tall, knee-high boots with rows of gold bells on either side (figure 1.1). Their shirt sleeves puff at the shoulders that enlarge their arm muscles, and many carry whips in their hands. Scattered among the rows of caporales are female dancers dressed in drag as men, known as *las machitas*, who act as queer figures of male power. The other women dancers, or *caporalas*, are sensual femme characters wearing revealing *mini-polleras* (miniskirts) and high heels, and long *trenzas* (plaits). They stand together in a large triangle, with eleven lines of caporales and machitas on two sides and rows of caporalas at the tip of the triangle. Together, they look like a thousand soldiers ready to march in a military parade (figure 1.2).

Suddenly, the patrons in the row in front of me burst out laughing as they point at six men covered in black paint standing behind the caporal carrying the banner in the front (figure 1.3).[7] Five of them are chained together, while another performer stands beside them with a scale on his shoulder and a watermelon in his hand. One wears a blond Afro wig, and two of them are wearing large silver and black top hats that match their silver pants. There is no racial ambiguity here, as these enslaved characters played by blackface performers stand directly in front of the other Sambos, who carry whips in their hands. Together, the scene creates a power play between the master or slave driver and the slaves. The blackface figures alongside the racially ambiguous Sambos performers create a juxtaposition between an identifiable blackness and the racially ambiguous bodies that stand in for whiteness, blackness, indigeneity, and racial mixture all at once. Suddenly, the drums start beating faster, trumpets blare, and the cry of "Zambo" shakes the entire stadium. A thousand dancing bodies come to life.

The drumbeats boom loudly and the sound of trumpets bursts into the air. There are whistles, screams, claps, and shouts. The rows of caporales suddenly move forward in military style, and they sway their hips in unison. The caporales and machitas raise their knees to their chests, then kick high into the air. The camera operators try to run around them but can only film a few squadrons of caporales at a time. There are too many jumping bodies to count.

As this dancing army moves forward, the sounds of the bells on their boots reverberate in our seats and on the stadium floor: Shhhhaaakkka shaakkka! They kick in circular motion, and when their feet touch the floor, they lift their shoulders up and down, then skip again to the drum's one-two beat. The caporales flirtatiously shout "Hey hey!" The women dancers sensually shake their behinds rapidly, crisscross their ankles, and screech "Ooo Ooo!" The men reply with loud barks. "Awoof Awoof! Siempre!" This is an ostentatious display of juvenile bravura.

The chained men in blackface dance just ahead of the caporales. The shhakka shakka sound of the caporales' boots match the sound of chains

1.1 *Caporales* and one of the blackface dancers from the performance troupe Sambos Illimani con Sentimiento y Devoción at La Fiesta de la Virgen de la Candelaria, Puno, Peru, in 2013. Author photo.

1.2 A *machita*, *caporal*, and *caporala* of Sambos Illimani at La Fiesta de la Virgen de la Candelaria, Puno, Peru, in 2018. Author photo.

1.3 Sambos Illimani's performance in Peru in 2020 featuring watermelon man and enslaved characters in blackface. Author photo.

that clang as the slaves move. From the distance, I can see the giant balls of the silver chains hanging around their necks sway to and fro. Their bright red lipstick gleams as the blackface performers grin wildly and excitedly stomp their feet to the beat. They hop and skip, moving their left feet twice and their right feet twice. The stadium erupts with laughter and applause. As the caporales move forward, they raise their whips above their heads, punch their fists in the air, and three or four rows of hundreds of caporales move to encircle the enslaved Africans. The dancing slaves in blackface skip and hop happily. The American tourists in front of me laugh heartily, and one points to an unchained slave carrying his watermelon. Three cameramen surround him. He stomps his feet delightfully, takes his watermelon to his face and bites into it wildly (figure 1.4). The laughter and cheers grow louder. The applause and reaction from the crowd roar throughout the stadium like thunder while countless voices join in shouting "Zambo!"

Sambos Illimani's deployment of blackface in their slave scene is exceptional and unusual, primarily because neither the use of blackface

1.4 Sambos Illimani's watermelon man at La Fiesta de la Virgen de la Candelaria, Puno, Peru, in 2018. Author photo.

nor explicit representations of slavery are typical features of the Danza de Caporales. Even though blackface is a part of indigenous performance traditions, it is more common for performers of the Danza de Caporales to briefly incorporate a black mask in theatrical scenes of their performances.[8] Of all the performances of the Danza de Caporales that I have witnessed in Bolivia and Peru, Sambos Illimani's performance in Puno is the only instance in which I have seen a dance troupe incorporate blackface in the dance.[9] Moreover, most investigations of Andean performance focus primarily on the deployment of the Andean mask, and blackface remains understudied.[10] I examine it in this chapter not only because Sambo Illimani's performance is unique, but also because it is a prime example of how blackface consolidates a nationalist fiction, in this case, of black invisibility in Peru, and it does so as the Peruvian state increasingly moves toward recognizing its black populations.

Discourses of mestizaje in Peru have created a national story that assigns designated roles or racial scripts to different racial groups in the nation. Grounded in fantasy and fiction, racial scripts are the popular mythologies that circulate around a particular racial group. As I explain in the introduction, these are not only state policies, but the stereotypes and ideas about racial others that are produced in popular culture. In Peru, where national identity is heavily associated with the image of the Incas, the racial scripts of mestizaje disappear blackness, thus relegating black people to the margins of national identity. In the Andean highlands, the tale of black disappearance is grounded in the popular story that black people died out during slavery. The scene of racial enjoyment in Sambos Illimani's performance serves as an example of how blackface sustains a racial script of black disappearance because it is a humorous recounting of the tragic disappearance of black people from the Peruvian Andes. Although Peru is on the outskirts of the multicultural turn in Latin America that I discuss in the introduction, in the 2000s, the country moved away from its official stance of colorblindness by formally recognizing the history of slavery, the contributions of Afro-Peruvians, and conducting a racial census. Despite this shift on the part of the state, Sambos's performance illustrates that the script of black invisibility proliferates on the ground. As I show here, summoning slavery's logics of racial subjugation enables people to redefine relations of racial power as the state reconfigures the national story. Because the Danza de Caporales is also a celebration of masculine power, I show how subjugation, as a domain of racial enjoyment, allows for the interarticulation of gendered, sexual, and racial power.

In Sambos Illimani's blackface performance, the marriage of symbolic possession with the material history of black bondage demonstrates how the racial scripts of mestizaje are entangled with memories of slavery. Re-enacting the slave past is a public ritual that keeps the racial script of black invisibility alive. For the narrative of black disappearance to be sustained, the fiction of their demise must be actively and constantly reproduced. As public rituals, these dances are acts of transfer, mnemonic reserves that transmit and construct social memory about the slave past. But the slave past that lives in popular performance is not about historical truth; rather, it is the province of a set of fictions about blackness. The figurations of blackness that emerge from these enactments of slavery are the convergent site of multiple and changing racial fantasies that performers and spectators actively cocreate and that change according to the needs of the conjurers. And these fantasies are not limited to the nation or its cultural patrimony. That this performance takes place in the transborder space of Puno, Peru, for example, is important because its rendition of blackness is tethered to a set of evolving racial fictions that emerged from the progenitor of the Danza de Caporales, the Tundique tradition in Bolivia. Sambos Illimani draws from a Bolivian blackface dance to activate a racial script about blackness in Peru. I show that the figurations of blackness in Sambos Illimani's performance are malleable devices, and that the fictions they stage are both reflections of an imagined past and the global images of race with which the performers and spectators come in contact. The enslaved black body on stage is inflected by and embedded in representations of blackness and imaginations of slavery that circulate in the hemispheric Americas. I track and critique these fantasies to destabilize the historical pillars upon which the script of black disappearance is constructed and transmitted. This chapter, then, not only seeks to discern how Sambos Illimani's act of racial conjuring reproduces the racial script of black disappearance in Peru. By mapping the hemispheric contours of the fantasies of blackness in the dance, it also underscores the limitations of the nation in unpacking the meaning of this blackface performance. I emphasize a shared history of slavery in the Americas because slavery produced a set of racial fictions whose imaginaries span multiple national borders. As I show here, scenes of subjection in Sambos's performance activated and drew from these diverse racial fictions circulating in the hemispheric fold.

Because carnivals are arenas of social transgression, they are popular spaces of racial enjoyment. It is important to note that in indigenous performance traditions, racial humor and masking are central features of all ritual practice, and all racial groups are subject to some form of racial parody.[11] The fact of the tradition, however, does not render Sambos Illimani's performance an act of innocent amusement. While carnivals are often seen as sites of social inversion, theorists have cautioned against simplistic approaches that define carnival as inherently liberatory or purely as sites of resistance, instead proposing we treat them as polysemic sites of contested meaning.[12] Studies of Andean fiestas affirm that they have always been arenas of fierce negotiation of dynamics of power between colonizers — or, later, the state — and indigenous people.[13] In my view, the temporary suspension of normative boundaries of race and gender does not magically erase the complex dynamics of power at play at a fiesta. Thus, I also pay close attention to the invocation of queer desire and the act of gender-bending in Sambos Illimani's performance to show how subjection, as a domain of racial enjoyment, keeps antiblackness intact even as normative boundaries of gender and sexuality are transgressed. The fictions that produce the figurations of blackness on stage not only sustain racial scripts but also delineate the gendered and sexual contours of racial power. Racial scripts also do sexual and gendered work.

My goal is not to parse the intentions or views of the individual performers. Performance and cultural studies treat embodied forms and cultural artifacts as epistemic practices that serve both as objects of analysis and as constitutive sites of knowledge production. I therefore focus on the meaning that the act of racial conjuring produced during the live performance. While members of Sambos Illimani indicated to me that they defined blackface as a US tradition and that their performance was an expression of their admiration, respect for, and fascination with blackness, as the performance circulates, their intentions are lost, while the performance of blackness continues to produce meaning.[14] As a central device of racial play, blackface activates and organizes a set of racialized and gendered relations of power that consolidate a long-standing nationalist fiction that has marginalized Afro-Peruvians. Tracing the persistence of this racial script in cultural practice is important as the nation turns away from colorblindness to the recognition of race, precisely because traditions are popular inventions that, in this case, enable publics to revise the renditions of blackness on stage according to their changing realities. To track these changes in narrative, I first examine the origin and nuances of the script of black invisibility as it emerged within Peru's nationalist discourse of mestizaje.

Black Invisibility and *Mestizaje* in Peru

Peru's international reputation as the "land of the Incas" has rendered its black population invisible and obscured the fact that the country was formerly a slave society with a large black population. During the colonial era, Peru was one of the major suppliers and traders of enslaved Africans along the Pacific coast.[15] Enslaved Africans came to Peru via two routes: they crossed the Atlantic Ocean and were then either re-exported to Peru via Cartagena or Panama or they came from Río de la Plata by land.[16] Upon arrival, blacks worked in haciendas, in silver mines, and in white homes as domestic workers, and they were heavily concentrated along the Peruvian coasts.[17] Blacks constituted half of Lima's population in 1593 and even outnumbered whites by 1650.[18] But by the twentieth century, it was largely believed that Peru's black population had "disappeared." The myth of black disappearance accelerated after the abolition of slavery in Peru in 1855 but had already been solidified during independence, when Peru developed a discourse of mestizaje that fundamentally reorganized the racial politics of the nation.[19]

When Peru gained independence from Spain in 1821, its leading intellectuals and politicians sought to unify and improve, as they saw it, the racial composition of the new nation. They produced a discourse of cultural mestizaje as the organizing national ideology that silenced race and disavowed the existence of racism in Peru. Cultural mestizaje was consolidated during the defining intellectual debates about race in the early 1900s between the highland intellectuals (*serranos*) of Cuzco and the creole elite of Lima. As anthropologist Marisol de la Cadena explains, the debates were largely centered on whether race was grounded in phenotypical, external appearance or in internal qualities such as morality, education, or intelligence.[20] The intellectuals who lived on the coast in Lima believed themselves to be white but considered their Indian counterparts who lived in the highlands to be inferior due to their brown skin color and their provincial origins. While Indians were seen as culturally distant denizens who lived in the far away highlands, the association of blacks with coastal culture meant that they were seen as more culturally proximate to whites.

Blacks were simply neglected in these formative debates. And since state policies focused primarily on acculturating indigenous people, Afro-Peruvians were also sidelined in state policies.[21] The fundamental logic of the state's emphasis on the indigenous population was that indigenous people could become mestizo citizens by way of abandoning indigenous languages, dress, and cultural practices. The purported backwardness of indigenous people could be cured through education, and they could be integrated into the national imaginary as modern mestizo subjects.[22] Afro-Peruvians simply did not figure in the development of national policies. The leading modernist thinker Manuel González Prada, for example, considered Indians to be the future of Peru who simply needed acculturation but saw blacks as mere relics of a colonial past, a dispensable presence for the development of the nation. As Golash-Boza writes, "Indigenous people were to be educated; blacks were to disappear."[23] And as the emphasis on culture ensured that race disappeared from the conversation, blackness then disappeared from the national imaginary. Cultural mestizaje was crucial to black invisibility because it used the language of culture to silence conversations about race, to deny the existence of racism, and to wield indigeneity in ways that furthered the whitewashing of the nation.[24]

Another factor in black invisibility is the fact that the Peruvian state did not conduct a racial census from 1940 to 2017. In 1961, the census director Pedro Gutiérrez defended the decision not to conduct a racial census by declaring, "The question about race is omitted because there is no racial problem in Peru."[25] Gutiérrez's stance is salient because it exemplifies a disavowal about the presence of racism in the nation. Because the state took a colorblind approach in 1940, it failed to document its Afro-Peruvian population until well into the twenty-first century. This was an obstacle to Black activists in the early 2000s seeking to identify and define the needs of the black population and to combat racism.[26] In 2002, Peru's Commission on Andean, Amazonian, and Afro-Peruvian Peoples (CONAPA) noted the harmfulness of the lack of ethnic data in the population and its contribution to the social invisibility of Peru. Afro-Peruvian NGOs began challenging the social invisibility of black people by noting the high number of black people living in poverty and the few white-collar jobs or high-ranking professional positions that they occupied. Despite the state's colorblind stance, through the twentieth century, Afro-Peruvians continued to face widespread discrimination.

As is common across Latin America, employers frequently seek candidates with *buena presencia* (meaning white features). Afro-Peruvians are stereotyped as fools who cannot think beyond midday.[27] There are even popular sayings in Peru such as, "I may be black, but I have a brain."[28] Afro-Peruvians also face economic stagnation and challenges accessing basic public services, and they are among the poorest of Peru's population.[29] In the 1990s and 2000s, media portrayals of blacks as criminal, buffoonish, or unkempt remained commonplace.[30] The popular blackface character El Negro Mama (Black Sucker), played by Jorge Benavides on the channel Frecuencia Latina, personified these representations as the character was rendered as a fool and a thief.[31] El Negro Mama first appeared on the Benavides television program *JBNews* in the 1990s. He was portrayed as a foolish black man constantly engaged in criminal activity. Throughout the programs he attempted to swindle and steal from those around him. Guests on the program typically referred to El Negro Mama using derogatory racial terms. In 2013, the Afro-Peruvian group LUNDU organized a successful media and legal campaign that led Peru's Ethics Tribunal for Radio and Television to deem the character discriminatory, to fine the television channel, and to mandate that they follow a code of ethics.[32] Racial discrimination persisted, even as Peru's nationalist discourse of mestizaje disavowed the problem of race and installed a structure of racial silence.

There are, however, nuances to black invisibility in Peru. Black cultural forms do enjoy some visibility today, even though Afro-Peruvians themselves have had to fight for social recognition and inclusion. Black culture has historically been celebrated on the national stage, but such celebrations have operated in tandem with the marginalization of Afro-Peruvians. Black folkloric groups like Peru Negro—an Afro-Peruvian dance and music group that has been performing since the 1970s—were and remain immensely popular in Peru today. But this fact does not contradict the notion that Afro-Peruvians are socially invisible. Heidi Feldman has demonstrated that from the 1950s to the 1970s, for example, Afro-Peruvian cultural forms were "revived" by the criollo elite and celebrated on the national stage. But this revival was grounded in the very logic of an absent or disappeared blackness in the nation that needed to be rescued.[33]

The renaissance of Afro-Peruvian folklore on stage was in keeping with the racial scripts of mestizaje that deem blackness a relic of the past. Latin American nations have long co-opted and exploited black cultural forms on stage to bolster nationalist discourses of mestizaje, and this is true for the historical celebration of black culture on the Peruvian stage.[34] The emergence of Peru Negro in the 1970s operated within a larger state project that elevated black cultural forms as emblems of the new national project.[35] Members of Peru Negro collaborated with white intellectuals and the Juan Velasco Alvarado regime in the 1970s to stylize and codify black cultural forms. The revival and subsequent visibility of blackness on stage was mediated by the needs and nationalist discourses of the regime, which sought to mine black cultural forms in its reimagination of national identity. The racial script of black disappearance served as the perfect justification for the celebration of black folkloric forms. Making black cultural forms visible did not contradict the social invisibility of Afro-Peruvians, nor did it trouble imaginations of black disappearance in the nation; rather, as was the case in the 1970s, it has historically been framed in ways that sustain it.

The discourse of black invisibility does, however, vary according to one's geographic location within the national imaginary. Peru is a site of competing racial formations where some imaginations of race exclude blackness while others do not.[36] For example, while blackness is excluded from the racial imaginary in Cuzco, which is centered on the tensions between highland Indians (*serranos*) and the creole elite in Lima, racial ideology in Lima acknowledges its African, European, and indigenous ancestry, even if it ultimately idealizes its Inca past.[37] This is due, in part, to the fact that race is organized by Peru's tripartite geography: *la costa* (the coast), *la selva* (the jungle), and *la sierra* (the highlands), and each racial group occupies a designated geographical zone. Blacks are associated with the coastal provinces of Lima, Ica, Lambayeque, and Piura while Amazonians and Andeans are associated with the jungle and the highlands. This geography of Peru's national imaginary emplaces blacks as people of the coast; in the highlands, then, blackness is configured as out of place.

In Puno, where Sambos Illimani staged their performance, the discourse of black invisibility is heightened in relation to other parts of the country. In the region, it is widely believed that enslaved blacks brought there to the Andes to work in the mines disappeared because they failed to adjust to the Andean cold, suffered from sickle cell disease, and were overworked.[38] But the fiction of black disappearance stands on shaky historical ground. Contrary to popular belief, blacks have not historically been strictly coastal people.[39] Blacks were sent to the highlands as workers, warriors, or slaves for the Spanish colonizers who assisted with the conquest of Cuzco in the sixteenth century. As colonization decimated the indigenous population along the coastline, the Spaniards sent enslaved Africans to the coast to replace the indigenous labor force.[40] Thus, the movement of blacks to the coast was largely a product of the economic imperatives of the colonial power. Nevertheless, the racial fiction of black disappearance in the highlands has been solidified in Peruvian lore through the popular saying, "El gallinazo no canta en Puno" (The turkey buzzard does not sing in Puno).[41] In indigenous communities of the highlands, where the Afro-Peruvian populace is minimal or non-existent, the negrito dances commemorate the historical presence of enslaved blacks there. Sambos Illimani's performance thus stages this racial fiction by re-enacting the origin story of black disappearance in the highlands.

Finally, although Peru is an outlier of the regional turn to multiculturalism that I discuss in the introduction, it has slowly made strides to acknowledge race. Former president Alberto Fujimori revised article 1993 of the constitution, which now recognizes the "ethnic and cultural plurality of the nation," and another article refers specifically to respecting the cultural identity of rural and native communities.[42] Even though the state offered a set of symbolic gestures, including formally apologizing for slavery and designating Afro-Peruvian Culture Day in 2006, the initial reforms privileged indigenous people over Afro-Peruvians, failed to specifically address experiences of discrimination, and did not meet the requests of Afro-Peruvian activists.[43] The limitations of the multicultural reforms aside, Black activist groups continue to organize to varying success against racism and discrimination. In 2015, for example, Peru had its first ever conviction for racial discrimination, and in 2017 the state finally conducted a racial census for the first time in decades. While the racial census itself is a victory for Afro-Peruvian organizing and the state has slowly moved away from official colorblindness to recognition, Sambos Illimani's performance shows how the fiction of black invisibility persists. Just as Afro-Peruvians have made strides in their fight against invisibility and colorblindness, Sambos Illimani's act of racial conjuring activates the very racial script that new state policies aim to leave behind. Staging black disappearance is embedded within larger public rituals that construct social memory about the nation's racial past. An apologist stance may suggest that Sambos Illimani's performance is simply part of an indigenous performance tradition, but as historian Eric Hobsbawm reminds us, traditions are often inventions "which seek to inculcate certain values and norms of behavior by repetition," and "normally attempt to establish continuity with a suitable historical past."[44] The negrería pantheon that Sambos Illimani's performance belongs to, like other traditions, are social constructions that, I suggest, produce an imagined racial past.

Impersonating Blackness: The *Negrería* Pantheon and the Imagination of the Slave Past

Sambos Illimani's performance belongs to a larger popular dance tradition at the Andean fiesta. In the Bolivian and Peruvian Andes, publics use embodied practice to pay homage to a Virgen or religious deity and to articulate collective understandings of race and difference, the colonial past, histories of slavery, and processes of globalization. Fiestas are celebratory, ribald events that are home to Andean genealogies of performance and public rituals: performances at the *comparsa* (dance competition), parades and the arrival of the Virgen to the community, acts of worship, and veneration of the deity. These are forms of collective representation that negotiate the sacred realm and processes of syncretism that emerged from colonial rule. The Virgen de la Candelaria, for example, known by Puneños as "La Mamita," doubles as the Catholic Virgen of the Candelaria of Spain and the Pachamama of Andean mythology. Embedded within the sacred realm, these genealogies of performance involve public re-enactments of past events. In these annual rituals, publics use their bodies to construct and transmit social memory, to negotiate their relationship to the past, and pay homage to a religious deity.

Its function within the sacred realm notwithstanding, the negrería pantheon indexes the role of embodied practice in constructing a racial past and remembering a history of slavery. The repertoire includes "negrito" dances such as La Morenada, Los Negritos de Huánuco, the Hatajos de Negritos, El Qhapaq Negro, the Danza de Caporales, and others. In the Bolivian and Peruvian Andes, they are danced by black, indigenous, and mestizo subjects alike. I do not dismiss the entire negrería pantheon as racist; rather, here I emphasize that the tradition is not static. Depending on the dance, the narratives of slavery and the dynamics of racial power differ. The negrería dances function as spaces for collective fictionalization by black, mestizo, indigenous, and white performers. Many of these dances commemorate the history of slavery by re-enacting slave scenes or referencing black bondage. The dances use acts of revision, repetition, and improvisation to construct a racial history based on kinesthetic imagination, popular lore, oral narratives, and fantasy.

Historically, Spanish colonists required indigenous populations to stage imagined versions of black dances, and many performances are, in fact, fantasies of blackness or imaginations of black subjugation.[45] At times, the slave scenes of the performances claim to reproduce the particularities of black subjugation. For example, the Baile de los Negritos that is danced in Lima's Fiesta de la Virgen de Cocharcas in September shows a line of four negritos holding whips given to them by a *cargoyuq*.[46] The negritos stomp their feet to represent the grape-stomping that enslaved blacks were required to do under the supervision of a foreman.[47] Imagination is crucial to dances that pay homage to the cultural practices of enslaved Africans, like in the Negritos de Huánuco celebrated at the end of the year, where the relationship of the dance to actual historical black practices is questionable.[48] Many are acts of remembrance, like the Hatajos de Negritos, which Afro-Peruvians dance in the coastal provinces in Peru at Christmas. In this dance, black performers dance in front of nativity scenes outside a church and adolescent black boys dressed as the Magi wear crowns on their heads, carry whips in their hands, and tie bells on their feet.[49] In Afro-Peruvian communities, the negrito dance both preserves and transmits histories of slavery and Christianization. The renditions of slavery on display may subvert or reinforce colonial dynamics of racial power, but in general these dances constitute a repertoire of historical racial invention. They produce a racial past through ephemeral acts of collective fictionalization and through the activation of racial memories that live in the popular imagination. The racial memories are themselves disparate and diffuse, and they always bear elements of fiction and fantasy.

As a central technology in the invention of the racial past, acts of impersonation—imitation of the other, racial play, and the conjuring of figurations of blackness, indigeneity, or whiteness—create culturally specific scenarios in which the fictions of racial others are made real. Sambos Illimani's performance perpetually restages the fictional origin story of the demise of enslaved Africans. The figurations of blackness that are conjured in their performance are the figments of a blackness in a state of perpetual disappearance, the sign of a tragic racial loss to be mourned and remembered. The affective structures that wrap blackness in regimes of nostalgia and loss produce a racial past and fix blackness as a thing that the region and the nation have left behind. The repetition of these dances in yearly public ritual, as Hobsbawm suggests, are not only how traditions come to be established but, in Sambos Illimani's case, it is also how a fictionalized slave past is brought into being, reaffirmed, and legitimized in the public domain as historical truth.

Sambos Illimani's act of impersonation demarcates black presence as the distant past, illustrating how impersonation marks the temporal coordinates of racial formation in the nation. The racial past is not a neutral entity; as Michel-Rolph Trouillot insists, "the past is a position," and it is not independent of the present.[50] Conjuring an enslaved black body is not just about faithfulness to a tradition or even about historical truth. Rather, I insist it enables performers to establish a fictional historical position from which they define the racial present. The enslaved black bodies dancing in chains of Sambos Illimani's performance represent a double temporality that simultaneously coproduces a racial past and racial present. Blackness is the spectral sign of a racial past whose presence on stage positions other racial subjects or groups as the stand-ins and representatives of the nation's present and future. And because performing stories of the past informs processes of racialization in the present, Sambos Illimani's renditions of black disappearance reproduce, consolidate, and maintain the racial script of black invisibility, especially when Peru has made strides toward formally acknowledging its black population.[51] As devices of historical invention, these acts of racial impersonation not only offer a fictional historical grounding and legitimizing narrative for the racial fictions of mestizaje, but they also ensure their endurance beyond the changing positions of the state.

While it is important to read Sambos Illimani's use of blackface within the specificities of the performance tradition, the cultural specificities by themselves do not free these traditions from animating and sustaining discourses of antiblackness. The tradition is neither neutral nor static nor fixed. In this tradition, the slave past figures as a site of historical racial invention, and the negrería dances are the province of collective racial fictions that are hardly limited to the nation. This is crucial for understanding the specificities of the Tundique—a blackface indigenous dance that predates the US blackface minstrel tradition and that Sambos Illimani's blackface referenced. The Tundique exemplifies the ways a set of evolving and shifting racial fantasies come to produce a racial past. Moreover, the renditions of blackness and the technologies of racial impersonation that have formed part of the dance are, in fact, deeply inflected by representations of blackness that circulate in the hemisphere. I turn to the Tundique to also emphasize that a nationalist frame does not adequately capture the multiple fictions of blackness that are mobilized in Sambos's blackface performance. Here I show how a blackface performance taps into a shared history of slavery across the hemispheric fold, even as the performers themselves seek to negotiate the changes to Peru's national story. It is this shared history that makes this scene of subjection legible for an international audience and that renders the figuration of blackness on stage malleable to multiple fantasies about blackness and different fictional imaginaries of the slave past. It is not only that the negrería dances fictionalize a racial past, but the racial fantasies and technologies that undergird these performances are themselves subject to renegotiation and evolution as they incorporate global representations of blackness.

The Tundique: Racial Fictions and Ventriloquizing Blackness in the Andes

The history of the Tundique is contradictory and nebulous, as the dance itself has multiple genealogies. It is associated with religious rites, popular culture, music, and carnivalesque representations of enslavement in the Andes. My purpose here is not to engage in what would be a doomed search for an original Tundique, but to trace how the representation of blackness from a colonial-era Catholic religious rite has held multiple and different fantasies of blackness that have been welded to different racial memories. These renditions of blackness correspond to global economies of representation because they have been inflected by multiple performance traditions over time.

The Tundique belongs to the tradition of the Baile de los Negritos, which emerged from Catholic religious rites and the celebration of the figure of the negrito. One of the central stories of the Catholic faith is that of the three wise men or three kings who visit baby Jesus. Each character represents a nation or race of the world. One of them is a black figure, referred to in Bolivia as Balthasar. In Spain, the representation of Balthasar as a white person in blackface predates Spanish arrival to the Americas and continues today in the Fiesta de Reyes, which occurs in January of each year. During the conquest of the Americas, the colonizers deployed the figure of Balthasar in colonial practices of religious conversion, using Balthasar's racial difference in the story of the Three Kings as an allegory for the conversion of the racial other.[52] Through performances and theater at Christmas time, colonizers presented a world where everyone—regardless of their ethnic or racial difference—would bow down and worship baby Jesus. Since impersonation of the other was already a central feature of pre-Hispanic performance traditions, the colonizers accommodated some indigenous public rituals and co-opted them as instruments of conversion.[53]

The Spanish tradition of impersonation in representations of Balthasar was fused with indigenous traditions of masquerade in the colonies. Colonizers often used *villancicos navideños* (Christmas carols) to proselytize to the native population, and these carols were eventually assimilated into Latin American folklore. In writings about celebrations in Sucre and La Paz, Bolivia, from 1913 onward, some of the rhythms and dances associated with these Christmas carols were referred to as *chuntunquis*.[54] It is believed that the word *tundique* is an evolution of the word *chuntunqui* and that it is an imitation of the onomatopoeic "tun-tun" sound of the rhythms associated with the song and dance of the earlier carols. As a blackface tradition embedded in religious practices, the Tundique is a fusion of Spanish and indigenous traditions of masquerade that emerged from the colonial encounter. The tradition has always been characterized by the fusion of different performance traditions.

While it remains common for people in La Paz and Sucre to dance as "negritos tundiques" to celebrate or represent baby Jesus, the Tundique has expanded from its earlier religious roots.[55] The terms *hacer tundique* or *bailar tundique* now refer simply to the act of blacking up, and by the turn of the twentieth century the Tundique encompassed general imitations of Afro-Bolivian popular dances. In his study of the Afro-Bolivian musical and dance form known as the Saya, Walter Sánchez explains that in the early twentieth century black dances from the Yungas—the subtropical zone and department of La Paz with a large black population— became increasingly popular. It was common for mestizo people in La Paz to imitate these dances and black up as *tundiques*.[56] One writer argues, "Los hombres de color introducidos en coloniaje en calidad de esclavos, tuvieron varios bailes particulares a sus costumbres y maneras de ser. De éstos, solo queda el de los *tundiques* y *mururatas* que ha llegado a popularizarse tanto que aún los imitan los mestizos con aplauso y embeleso del vulgo" (Men of color introduced to the colonies as slaves had various dances that were particular to their customs and ways of being. Of these, only the *tundique* and *mururatas* remain and have become so popular that even mestizos imitate them to the applause and fascination of the masses).[57] The Tundique ceased to simply refer to religious rites and came to be the general term for mestizo or indigenous imitations of black popular forms.

At the time of writing, it remains unclear when the Tundique came to represent African enslavement in Bolivia. Since the term refers to general imitations of blackness, new and varying stories about the origins of the dance frequently emerge. Some contend that the Tundique was historically an Aymara imitation of enslaved blacks who used to work in the mines.[58] Some theorists and practitioners describe this Tundique as a dance that commemorates the history of enslavement in the Bolivian sub-tropical zone known as the Yungas. In this version, there is a *negra zamba* (black woman), slaves, and a cruel *capataz* acting as the slave driver.[59] Others claim the Tundique was an imitation of the Afro-Bolivian Saya dance.[60] The Black activist group Movimiento Cultural Saya Afro-Boliviano, however, is adamant that the Tundique has no relation to the Afro-Bolivian Saya, is not part of the Afro-Bolivian cultural repertoire, and that it was never performed by black people.[61] The notion that the Tundique is an indigenous imitation of black dance or grounded in the actual history of black enslavement remains the subject of contention among local practitioners, activists, and experts in Bolivia and Peru. If anything, the racial memories the dance purportedly represents are the confluence of different collective fictions and racial fantasies. This controversy notwithstanding, the Tundique is also known as a dance that represents African enslavement in the Andes.

Despite its nebulous origins, the Tundique has remained a popular feature of street carnivals in Bolivia. It represents both the negrito of Catholic religious rites and imitations of popular black dances. The Tundique gradually became more formalized as a dance at carnivals between the 1920s and the 1960s. The dance's popularity reached its zenith after Bolivia's National Revolution of 1952, which led to a renewed investment in folklore and cultural production and occasioned the emergence of many performance troupes specializing in the Tundique or negrito dances.[62] The most notable group is Walter Yugar's folkloric group Centro Tradicional Negritos del Pagador, founded in La Paz on October 12, 1956, which was dedicated to the Baile de los Negritos. As the Tundique dance became more formalized, its blackface representation was quickly inflected by transnational images of blackness. The founding of Yugar's group, for example, coincided with increased exposure to Afro-Cuban performance, and the Tundique began to incorporate tropical images of blackness. At the first performance of Negritos del Pagador at the Carnival de Oruru in 1957, they fused images of Afro-Cuban dancers with carnivalesque representations of the negrito from the Black Magus Balthasar. Mimicking the image of the Afro-Cuban dancer, the Negritos del Pagador danced in blackface, painted their lips bright red, wore mambo shirts with *guarachas* (large, colorful ruffles), and carried small drums in their hands that they beat as they danced. Some also wore large Afro wigs and adorned their ears with fruits to reference the tropical images of Cuba (figure 1.5–1.6).

1.5 & 1.6 Members of the Fraternidad Saya Negritos de Ayacucho performing at La Fiesta de Gran Poder, La Paz, Bolivia, in 2017. This is a modern derivative of the Tundique dance. Author photos.

By the 1960s, women dancers of the Tundique created a new set of characters, including a negrita with a baby on her back.[63] Blackface performers would walk behind a caporal who carried a whip as they all danced and sang. Sometimes performers wore masks, but often they simply blacked up. The blackface representation in the Tundique and the racial pasts it supposedly represented had been revamped to accommodate transnational tropical images of blackness circulating the hemisphere. By the 1960s, the Tundique was an amorphous form fusing colonial and modern as well as local and transnational images of blackness.

Following the Tundique's popularity in the 1960s, new musicians dedicated to Andean folklore transformed the dance's *tun-tun* rhythm into commercial musical hits. The most notable example is the song "San Benito," recorded in 1968 by Yayo Jofré of the Bolivian folklorist band Los Jairas. A fictional racial memory persisted. The lyrics of Los Jairas's song reference Catholic religious rites in that they tell the story of a negra zamba who is dancing the "Saya de Tundiqui" with her baby and receives a little bird from Saint Benedict for the Fiesta de los Negritos. While the song conflates the Afro-Bolivian Saya with the Tundique, it maintains the dance's association with representations of blackness from Catholic religious rites in its discussion of St. Benedict and the black woman. Its invocation of the dancing black Andean woman with her baby on her back may, perhaps, refer to the association of St. Benedict with black communities in Bolivia, but the affective tone of "San Benito" lays somewhere between celebrations of and nostalgia for blackness. This song became a local and international hit at the height of the New Song Movement in Latin America.[64] Los Jairas toured with the movement's founder, Violeta Parra. "San Benito" was soon covered by other groups in the region, most notably the Chilean folkloric group Inti Illimani, and it became a hit in Bolivian street carnivals. Local Bolivian groups including the Banda Pagador de Oruru often covered "San Benito" at the carnival in Oruro in the 1960s. The Estrada family, who later invented the Danza de Caporales, claim to have been inspired by the band's performance.[65] They used the Tundique as the foundation of a new dance.

The Tundique thus emerged from Catholic practices, popular culture, street carnivals, and imitations of black popular forms. Today, representations of slavery and imitations of black people in the Tundique are the subject of controversy in Bolivia. In contemporary performances, dancers represent black people with gorilla masks, or they black up, don chains, and play out a master and slave scene. Afro-Bolivian groups launched a successful campaign decrying such representations as racist and have called for the prohibition of racist representations in the Tundique. They rightly claim these representations distort the Saya, humiliate black people, and mock black cultural forms.[66] In 2014, the state prohibited the Tundique, but when I was in La Paz, Bolivia, in 2017, I continued to see people performing the dance in blackface at the Fiesta de Gran Poder.[67] Recently, the state has banned the use of blackface and whipping in the dance.[68] This controversy underscores how blackface continues to enable the articulation of racist fantasies of blackness and of black subjugation, and ultimately produces antiblack racism in a local context. It also undermines any presumption of a local consensus about the racial politics of a historical indigenous performance tradition.

That so many fictions of blackness cohere in the Tundique demonstrates how the dance transforms the "negrito" into an open-ended stand-in for Balthasar the Black Magus, baby Jesus, a Cuban "negrito," and an enslaved African. As a porous form, blackface representation in the Tundique is the confluence of colonial and contemporary, local and transnational, popular and religious representations of blackness in the hemisphere. Far from a static cultural tradition wedded to historical truth or even the nation, the memories of blackness emanating from the dance are themselves fictions that are constructed, negotiated, and fought over. These historical fictions, in turn, become the ground upon which fantasies of power are articulated. And in the Danza de Caporales, these fantasies work in gendered ways.

The Danza de Caporales: Racial Fantasy and the Gendered Dimensions of Racial Power

If the Tundique facilitated the articulation of fantasies of blackness, then as its progeny, the Danza de Caporales marries ideas of blackness to fantasies of male power. The Estrada family from La Paz, Bolivia, had a performance troupe called Urus de Gran Poder that specialized in folkloric dance, including the Tundique, and they invented the Danza de Caporales in 1969. While the entire family played a role in its invention, Víctor Estrada is recognized as the main founder. The Danza de Caporales became an instant hit when Estrada and his brothers debuted it in 1972 at La Fiesta de Gran Poder.[69] The Estrada brothers propagated various myths about its invention that scholars have since debunked. In several interviews before his death, Víctor claimed he was inspired to create the Danza de Caporales after observing black people during a trip to Tocaña, a department of La Paz with a large black population. Since Víctor's uncle Alberto Pacheco typically contracted black performers, Víctor traveled with him to learn more about black musical traditions, including the Saya. In the Saya, a caporal or capataz marks the rhythm with a bell, and Estrada claimed to have been inspired by the town caporal.[70] He described this caporal as an older black man who wore a straw hat, large belt, and bells on his boots.[71] Scholars, however, have cast doubt on the notion that the dance is tethered to an actual black man, suggesting Víctor's racial memory to be mere fiction. Instead, they suggest that the caporal emphasizes masculine strength and is a fusion of the carnivalesque images of the negrito, the figure of a capataz, and the caporal, who typically dances alone when he acts as the foreman or guide of a dance troupe.[72] They read his dictatorial nature in relation to Bolivia's turn to authoritarianism in the 1950s.[73]

The Estrada brothers built on preexisting representations of blackness in carnival to ultimately create an open-ended figure of male power. Theorists Eveline Sigl and David Mendoza Salazar explain that the caporal symbolizes a violent oppressor and the backwardness of an ethnic or racial other.[74] When the Estrada brothers invented the Danza de Caporales, the caporal's racial difference, however, was hardly obvious. While many folkloric dances represented blackness through black masks with African features, neither masking nor blacking up is a feature of the Danza de Caporales. This may be because the dance emerged when the Tundique's popularity was waning, and the comedic negrito simply would not fit the image of an authoritarian male power figure. Nevertheless, blackness was important because the Estrada brothers wielded the idea of a figure of racial difference in their invention of the caporal. The caporal is therefore a racially ambiguous authoritarian oppressor. His strength and power are conveyed through high kicks, jumps, and the flashing of his whip—all of which I witnessed in Sambos Illimani's performance at the fiesta. He is a military commander of a squad, the exuberant leader of the performance troupe, a *mandamás* (big boss), or a slave driver whose power was constituted through the enforcement of racial subjugation. He is simultaneously the black or zambo slave driver, the Spanish/white oppressive colonizer, and some performers even claim he is merely Spanish or mestizo. The caporal operates at the intersection of male power and racial differ-

1.7 Víctor Estrada, the first *caporal*, in Bolivia. Photo dated 1973 from the family collection of Carlos Estrada. Reproduced by permission of Alejandro Estrada.

ence. He is a subject of double or multiple racial coding acting as an open-ended stand-in for or enforcer of oppressive power.

The caporal was imagined as the quintessential macho man. A photograph of Víctor Estrada as the first caporal at the Teatro al Aire Libre in La Paz in 1973 shows him dressed in tall black leather cowboy boots with gold stripes and silver bells; wide, white or silver pants and a black sash across his waist; and a bright red long-sleeved shirt (figure 1.7). He wears a hat on his head and is looking off into the distance with his arms crossed. Members of Urus de Gran Poder wore this same costume, which bears similarities to the Argentinian gaucho outfit, at the Fiesta de Gran Poder in June of that year.[75] The vibrant aesthetic and defiant posture in the photograph of Víctor Estrada dressed as the first caporal capture the bravado and masculine virility that has come to characterize the dance, in the form of high kicks and displays of athleticism. This was the image of the macho male sex symbol. For the most part, the Danza de Caporales was imagined as a decidedly masculine space, and the macho aesthetic that inaugurated the first caporal was that of the gaucho—a masculine or cowboy figure epit-

1.8 Lidia Estrada, the first *macha*, Bolivia. Courtesy of Alejandro Estrada.

omizing strength and virility. The modern-day costume of the Danza de Caporales would later be heavily influenced by the vibrant aesthetic style of the performance troupe Caporalistas de San Simón in Cochabamba, Bolivia, but the celebration of an ideal of masculine power remains. It is not surprising, then, that today the dance is so popular among politicians, CEOs, and men of Bolivia's white upper-class elite. Unlike in Peru, where the dance is associated with blackness, its popularity among the Bolivian elite has contributed to the erasure of the historical relationship between blackness and the Danza de Caporales and to the ostensible whitening of the dance in Bolivia.[76] This racial erasure is not incidental but, rather, central to the transformation of the dance into an expression of upper-class masculine power.

Recently, the Danza de Caporales has also served as a space for the expression of female masculine power. At the dance's inception, the caporal was a traditional heteronormative macho male sex symbol. Female stock figures did not appear until much later. It did, however, include the expression of female masculinity when it was founded. In 1975, Víctor Estrada's sister Lidia Estrada danced as the first *macha* with her brothers (see figure 1.8). Lidia's outfit was identical to her brother Víctor's. She wore a large sash around her waist, carried a whip in her hand, and large silver bells adorned the top of her boots. This queer history has been forgotten because the dance was a decidedly macho, heteronormative space for so long; the macha or machita only became a stock figure of the Danza de Caporales in the 1990s. The word *machita* is the diminutive of a Spanish term for tomboy, or for a masculine woman. As it evolved, the Danza de Caporales made space for women to perform, and machitas, or female performers dressed in drag as men, danced either in their own lines in performance troupes or alongside the male caporales. The Danza de Caporales is now characterized by the expression of multiple types of masculinity and of femininity. Today, as the dance's emblem of female masculinity, the machita has access to the celebration of masculine prowess and virility. While the movements of the machita dancers are softer than that of the male caporal, their kicks and turns also express female athleticism or female masculine strength. When placed alongside the femme caporala, the machita expands expressions of femininity, and both characters widen the spectrum of feminine and masculine performance in the dance. The racial fantasies of blackness that underwrite the creation of the caporal enabled the gendered expressions of power that are now sutured to queer and heteronormative fantasies alike.

After Víctor Estrada debuted the Danza de Caporales, it took on a life of its own. By 1975, the dance had arrived in Peru. Bolivians and Peruvians alike seek to proclaim the Danza de Caporales as a cultural patrimony and symbol of the nation.[77] While its blackface origins have disappeared, some performers find ways to represent its Bolivian Tundique origins, as is the case in Sambos Illimani's performance that I witnessed at the Fiesta de la Virgen de la Candelaria. Its relationship to the Tundique is important precisely because it demonstrates the way historical fantasies of blackness demarcate the sexual and gendered codes of racial power. Indeed, we can see the interarticulation of constructs of race, gender, and sexuality in the staging of these fantasies of power in Sambos Illimani's performance at the fiesta in Peru.

Sambos Illimani, the Watermelon Man, and
Hemispheric Fictions of the Slave Past

The figurations of enslaved black bodies that Sambos conjured in its slave scene both emphasized fictions of black disappearance while also activating memories of slavery for spectators at the fiesta. Carnivals are mediatized tourist spectacles produced for a global audience and retransmitted via mass media. The figure of the enslaved African that circulated in that mediatized event conjured racial memories that exceed those of the live performers and spectators at the carnival. Sambos Illimani's performance also gestured to the other fictional imaginaries of slavery in the hemisphere through the troupe's incorporation of the figure of the watermelon man. When the performer of Sambos Illimani said he had *always* seen a crazy little black with his watermelon, I initially wondered if the watermelon man was part of the Tundique tradition, only to discover that it was not. The directors of the troupe explained that they decided to black up to recognize the dance's Tundique origins, but that the open-ended nature of carnival performances enable participants to incorporate other traditions.[78] When I inquired about the watermelon man, they claimed it was the idea of one of the participants, and they decided to keep the figure in special performances of the dance. Until recently, my questions about the association of blackness with the watermelon and whether there was a historical relationship between black people and watermelons in Peru remained unanswered. My search for a historical referent for a black man with his watermelon initially yielded nothing. But in 2020, Afro-Peruvian feminists decried early associations of black women with watermelons in the poetry, published in the 1940s, of the iconic Peruvian feminist Blanco Varela. These feminists and scholars insist that US minstrel archetypes circulating in Peru and Latin America influenced these depictions.[79]

The ongoing recognition of this hemispheric history suggests that the blackface figure with a watermelon is a riff off the US minstrel Sambo. Indeed, theorist Miguel Becerra has noted how the arrival of minstrel archetypes in Peru impacted representations of black people in cartoons in the 1950s and had a lasting influence on representations of Afro-Peruvians in popular culture.[80] Sambos Illimani's incorporation of the watermelon man demonstrates how indigenous blackface traditions have absorbed and integrated the efficacious tropes of blackness from the Global South and North to sell in the global marketplace. Their performance exemplifies the encounter of performative idioms within the network of hemispheric blackface. It recycles tropes from different coordinates of the hemisphere, blending two Sambos from the Americas: the Latin American zambo, an intermediate racial archetype, and the infantile US minstrel Sambo buffoon who carries a watermelon. In this performance, the Latin American zambo signifies on the US minstrel Sambo archetype. In this act of double surrogation, the US minstrel Sambo and the Latin American zambo stand in for each other, and the audience reads two hemispheric archetypes through a prismatic field of signification.[81]

Hemispheric blackface is a site of racial doubles where spectators may interpret the representation of blackness in one blackface tradition through the valence of another. In these moments, the specific historical context of a given representation will be lost, but the racial sign of blackness will remain legible to the audience. Its legibility is grounded not only in the shared tropes of blackness, but in their representation of the enslaved body, they also underscore a shared hemispheric history of black enslavement and the fictional racial imaginaries of the slave past it has produced. The Sambo archetype of the US blackface minstrel tradition is the floating signifier of another tradition of historical racial invention. It is the symbol of a slave past and an economy of popular racial memory built on racist fiction and fantasy. This racial double points to not only the embeddedness of Sambos Illimani's performance in hemispheric economies of representation, but it also exemplifies a moment of collision of the different imaginations of the slave past that circulate and make themselves present in a given locale. The question at hand, however, is not "Which Sambo is this?" but how is this act of hemispheric doubling producing meaning about blackness in Sambos Illimani's performance?

Since the Danza de Caporales is a power fantasy, Sambos stages a scene where power is constituted through racial subjugation. In self-identifying as sambos, the performers are authorized to live out fantasies about blackness and its relationship to slavery. While the performers masquerade under the auspices of a racially ambiguous figure, blackface operates as a differentiating marker between the enslaved black body or the black buffoon and the racially unmarked slave driver or caporal. So, though everyone proclaims to be "part black" or to be "zambos," in the performance, blackface sets up a racial hierarchy by way of marking a visible power imbalance between differentially racialized subjects in the performance. For even if they were all sambos, the power fantasy being enacted by both the performers and the tourist audience relies on a scene of consensual subjugation whereby black subjects are complicit in their own oppression either as slave drivers or as happy dancing slaves. Indeed, the presentation of the black buffoon wildly eating his watermelon alongside happy, dancing slaves enables performers and the audience to collectively imagine black subjects as content in their own subjugation.

Even with slavery in the backdrop, the black buffoon is impervious to his own pain and engaged in unadulterated fun. When the performer described the black subject as a "negrito loco," or a crazy little black, he rendered blackness as a crazy child who is endearing but ultimately different. His difference lies in his purported craziness, his infantilism, and his capacity to operate outside normative models of behavior. Moreover, if black subjects are imagined as invisible in Peru, then they become visible only to be fixed within the idiom of servitude and complicit in their own oppression. This performance also captures the paradoxes of investing a scene of antiblack violence with humor. For in this performance, the spectacle of black enslavement becomes "funny," a mere object of entertainment for a global audience. While it is certainly common in Andean performance traditions to represent black enslavement through masking or the donning of chains, and to do so humorously, my contention is that unlike other dances, the Danza de Caporales is designed to *celebrate* the agent of violent oppression. In this instance, racial domination is the apparatus through which the caporal's power is enacted and through which the dance praises its central protagonist.

But subjection, as a domain of racial enjoyment, also mediates the specter of queer desire in Sambos performance. The black buffoon with his watermelon represents an infantile, childlike black body and a desexualized masculinity. His desexualization functions as a counterpoint to the caporal's expression of masculine prowess, athleticism, and virility. The black buffoon thus not only serves as the object of racial subjugation, but he is also the instrument through which the caporal's masculine power is consolidated. This is salient because the caporal must also contend with the presence of the machita, a figure of female masculinity. The machita destabilizes the gendered norms that are associated with the Danza de Caporales, and she also troubles the expression of heterosexual desire of the dance. That she participates in the flirtatious call and response between the caporal and femme caporala in Sambos Illimani's performance, for example, is salient because it creates a space for the expression of queer desire in a performance traditionally scripted in patriarchal and heteronormative terms. In Sambos Illimani's performance, when the caporales and machitas shout or bark, the caporalas respond flirtatiously with high-pitched screams, shaking their hips and delicately moving their legs to and fro. The normative flirtatious script between the caporal and caporala is disrupted by the figure of the machita, who represents female masculinity or the queering of the macho man.

The machita's participation in the flirtatious call and response with the caporala creates a triangulation of desire in the performance among the caporal, the machita, and the caporala. For she, like the caporal, dances as an expression of her own virility and/or desire for the caporala. The machita raises the specter of queer desire between the "tomboy" or butch woman and the femme caporal, undermining any notion that the dance is merely an expression of patriarchal power and heterosexual desire. Far from being a passive participant, the caporala as femme figure of the dance engages in a flirtatious game with both the male caporal and the queer machita. The Danza de Caporales, therefore, makes space for the articulation of queer desire in a dance traditionally imagined as merely a heteronormative celebration of masculine virility.

The enslaved black body, therefore, appears as a mediating force amid the shifting gendered and sexual dynamics of dance. In the context of Sambos Illimani's performance, the machita is both a symbol of queer gender performance and a zambo acting as an agent of oppression in relation to the conspicuously black bodies in the performance. The machitas all dance with whips in their hands and act as queer enforcers of racial domination over the blackface characters in the performance. The placement of the male caporal alongside the machita means that, in Sambos Illimani's performance, the caporal's power becomes contingent on the interplay of expressions of racial power and queer desire. The machita's queering destabilizes the power that ordinarily resides in the caporal's heteronormative masculinity, but power is restabilized and affirmed through the subjugation of an enslaved black body and the buffoonery of the blackface character with his watermelon. He is a counterpoint to the expression of masculine prowess, athleticism, and virility of the caporal and the machita alike.

Blackface, functioning as the sign of the enslaved black body and the black buffoon, is the recuperative power force where hierarchies of gender are unsettled and redefined. It animates and shores up racial power in the face of gender trouble, queer desire, and the potential threat to heteronormative power. In hemispheric blackface, the tropes of blackness and masculinity are open-ended in nature and acts of impersonation shore up the racial and gendered dynamics of power. But most importantly, the collective fictionalization of the slave past serves as a foundation for codifying and defining the sexual and gendered regimes of racial power in the present.

Staging the Slave Past and Black Subjugation

While the staging of black subjugation is central to the dynamics of racial, gendered, and sexual power within the immediate context of the performance, Sambos Illimani's enactment of slavery resonated with spectators because it also shores up collective understandings of blackness as a disappeared trope or artifact of the past in the Andean context. Since in Peruvian popular lore, black subjects are imagined as never having survived enslavement in the mines, this performance of enslavement enables the audience to revisit blackness as a trope of the colonial past. This performance is an ostensibly nostalgic one animating popular discourse among local spectators about enslavement as the foundational site for the disappearance of blackness from the Andes. The spectators live out and participate in a fantasy about the tragic tale of black disappearance, and the tale of the African slave's demise is transformed into the object of entertainment and consumption. Blackface, as tethered to the enslaved body, not only functions as an instrument for consolidating power where gendered norms are destabilized, but it also does so in ways that affirm the racial script of black invisibility in the Andes and in the national imaginary. The collective fictionalization of the slave past that takes place in these performances defines a historical position from which regimes of racial power in the present can be articulated, defined, and codified.

The racial fantasies and fictions that produce the slave past and the collective memories of them are inflected by and embedded in the representations of blackness that circulate in the hemisphere. The shared history of enslavement in the hemispheric Americas has also spawned an ecosystem of fictional racial imaginaries that circulate as entertainment and encode black subjugation as a common trope of racial enjoyment. Sambos Illimani's rendition of African enslavement and black buffoonery also resonated among the tourists sitting in the stands because it animates fantasies of enslavement among tourist spectators. For it is the shared history of enslavement, as well as its centrality to the foundation of Western modernity, that makes the spectacle of enslavement in this performance legible for the fiesta's global audience. That this history extends beyond national borders and that some blackface tropes have global weight ensure that this act of impersonation resonates widely. In tethering the blackface body to the enslaved body, Sambos Illimani's performance gestures to how the figurative possession of blackness in acts of impersonation is tied to histories of enslavement. As Saidiya Hartman declares, "The desire to don, occupy or possess blackness or the black body as a sentimental resource, and/or locus of enjoyment is both founded upon and enabled by the material relations of chattel slavery."[82] African enslavement functions as the historical ground upon which blackness is rendered available for possession. It is the history of slavery that underwrites this figurative possession of blackness at the fiesta and that connects imaginations of blackness across the hemisphere. Fantasies of black subjugation that are grounded in a slave past and the mining of blackness as a source of entertainment are neither unique nor singular to the Andes or the Peruvian national imaginary.

While Sambos Illimani's use of blackface is grounded in a larger historical tradition that predates the US blackface tradition and commemorates the history of slavery in the Andes, the cultural specificities of the tradition do not render it immune from antiblackness—a common argument of those who deploy and enjoy it. In fact, the tradition is itself the province of evolving racial fictions and fantasies, and the memories of blackness they produce are constructions that are not limited to the nation. Lurking beneath the racial scripts of mestizaje in the chapters that follow are often a set of historical fictions about the racial past that blackface brings to the surface. And because, as I argue, these acts of impersonation are vectors of cultural and racial memory, they facilitate a type of identification and sense of belonging among different publics living in the hemispheric fold.

Doing Antiblackness in the Hemispheric Fold

Blackface Performance in Miami
in the Age of Obama

In an episode of the Spanish-language program *Esta Noche Tu Night* that aired on June 19, 2009, the Cuban host Alexis Valdés welcomes the famous New York–based merengue group Grupo Oro Sólido to the show to discuss their new album *Fantasía Urbana*. After a discussion about the album with the lead singer, Afro-Dominican artist Raúl Acosta, Valdés explains that there is a compatriot from the Dominican Republic that he would like the band to meet. Valdés asks them if they know Yeyo Vargas, leader of the Unión Latinoamericana de los Partidos Obreros (ULPO; Latin American Union of Workers' Parties). "What?" the group laughs and asks in surprise. The audience cackles and laughs as Acosta repeats, "What? What is the name of the party?" Valdés says it again, more slowly, "The Latin American Union of Workers' Parties?" Acosta turns his head and exclaims, "Wow!" Valdés continues, "He is a leader. He's emerging right now. According to him, he is very related to Obama because he is a leader. He is black. He says he wants to create the link between Obama and Latinos. Let me introduce him to you... Here comes YEYYYOOO VARGAAAASS!"

The show's band breaks into song. The drummer strikes his sticks four times, and the pianists abruptly begin to play the ULPO anthem on the keyboard. The drum beats faster, marking the marching rhythm of a lively merengue beat. The back-up singers chime in and chant the ULPO's catchy, infectious anthem: "¡*Este es el partido, partido ULPO! Este es el partido, partido ULPO!*" (This is the party, the Latin American Union of Workers' Parties. This is the party, the Latin American Union of Workers' Parties!).[1] Yeyo enters the stage. Played by the white Cuban actor Carlos Marrero in blackface, Yeyo is flamboyantly dressed in an oversized bright yellow suit, a colorful green shirt, and white and black shoes.

He wears a large Afro wig that shakes as he rushes onstage with a *güiro* in hand, dancing wildly to the beat of the theme song. The studio audience roars with laughter, and it seems everyone is singing the ULPO song. The music fades as the studio audience shouts: "Yeyo! Yeyo! Yeyo!" Valdés embraces Yeyo and members of Grupo Oro Sólido before he takes a seat.

Yeyo's immediate appearance on stage is striking. Valdés introduces Yeyo as a leader of a fictional political party, a figure of black authority, and in other episodes he proclaims Yeyo an expert and "the most important Latin American politician." But as he enters, Yeyo is the symbol of fun and black buffoonery. He is the dancing, joyful black body on stage and a lighthearted entertainer. The theme song and the chants, along with his vibrant lighthearted dancing, portray a character that doubles as the embodiment of a black leader and, simultaneously, as the incarnation of stereotypical tropes of blackness and of Latinos. Shown with güiro in hand, this is a black political figure who is musical, an entertainer, the life of the party. And in interviews about his role as Yeyo, the Cuban actor and impersonator Carlos Marrero has described the character as a *loco* or a crazy person.[2] So what exactly is the function of this blackface character, and what does it mean that they conjured Yeyo precisely as President Barack Obama rose to power in 2008?

Yeyo, I argue, is conjured to negotiate the shifts in the racial politics of the two Americas (figure 2.1).[3] This figuration of blackness mediates Obama's ascendance to power as the first black president of the United States, which prompted the production of a postracial fiction in the country, and it negotiates the racial politics of Miami and the fissures of the Cuban diaspora living there. That Alexis Valdés and Carlos Marrero are Yeyo's conjurers is important because they are symbols of a younger generation of new Cuban immigrants in Miami. Obama's election marked a slow re-establishment of the relationship between the United States and Cuba, as well as a recalibration of a diasporic imaginary that, since the 1990s, had been moving away from the hallmark hardline stances of Cuban exiles living in Miami. Throughout this book, I argue that acts of racial conjuring mediate shifts in racial formation and moments of new political articulation. In this chapter, impersonation mediates the hemispheric politics of the two Americas—specifically Cuba and the United States—and surpasses national differences. This illustrates the importance of thinking with and across national silos for discerning the multiple workings of blackface performance and its relationship to nationalist fictions and discourses of postracialism in the hemispheric fold.

2.1 Yeyo Vargas on *Esta Noche Tu Night*. Video still, Carlos Marrero, YouTube, May 7, 2013.

Esta Noche Tu Night was a late-night variety and comedy show produced in Miami. It debuted in 2007 on MegaTv, a Spanish-language television station that specifically caters to Latin American immigrants and diasporic communities based in the United States. MegaTv forms part of Spanish Broadcasting Inc. (SBS)—one of the largest minority-owned companies in the United States dedicated to Spanish-language programming. Grounded in Cuba's exile imaginary, SBS was founded by father-and-son partners Raúl Alarcón Sr. and Jr. The family fled as political refugees from Cuba to New York in the 1960s. The company first found success as a radio station producing Spanish-language music in New York in the 1980s, but it has since expanded and is one of the largest media conglomerates offering Spanish-language entertainment to communities in New York, Miami, Los Angeles, San Francisco, Texas, Chicago, and Puerto Rico. MegaTv is one of the major Spanish-language television stations in South Florida, and its presence is rivaled by the Argentine-owned station AméricaTeVé.

Esta Noche Tu Night was broadcast on DirectTV through the company's satellite and cable services. From 2008 to 2012, the show aired Monday to Friday at 9 or 10 p.m. in South Florida. The show's format is typical of late-night television programming. It opened with a stand-up performance or monologue by Valdés or comedic sketches by one or more rotating comedic characters, followed by an interview segment with guests and performances by invited artists. The producers marketed *Esta Noche Tu Night* to Spanish-speaking adult audiences over the age of fifty.[4] This niche audience is distinct from younger bilingual, first-generation American audiences in the United States who are likely to consume more English-language television than do the older Spanish-speaking audiences who migrated to the United States.[5] The show, like other Spanish-language programs produced in South Florida, also circulated in Cuba through *el paquete semanal*—a weekly package sold by local vendors in Cuba that includes US TV shows, Hollywood blockbusters, YouTube videos, and programming from Cubans in the diaspora.[6] Many Cubans download the package on thumb drives, computers, and the like, and Valdés is a very well-known comedian in Cuba. Television thus operates within a larger "Caribbean mediascape" that transcends national borders and creates an echo chamber for images of blackness circulating in the hemispheric fold.[7] Yeyo's place in Miami, a geographic site of encounter par excellence, perfectly encapsulates the transnational flow and collision of performance practices and cultural artifacts in an interconnected hemispheric network.

More importantly, as I contextualize in this chapter, Yeyo's function and meaning are conditioned by the social and racial politics of the Cuban diaspora in Miami, a hemispheric city that has historically served as a bastion of the Latin American Right, stronghold of the Republican Party, and the capital of Cuban whiteness. This enclave had to contend with Obama's ascendance to the presidency of the United States in 2008, along with his administration's relaxation of restrictions toward Cuba that had been the hallmark of US foreign policy with Cuba. Furthermore, the arrival of Cubans who grew up under the revolution has occasioned a shift away from the exilic hardline stances for which the diaspora in Miami was known. I suggest that through his lampooning of a black leader, Yeyo mediates the demographic shifts, generational tensions, and conflicting political orientations toward the revolution among older Cuban exiles and younger Cuban immigrants that these political changes have spawned. Humor and Cuba's ludic traditions serve as the instrument for wrestling with and uniting the diaspora amid a moment of political articulation.

Despite being coded as Afro-Dominican, Yeyo doubles as a negrito from Cuba's teatro bufo tradition. Heralded as the iconic figure of Cuban national theater, the negrito is a figure of diasporic and nationalist investment who animates a set of nationalist fictions, cultural memories, and facilitates identification among various sectors of the Cuban diaspora, while it also reconsolidates the hegemony of Cuban whiteness. While I underscore Yeyo's cultural significance as a negrito of Cuba's bufo tradition, I also go on to explain how his place in Miami, a hemispheric city, highlights the limitations of the nation as a discrete category for discerning the workings of blackface. Yeyo, along with other characters on the show, taps into various registers of antiblackness that are at once local and transnational. Scholars have written about Miami as a transnational field, and I further suggest that the city is an example of the hemispheric fold—a place of encounter for the geopolitical and racial histories, performance traditions, and registers of antiblackness of the two Americas.

Yeyo highlights the role of *doing antiblackness* in forging a sense of diasporic belonging in the hemispheric fold. Throughout the chapter, I locate Yeyo and doing antiblackness more broadly within larger ludic genealogies of Cuba and the diaspora: *choteo*, teatro bufo before the revolution and during the Special Period, exilic humor and histories of blackface performance in Miami, and the emergence of Obama impersonators during Obama's rise to power. Doing antiblackness refers to the whole gamut of racial practices in a comedic space, from the conjuring and enactment of racial stereotypes through the characters on stage to the social ritual of laughter and its consumption by the exile audiences at home. The "doing" refers to the active participation and gestures of social sanctioning by performers and audiences that are produced through the call and response taking place on stage. As I show here, Yeyo enables people from all racial backgrounds on the show to participate in doing antiblackness. While doing antiblackness is hardly unique to a comedic space, I seek to discern how interacting with this blackface character enables people to do antiblackness in ways that paper over the fissures of the Cuban diaspora and to define or recalibrate racial hierarchies in Miami amid Obama's emergence as the first black president.

Furthermore, Yeyo is another type of hemispheric double akin to the zambo/sambo examined at the Andean fiesta in Peru in chapter 1. Understood within the complexities of the hemispheric fold, I trace the multiple racial fantasies and significations that cohere around this figuration of blackness. I also attend to the polyvocal nature of this racial caricature, delineating his capacity to speak through multiple traditions and temporalities and therefore be legible to hemispheric audiences. This multiplicity is important, for he mediates two repeating nationalist fictions: Cuba's nationalist discourses of racial fraternity, and US postracial fiction occasioned by Obama's election as the first black president of the country. Despite its history of de jure segregation, Obama's rise led to the circulation of a postracial fantasy that the fraught history had been overcome. For the first time in recent history, the repeating nationalist fiction emerged in the United States. Hemispheric blackface therefore attends to the role of impersonation in mediating versions of postracialism in the two Americas.

Doing antiblackness is a ludic ritual that transcends the nation and, instead, facilitates an integration into the racial hierarchies of the hemispheric fold. Where other studies of Yeyo have centered around his function within the Cuban diaspora, I wield this hemispheric frame to show how this figuration of blackness enables the Cuban enclave to orient itself toward the different formations of whiteness across Latin American and Caribbean immigrant groups in Miami and to respond to political shifts in Latin America.[8] Doing antiblackness is how subjection, as a domain of racial enjoyment, is consolidated regardless of the political, national, and social differences of the conjurers and spectators. Yeyo is part of a longstanding tradition of using the ludic to forge diasporic identification, to consolidate formations of a transnational Cuban whiteness, and also to forge alliance across different immigrant enclaves in Miami. Through the character of Yeyo, we see how hemispheric blackface is constituted by moments where acts of racial conjuring mediate an encounter of structures of racial formation in the two Americas.

Cuban Whiteness in the Hemispheric Fold: Exile Imaginaries and Racial Politics in Miami

Since its founding, theorists have described Miami as "the city of the future," "the magic city," and "the Harlem of the Hemisphere"; I would add, it is the exemplar of the hemispheric fold.[9] Located in Florida, "the fork between two hemispheric Americas," Miami has been completely transformed by the major historical events of the twentieth century for the two Americas: the Cuban revolution, the fight against Jim Crow, the 1968 race riots in Liberty City, the Nicaraguan Sandinista revolution in 1979, the 1980 race riots, the 1980 Haitian and Cuban Mariel boatlifts, and the *balsero* crisis in the 1990s.[10] A truly international city, 93 percent of its population is foreign.[11] As symbol of the hemispheric fold, it is a geographic space in the hemispheric Americas where competing processes of racial formation coexist and at times collide, where one feels and lives in real time the social, economic, and political ramifications of the US imperial project and its foreign policies in Latin America and the Caribbean: the influx of refugees, exiles, and migrants—and its resulting reconfiguration of bodies, languages, and space. Miami is a contact zone, a busy intersection where multiple registers of antiblackness from the two Americas fold into and rub up against one another and coexist within the distinct nationalist silos of immigrant communities.[12] The racial politics of its residents therefore operate through a multivalent orientation; they position themselves in relation to the racial hierarchies of the United States and their diasporic communities by reproducing the systems of racial stratification of their countries of origin in Miami. They also orient themselves in relation to other immigrant groups in the city and to the geopolitics of US foreign policy in their countries of origin.

This multiple orientation is crucial for understanding the racial politics of Miami's Cuban enclave, which has long enjoyed hegemonic status in the city. While this is now rapidly changing, the Cuban enclave's racial ideologies have been historically grounded in an antiassimilationist paradigm and rejection of US racial categories. Fidel Castro's rise to power in 1959 fundamentally altered the social and political landscape of Cuba and of Miami. In earlier waves, these immigrant demographics played a crucial role in making Miami a site of "acculturation in reverse" by infusing foreign customs and languages into the native population.[13] Following multiple waves of migration and immigration policies that granted Cubans a fast path to citizenship and government assistance for resettlement, access to capital, job-placement assistance, English-language training, housing assistance, and a lack of immigration-quota restrictions, the Cuban ethnic enclave emerged as one of the strongest and most politically significant groups in South Florida.[14] White Cubans constituted the majority of Cuban exiles from the early waves because the racial hierarchies of prerevolutionary Cuba granted them more social and economic access, and they had larger familial networks in the United States than their Afro-Cuban counterparts.[15] This ultimately proved favorable for US refugee policy. Upon arrival to Miami, Cubans slowly became a reliable voting bloc of the Republican Party. White Cuban immigrants quickly usurped the hegemonic position of Miami's Anglo-white native population and ascended to the throne of racial power in the city. In the decades after the first wave of immigration in 1959, Miami was transformed into the "capital of Cuban whiteness."[16] By 2010, Cubans constituted 57 percent of Miami's local population.[17]

But acculturation in reverse is only one facet of the larger antiassimilation paradigms that underwrite Cuban whiteness in the hemispheric fold.

Cuban whiteness in Miami has historically differed from Anglo-whiteness in its emphasis on an exilic experience of "forced departure and the fantasy of return."[18] Nevertheless, Cuban whiteness in the city is grounded in multiple regimes of antiblackness in the hemispheric fold. Upon their arrival in 1959, white Cubans built on Miami's preexisting structures of antiblackness that were typical of the Deep South: Jim Crow segregation, a vibrant and active Ku Klux Klan whose members dominated Miami's police force, housing segregation, racial zoning, and so on.[19] White Cubans often served as agents of antiblackness, and some joined Miami's police force.[20] Although white Cubans faced discrimination from Anglo-white Miamians who were resentful of the perceived Cuban takeover of their city, as evidenced by the launch of English-only campaigns, white Cubans distanced themselves from African Americans.[21]

Moreover, white Cubans also wielded racial power over their Afro-Cuban counterparts who, upon their arrival to Florida in the 1960s, were relocated from Miami to the Northeast, especially New York. Afro-Cuban experiences of antiblack racism from US officials and white Cubans created formidable obstacles to their resettlement in Miami: they faced widespread discrimination from the police, in housing, and in the workplace from fellow white Cubans.[22] Furthermore, the Cuban enclave clung to the notion of a racially democratic or race-neutral society through concepts of *fraternidad racial* (racial fraternity) that celebrated a colorblind conception of Cubanness that rendered Afro-Cubans and the racism they faced from their white counterparts invisible.[23] Many Afro-Cuban exiles lived on the margins of Cuban enclaves and moved into the historically black neighborhoods in Miami.[24] The nationalist fiction of racial fraternity has been foundational to both the enactment and disavowal of racial power within the Cuban diaspora in Miami. Cuban whiteness in Miami is a deeply hemispheric position that distinguishes itself from US-Anglo ideals of whiteness while grounding itself in structures of antiblackness against African Americans, Afro-Cubans, and other black people in the city.

Indeed, Cuban whiteness occupies a hegemonic position in the city, but its racial politics are oriented toward and overlap with broader notions of Caribbean blackness and whiteness in Miami that are inflected by other Latin American and Caribbean immigrant communities. Cuban whiteness is also aligned with the newly emerging white Latin American enclaves of economic and political power of Venezuelan, Colombian, and Argentine immigrants to the city. These alliances have led to what Donette Francis and Allison Harris refer to as practices of "hemispheric creole whiteness," which reject "the assimilation into the US-national Anglo model of becoming American and maintain connections to centers of power in Latin America and the Caribbean."[25] Like Venezuelan, Colombian, and Argentine whiteness in Miami, Cuban whiteness is a transnational formation that continues to be tethered to structures of racial, economic, social, and political power on the island. In real terms, these look like the economic advantages that white Cubans in the diaspora bestow upon their relatives on the island through remittances and financial support, for example, to local businesses or for living costs.[26] Hemispheric creole whiteness also emphasizes the place of Cuban whiteness within larger transnational networks of white supremacy lurking beneath celebrations of racial fluidity, hybridity, and creoleness in the hemispheric fold.

US refugee and immigration policies have only bolstered the hegemonic power of white Spanish-speaking immigrant enclaves, because other racialized immigrant groups like Nicaraguans and Haitians encountered far more hostile immigration policies.[27] Haitians, for example, frequently faced accelerated deportation proceedings, were subject to torture and imprisonment, stigmatized as vectors of disease, and pejoratively dismissed as "boat people."[28] In Miami's racial landscape, the black immigrant and Afro-Caribbeanness are symbols of abjection. Grounded in a shared hemispheric history of slavery, distinct and overlapping registers of antiblackness in the hemispheric fold exceed the borders of a single nation. And yet these registers of antiblackness are often disavowed because Miami's racial politics are heavily shaped by US-Anglo race structures and Latin American discourses of mestizaje and myths of racial democracy.[29] Within the hemispheric fold, distinct modalities of a repeating postracial fiction and their concomitant celebrations of racial mixture and national identity proliferate. Since Spanish-speaking immigrants constitute the majority, the terms *Hispanic* or *Latino* are virtually meaningless.[30] Latin American–born immigrants and their descendants tend to overwhelmingly identify either as white or according to their nationality on censuses.[31] For most Latin American immigrants, a claim to a national identity rather than a racial one erases and silences hierarchies of race in Miami.

This embrace of the national is crucial to the anti–Anglo assimilationist paradigms that have defined the racial politics of Latin American and Caribbean immigrants in Miami. As an exemplar of the hemispheric fold, Miami not only represents a site where distinct registers of antiblackness coexist and collide, but also these structures operate in tandem with several nationalist fictions that obfuscate the structural power of race in the city. In this context, acts of hemispheric blackface—the conceptual frame for instances where acts of impersonation rub up against nationalist structures of racial silence—thus negotiate the particularities of Cuban whiteness and multiple modalities of a nationalist fiction circulating in the hemispheric fold.

Blackface is also mediating major demographic and political changes that have transformed the Cuban enclave in Miami. In the decades prior to Obama's election, the intraracial tensions of the enclave had been amplified, first when a more racially diverse group of Cuban exiles known as *marielitos* arrived in the 1980s, a moment seen as the "blackening of Cuban America."[32] Castro labeled this wave of Cuban migrants he had released from prisons and mental hospitals *escoria* (scum, dregs), the US media portrayed them as social deviants and criminals, and they were "loathed as [a] timeless infestation" in Miami.[33] When these exiles arrived, they had less access to state assistance than previous Cuban immigrants, which would have served as a cushion from racism. So unwelcome were they that the popular expressions of *Cuba de ayer* (Cuba of yesterday), which expressed the nostalgia and longing for Cuba's prerevolutionary time, was quickly accompanied by reminiscences of *Miami de ayer* (Miami of yesterday)—nostalgia for a white Cuban exile imaginary that predated the arrival of the marielitos in Miami.[34] The second transformation of the enclave took place during the balsero crisis of 1994, wherein some 30,000 Cubans came to Miami on makeshift rafts from Cuba, fleeing the economic crisis and hardships in Cuba during the Special Period.[35] To mitigate the crisis and the rapid influx of immigrants, the United States and Cuba agreed to a set of provisions that allowed some 20,000 Cubans to migrate to the United States. In 1994 and 1995, more Cubans arrived than had come during the first freedom fights, and for the first time ever, Cuban exiles of the prerevolutionary era living in Miami were outnumbered by those who grew up under the revolution.[36]

These "New Cubans" differ from the older generations of Cuban exiles and are more similar to other Latin American immigrants in Miami who migrate to the United States for economic reasons.[37] They are less likely to support the embargo, are often in favor of strengthening relations with Cuba, maintain kinship ties on the island, send remittances frequently, and will even send their children to Cuba for the summer.[38] As has always been the case, Miami Cubans of the earlier waves view new Cubans who grew up under the revolution as too tainted by communism, "less authentically Cuban," and frequently demanded they prove their anti-Castro credentials. The pejorative moniker *balsero* not only refers to people who came on improvised rafts, but it also connotes a presumed unwillingness to assimilate or "shake off" a communist upbringing.[39] While the exilic identity and its concomitant associations with a right-wing political ideology, Republican politics, and celebrations of a prerevolutionary Cuba as the ideal may apply to Cubans in Miami who arrived pre-1980s, the post-1990 generations are far more politically diverse and increasingly removed from both the hardline political stances that have defined the relationship between Cuba and its diaspora in Miami, and from a prerevolutionary Cuban society. These political differences regarding how the United States ought to relate to Cuba were the central bone of contention among members of the diaspora when Obama came to power in 2009. To account for these complexities and tensions, I limit the term "exile" to refer to those who came before the 1980s and privilege "Cuban diaspora" as an umbrella term that includes both the earlier generations and those arriving in Miami from the 1990s onward. These tensions do not, however, undermine the hegemony of Cuban whiteness in the city. Only 4 percent of South Florida's Cuban population identifies as black, so the core audience of *Esta Noche Tu Night* remains overwhelmingly white.[40] Yeyo is thus conjured to mediate these political and generational differences within the Cuban enclave, the shifting definitions of *cubanía* after 1994, and to re-consolidate the hegemony of Cuban whiteness amid a variety of political and demographic changes.

The age of Obama refers to the cultivation of the postracial fiction in the United States during and after Obama's ascendance to the presidency. His association with aspirations of a postracial future began with his speech at the 2004 Democratic National Convention where he famously declared "There's not a black America and white America and Latino America and Asian America; there's the United States of America." Like José Martí, Norman Manley, Eric Williams, and other thinkers, Obama rejected the racial divisions and silos of the nation and instead appealed to a unifying, universal national identity to transcend the problem of race. This speech proved foundational to his image as the symbol and harbinger of a postracial nation. The media immediately touted him as a potential future presidential candidate and antidote to racial division.[41] By 2008, when he was the official presidential nominee of the Democratic Party, this discursive postracial frenzy surrounding his meteoric rise only increased. While Obama explicitly distanced himself from proclamations that his candidacy solved racial division, his race-neutral language, malleable campaign slogan of "Hope and Change," and international personal story rendered him the perfect screen on which the media and the nation could project a set of postracial dreams.[42] Though short-lived, the veneration of Obama as the mixed-raced protagonist of the media-produced postracial frenzy represents the type of repeating nationalist fictions that I insist have defined processes of racial formation in the hemispheric Americas. Despite the emergence of the new nationalist fiction, doing antiblackness on *Esta Noche Tu Night* formed part of what scholars actually noted to be the increase in explicit expressions of antiblackness across the country as Obama rose to power.[43] That Yeyo was conjured as an inept black leader in 2008 until early in Obama's second term shows how blackface mediates both enduring and emerging nationalist fictions of both Cuba and the United States.

Moreover, the age of Obama also denotes the reconfiguration of a set of geopolitical relationships in the hemispheric Americas. Obama's rise to power coincided with what the US media dubbed "the Pink Tide"—the emergence of a bloc of progressive leftist leadership in Latin America.[44] During the first decade of the twenty-first century, Latin Americans voted for a set of socialist democratic and progressive governments ranging from the authoritarian populism of Hugo Chávez in Venezuela to the horizontal electoral processes that produced Evo Morales, the first indigenous president of Bolivia, to the radical leftism of Uruguayan president José Mujica.[45] The anti-Obama right wing inaccurately touted Obama as a socialist and Marxist leader, and so his election consolidated the Right's perception of the new rise of social democratic governance in the hemispheric Americas. In quotidian life in Miami, Obama was pejoratively referred to as *el negro comunista* (the black communist)—a symbol of an emergent Left in the hemispheric Americas. This perception was reinforced when Obama and Raúl Castro announced the reopening of relations in 2014 and lifted travel restrictions. But from the early years of his administration, Obama had already encouraged "people to people" travel and cultural exchange with the island. By 2013, his administration granted five-year visas with multiple entries to Cuban nationals visiting family or for personal and medical travel, and this coincided with the Cuban government's suspension of the unpopular *tarjeta blanca* (exit visa), which allowed Cubans to leave the island more freely.[46] The lifting of these restrictions completely transformed popular culture in Miami and certainly in Cuba. The moment marked a turn away from the hardline exilic stances in the city and occasioned a far more porous relationship between those on the island and in Miami. Amid the rise of a hemispheric left, Obama's changes exacerbated divisions between a diasporic community that had different political orientations toward Cuba.

The Obama administration reconfigured the geopolitical relationship between the United States and Cuba, between Cubans on the island and in the diaspora, and the transnational flow of popular culture. Indeed, these policy changes also had a profound impact on the comedy scene. Comedians residing in Cuba were now able to work and earn money in Miami, and they flooded the city in 2009. Whereas in the 1990s, Cuban artists based in Cuba who occasionally performed in Miami were greeted with vociferous protests from those in the city and were granted very little airtime on television and radio in Miami, from 2009 onward this changed.[47] When the famous actor Osvaldo Doimeadiós came to Miami in 2010 to perform stand-up comedy and to fill in as host of *Esta Noche Tu Night*, it was the first time that an artist residing in Cuba hosted a local TV program in Miami.[48] Despite minor grumblings in the press, he was well received by TV audiences, and the city's entertainment industry took note. They decided to make use of the potential profitability of tapping into the transnational network of Cuban entertainment on the island and in the diaspora.

Both Alexis Valdés and Carlos Marrero—Yeyo's conjurers—belong to the generation of new Cubans who came of age under the revolution and moved to Miami in the 1990s. Their success in Miami operates within the context of policy changes and the burgeoning transnational expansion of the city's cultural industry that caters to those in the diaspora and on the island. The antiblackness they animated on the show therefore spoke to a transnational whiteness and transcended the diverse constellations of racial power in the hemispheric fold. The ludic ritual they performed encouraged a sense of belonging amid the geopolitical changes in the hemispheric fold as well as the emergence of a postracial fiction in the age of Obama, and within a fractured Cuban diasporic community. I go on to show how subjection, as a domain of racial enjoyment, papered over a set of internal fissures amid the political changes of the time.

Esta Noche Tu Night: Choteo, the Ludic, and Cuban Whiteness

Esta Noche Tu Night belongs to a larger comedic tradition of Cubans in Miami who have used the ludic to dramatize the Cuban diasporic condition, address the cultural differences between the United States and Cuba, invoke nostalgia, preserve cultural memory, and comment on contemporary life in Cuba.[49] Comedic practices like those on the show belong to Cuba's broader, culturally specific tradition of choteo. In his influential essay *Indagación de choteo*, which was first delivered as a lecture in 1927 and then published in 1928, Jorge Mañach explains choteo is a distinctly Cuban form of irreverent humor that mocks authority. Choteo entails a refusal to take things seriously. It is the "enemy of order," a negation of hierarchy, and its power lies in its "leveling tendencies," which balance the uneven power hierarchies of a given context.[50] Mañach theorizes choteo in relation to the crisis of a bourgeois high culture and as part of a larger project wherein intellectuals sought to define Cubanness and to articulate the idiosyncrasies of a Cuban national identity soon after the country gained independence.[51] As a distinctive Cuban form of mockery and irreverence, choteo is frequently invoked in studies of Cuban cultural production at home and in the diaspora.[52] Irreverence, humor, and mockery have been integral to the psychic functions of the exilic generation for articulating a sociopolitical space, fortifying a Cuban exile identity defined as anticommunist, preserving cultural tradition, and resisting assimilationist paradigms of the US.[53] This was exemplified in the comedic work of Cuba's most famous comedian of the 1960s, 70, and 80s, Álvarez Guedes, and has continued in the humor of contemporary Cuban comedians like Alexis Valdés, Robertico Riverón, Zulema Cruz, and others.

Esta Noche Tu Night functions as a space of ludic sociality for Cubans living in the diaspora, where culturally specific forms of play unify the Cuban community. In what is the most extensive study of Cuban humor or *diversión* in Miami from the 1960s to the 2010s, Albert Laguna brilliantly explicates the role of the ludic for Cubans in the diaspora in theorizing their own experiences, engaging the geopolitical realities in the hemisphere, unifying a divided Cuban enclave, and consolidating a heteronormative Cuban whiteness. This is true for the show, which was both a meeting ground for Cuban artists and a launching pad for the careers of many upcoming comedians from the Caribbean who were seeking to establish themselves in the TV, theatre, and film scenes in Miami. But the orchestration of the space as a site of Cuban signification relied heavily on its host, Alexis Valdés. It is important that Valdés serves as host, main writer, and producer of *Esta Noche Tu Night* because of his popularity on the island and in the diaspora. An international and cosmopolitan figure, Valdés enjoyed a successful acting career in Cuba for ten years before pursuing a stand-up comedy and theatre career in Spain. He moved to Miami in 2001, where he served as host of *El show de Alexis Valdés* and *Seguro que Yes*. He worked at AméricaTeVé from 2005 to 2007 until he joined MegaTv in early 2008 and promptly renamed his show *Esta Noche Tu Night*. Valdés's cosmopolitanism and popularity in Cuba appealed to Cuban audiences and to a larger pan–Latin American, urban, international audience as well as other Latin American exile imaginaries and immigrant groups in South Florida.

Valdés is particularly well known in South Florida for his popular comedic persona, Cristinito Hernández. Inspired by his character Bandurria, who was popular in Cuba, Cristinito is a fool who thinks he is a genius and regularly offers philosophical musings on life. Valdés has made cameos as Cristinito on other Spanish-language television programs in South Florida and sometimes did monologues as Cristinito on *Esta Noche Tu Night*. Cristinito, Yeyo, and many of the comedic characters on the show exhibited the trademark features of Valdés's comedic style, which relies on malapropisms, buffoonery, non sequiturs, and humorous musical performances. Valdés was also known in South Florida for his celebrated theatre show, a trilogy titled *Oficialmente Gay* (2014), about a macho man who decides to pass as gay to get a job at a hotel in Cuba, but who is ultimately seeking to escape the island for the United States through the cultural-exchange program. In general, Valdés's humor caters to the diasporic condition by engaging questions of hardship, escapism, and truth-telling about life under the dictatorship.

As the host of *Esta Noche Tu Night*, Valdés also wielded humor for cultural preservation. He commemorated important events in Cuban history such as Grito de Baire (Cuban independence from Spain) and el Día de la Cultura Cubana (Day of Cuban Culture). In doing so, he turned the show into a venue of cultural memory for people living in the diaspora. Valdés's individual monologues addressed the realities of living away from home, and he used humor to stage the complex affective relationship the diasporic has in relation to home. In one episode, Cristinito laments that he was not included in Cuba's official celebrations for el Día de la Cultura Cubana, proclaiming that what he has contributed (to Cuban culture) would not fit in an encyclopedia. The monologue begins as a self-deprecating mockery of Cristinito's delusions of grandeur, but it becomes a general meditation on the lack of recognition of the contributions of artists living outside Cuba. He insists that most artists have left Cuba, and that those who remain do so for their families, for their roots, and "for their own good!"[54] Cristinito proclaims, "There are more artists outside than inside Cuba. There is Arturo Sandoval, Papito Rivera, Willy Chiringuito, Gloria Estrella.... Are you going to tell me that Sarita is not a part of Cuban culture because she lives in Miami Beach?" He ends the monologue by calling for a celebration of global culture instead of Cuban culture.

Cristinito's monologue is an expression of diasporic blues—the feelings of exclusion or missing out from the events of home. His lament of the lack of national recognition for diasporic artists is a meditation on questions of belonging and inclusion for a diasporic subject living abroad. It also affirms the way Cuban culture, as produced in the diaspora, is either ignored or dismissed as a failed copy of an authentic national original.[55] This lack of recognition also gestures to the way nationalist discourse conceptualizes the diaspora as "the abjected and disavowed Other to the nation."[56] For the diasporic subject lives between acceptance and rejection as well as inclusion and exclusion in relation to the national polity. Yet Cristinito's lament is also a defiant rejection of his own diasporic abjection as either not Cuban enough or as the nation's rejected other. His privileging the global over the national at the end of the monologue rejects the notion of borders as the anvil upon which imaginations of the nation rest.

As the conductor of the ludic space, Valdés wielded diasporic humor as a therapeutic device for those facing the loss and pain of exile. In his segment titled *risa terapia* (laughter therapy), Valdés and a group of comedians told *chistes cubanos* (Cuban jokes). Valdés sat in a circle alongside other popular Cuban comedians Boncó Quiñongo, "Robertico" Riverón, and Nenita on stage. As they sang together, he invited each comedian to tell a joke during the breaks in the song. Some jokes appealed to a general audience while others specifically spoke to life in Cuba. Reflecting on scarcity and poverty on the island, Valdés told a joke of two Cubans talking in a corner in a barrio: One Cuban says to the other, "*Muchacho*, the other day I was eating a steak at home. Suddenly, I look out the window, and a UFO passes by (the window)." He continues incredulously, "A flying object! It passed right in front of my house!" The other Cuban replies, "You are such a liar! A liar, *compadre*! Who is going to believe that you were eating a steak in Cuba?!"[57] The audience and comedians on stage laugh loudly. The joke uses misdirection, as one assumes that the UFO is the impossible phenomenon, but it is in fact the idea of eating a steak amid the economic hardship in Cuba that is marked as improbable. The laughter at the joke constitutes moments of diasporic identification and of communal bonding for Cuban audiences on stage and at home. Humor is also a mnemonic reserve that relies on acts of diasporic recall, a backward-looking glance that Stuart Hall writes about, to summon shared memories of home.[58] But the reference to Cuba's economic hardships and Miami's long-standing reputation as a space of opposition to the Cuban revolution suggests that the joke is both a critique of life under the dictatorship and a therapeutical device for engaging the stark economic deterioration of the island. In highlighting the failures of Castro's revolution, the joke also implicitly affirms the anti-Castro and anticommunist sentiment as one of the defining characteristics of Miami's Cuban diasporic community.

Choteo not only cemented anticommunist sentiment as a means of bolstering Cuban diasporic identity, but it also oriented the political space toward other immigrant enclaves in Miami by lampooning the emerging Latin American Left. Indeed, *Esta Noche Tu Night* corresponds to Miami's hemispheric politics as Latin American enclaves in the diaspora responded to the wave of leftist leadership in the region. The show's international cast and guests reflected the cosmopolitanism of the city, featuring a cadre of internationally renowned actors and artists from across the globe including the Mexican artist Paulo Quevedo, Cuban singer Nelson Llompart, Dominican singer Johnny Ventura, Spanish artist Enrique Iglesias, Puerto Rican singer La India, the Colombian musician Manu, and so many others. The program's targeting of politicians and famous figures across the hemispheric Americas exemplified the use of choteo to engage the relationship between the United States and Latin American countries and to critique authority figures. It featured impersonations of famous politicians, including former presidents Hugo Chávez of Venezuela, Danilo Medina of the Dominican Republic, and George Bush and Barack Obama of the United States. For example, played by the Venezuelan impersonator Gustavo Ríos, Chávez frequently sends revolutionary greetings to everyone except the United States. A mockery of Chávez's anti-imperialist rhetoric, the character frequently quips, "I hate you, Mr. Bush!" "I hate you, Snoopy! I hate you, Colonel Sanders, with your extra, extra crispy Kentucky style!"[59] These segments also frequently alluded to Chávez's close relationship with Fidel Castro, as Chávez dismissed speculation about his health by claiming he had learned his exercise regimen from Fidel. Here, choteo and its trademark irreverence and mockery of authority figures is wielded to lampoon a Latin American Left and to cement the show's relationship to Miami as the bastion of the Latin American Right. Choteo was, therefore, a site of Cuban enunciation toward the political establishments of the United States, Latin America, and even Miami. The politics of belonging in this ludic space are thus grounded in a hemispheric political sensibility that forges political alliances with other diasporic imaginaries.

But the politics of belonging, as articulated in *Esta Noche Tu Night*, are also codified along racial, sexual, and gender lines. This is in keeping with the tradition of Cuban comedy in Miami, which, as Laguna has insisted, works to consolidate a heteronormative Cuban whiteness both in the city and on the island.[60] The humor on the show generally trafficked in discourses of homophobia, misogyny, ableism, and classism, frequently making women, queers, and disabled people objects of ridicule. Yeyo shared company with an array of other characters: the queer pirate Jack "el Pájaro," Magdalena la Pelúa, Mónico Pino, José Feliciano, Elvis Conde (*el vizconde*), El Serguei "el niño de sevilla," Cristinito Hernández, and many others. At times, the characters had individual segments, or they appeared in sketches with Valdés and in interviews with guests. For my purposes here, I highlight the characters who appeared most frequently and who played key roles in determining the sexual and racial politics of the diasporic imaginary. For example, Valdés had skits with the *enfermera*—a nurse character played by the Puerto Rican actress Karelys Tosado—a scantily clad seductress who frequently carried a stethoscope around her neck and a bag of medical supplies. In her scenes, the nurse attempted to seduce Valdés and other guests on the show. She bent over provocatively in front of male guests and before the camera and often used sexual innuendos in comedic dialogues with the host. Alternately, the popular female character Magdalena la Pelúa, played by Cuban actress Judith González, was a disheveled peasant woman whose hair was frequently unkempt, had missing teeth, and who played a clueless country bumpkin or fool. These comedians' appearances both as fools and as titillating objects of desire bolstered the gendered and patriarchal dynamics of power in the show.

The humor on *Esta Noche Tu Night* also relied on discourses of homophobia in mocking the queerness of the character Jack "el Pájaro," played by the Venezuelan actor Gustavo Ríos, who claimed he was the inspiration for Johnny Depp's bombastic character Jack Sparrow in the hit movie

Pirates of the Caribbean. Jack "el Pájaro" is an effeminate and flamboyant captain of a ship who dresses like Jack Sparrow and declared himself the "manliest" man of his crew. The humor of his statement resided in the presumption that a queer man's masculinity is compromised by virtue of his sexuality. The sobriquet *el pájaro* (the bird) is a derogatory term for a gay man, making the character's queerness the butt of the joke. The show also poked fun at people with disabilities. This was exemplified by the character Mónico Pino, played by the Cuban comedian Ernesto López Pino, who appeared in different segments including one titled "El día como hoy" (On this day) that celebrated historical events. Pino's speech impediment and his constant stuttering often prevented him from clearly announcing details about the historical event, and he frequently either misused words or misstated historical facts.[61] His stutter was both the object of ridicule and the presumed sign of his lack of intelligence. As with Jack "el Pájaro," Pino's masculinity was also compromised in that his stutter rendered him stupid, undesirable, and outside the boundaries of the normative.

While Yeyo was certainly more of a protagonist, the blackface female character Mañeña played by the actor Osvaldo Doimeadiós also appeared on *Esta Noche Tu Night*. Although her scenes were filmed in the studio in Miami, Valdés usually introduced Mañeña as joining the show live from Cuba. In some ways, Mañeña was Yeyo's female double, for she, too, was a black woman with comic pretensions of erudition. She claimed to be a scientist and inventor in Cuba. Throughout the conversations, Mañeña is shown to be uneducated and clueless, begging the host for a *carta de invitación* (letter of invitation) so she can migrate to the United States. Mañeña also has an African American boyfriend in Liberty City—a predominantly black neighborhood with high levels of crime and poverty—who was frequently portrayed as a criminal. In one episode, for example, she boasts proudly that her boyfriend "se graduó ... de pro ... bay ... shon" (he graduated from probation), thinking that probation is a university.[62] Her stupidity and incompetence combined with her delusions of grandeur affirmed the "familiar trope of black femininity as incompatible with modernity," and her pairing with the African American boyfriend also reinforced stereotypical tropes of black criminality in Cuba and Miami.[63] In reproducing discourses of antiblackness that are both local and transnational, the show laid bare those overlapping registers of antiblackness organizing the hemispheric fold.

The targeting of difference across race, sexuality, gender, and ability in the show's humor underscores that choteo is not only about the leveling of unequal power relations by critiquing the political class, but it also entails the articulation and enactment of racial, sexual, and gendered hierarchies within the Cuban diaspora and the hemispheric fold. Humor dictates the politics of belonging by laying bare the conceptual registers of difference and internal borders of the diasporic community. These conceptual registers are not incidental to the sense of belonging that the show sought to cultivate; rather, they are constitutive of it. Humor thus enables acts of remembering and communal bonding; it is a therapeutic device and a means through which those in the diaspora negotiate their complex relationship to home and to cubanía; and it is an instrument for consolidating a relationship and forging political alliances with other immigrant enclaves while critiquing political establishments in the hemispheric Americas. And in this case, these ludic practices also demarcate the gendered and sexual contours of antiblackness. Yeyo, I argue, operates within the show's larger articulation of the terms of belonging and citizenship for a divided Cuban enclave navigating geopolitical changes. He is also a device that works to assuage racial anxieties by fixing the figure of the black leader within stereotypical tropes of black buffoonery.

Yeyo Vargas: Lampooning the Black Leader

Yeyo Vargas was played by the Cuban impersonator Carlos Marrero, who arrived in Miami after the balsero crisis. Marrero was born in 1971 in Matanzas, Cuba, and he moved to Miami in 1999 during the Special Period. Unlike Valdés, Marrero had no formal training in acting or theatre, but he had a childhood penchant for imitation. He got his big break in Miami by appearing on the Cuban comedy show *El Mikimbin de Miami* for playing the character El Pillín—a *pinareño* (a native of Pinar del Río) who was critical of Castro. While Marrero was temporarily denied entry to the island for playing the character, he has since become known in Miami for his impersonations on Spanish-language television of Queen Elizabeth, Donald Trump, the Pope, and other famous figures. On *Esta Noche Tu Night*, Marrero appeared as the characters El Vizconde (The Viscount) and the Russian character El Serguei "el niño de Sevilla," but Yeyo was by far Marrero's most popular character on the show. On occasion, the actor even stepped in for Valdés and hosted the show as Yeyo. Yeyo was first conjured on *Esta Noche Tu Night* during the latter part of then–presidential candidate Barack Obama's campaign in 2008, and he became a much more frequent figure on the show after Obama's inauguration. Returning to the scene at the start of this chapter, we can see how Yeyo's legitimacy as a black leader was immediately undermined.

Yeyo's proclaimed relationship to Obama was cast as the delusions of a mad buffoon. For example, after Valdés introduces Yeyo to Grupo Sólido, Yeyo's delusions quickly unravel before the spectator's eyes. Throughout the interview, Yeyo asks Valdés to tell him which camera to look at and Valdés explains that Yeyo is a novice who is unfamiliar with the protocols of being on television. As the interview progresses, Valdés confesses to Yeyo that he found it strange not to have seen him at Obama's inauguration. Yeyo insists he was there and offers to show proof of his closeness to Obama. The camera cuts to a video of the inauguration. As Obama gives his inaugural speech, Yeyo emerges in front of him with a US flag draped across his shoulder. He smiles at the camera and then laughs. His face almost blocks Obama from view. Yeyo looks the part of a thrilled fan as he excitedly points to Obama in his background. He looks to the left, and suddenly a bodyguard jumps and pushes Yeyo off screen. There is a loud noise off camera, and the audience roars with laughter yet again. Yeyo's cluelessness about TV protocols suggests that he is a ludicrous interloper. This is an inadequate political figure who suffers from delusions of grandeur, and the dialogue suggests that the audience and performers on stage know from the very outset that his proclaimed relationship to Obama is a farce.

But Yeyo's inadequacy was emphasized mostly through his speech. On the show, the character frequently deploys malapropisms, unnecessary grandiloquence, or circumlocution in his dialogs with Valdés. Yeyo had a set of trademark responses and quips to the host's questions. He typically replied, "Alexis, te voy a respondel in fragante. Primero que nadie, antes y después." ("Alexis, I am going to respond to you in flagrante. First of anyone, before and after.") Throughout the show, Yeyo frequently and comically misused words. Following the election of a new president in the Dominican Republic, Yeyo Vargas proclaimed him "el excrementísimo, el extinto: Danilo Medina" (the most excremental, the extinct Danilo Medina).[64] Yeyo's failed attempts at grandiloquence were a steady staple of comic relief during his appearances on the show. He also had a particular accent that indexed his Dominican and peasant background as he claimed himself to be *cibaeño*—of the region of Cibao in the Dominican Republic. As is typical of the Dominican accent, he pronounced his *r* as *l* or he ended the infinitive forms of Spanish verbs with a *y* instead of an *r*, which is typical of inhabitants of Cibao. In his expression of adoration for Dominican comic Jochy Santos—a guest on the show—Yeyo remarked, "Yo quisiera aprovechay de esta oportunitú de que Jochy está aquí. Y lo quiero hacey y lo quiero day hacerle en nombre de la ciudad de Miami, darle algún obsequio y ofenda . . ." (I would like to take the opportunity, since Jochy is here, to give him, in the name of the city of Miami, a gift and an offense"). When Alexis Valdés corrected him to say an "ofrenda," meaning "offering," Yeyo replied in the typical Dominican colloquialism: "¿Cómo es la vaina?" ("What is that thing?" or "How do you say that thing?").[65] The accent that betrays a rural peasant background, the misuse of Latin phrases, and the malapropisms combined with the failed attempts at grandiloquence cemented Yeyo's status as a black, uncivilized, country bumpkin with comic pretensions of erudition. Codifying Yeyo as backward, unrefined, and primitive delegitimized the notion of a black authority figure. For Miami's cosmopolitan urban audience, mocking Yeyo's rural background marked the class pretensions and hierarchies of the diasporic imaginary.

Even Yeyo's political posts and areas of expertise are questionable. Throughout the show, Yeyo is in fact constructed as a jack-of-all-trades (figure 2.2).[66] On *Esta Noche Tu Night*, his title shifted from being the right-hand man to Obama, to an adviser to Dominican president Danilo Medina, to a consultant on all issues Latino or concerning Latin America and the Caribbean. Over the years, Yeyo also acted as a salesman who came on the show to advertise his products—including a "zap" telephone that transforms gringa women into hot Latinas. Yeyo, at times, used Dominican slang, calling himself "el tigre" which refers to "brotherhood, macho sexual prowess, and street smart behavior" and by extension, conferred *tigeraje*, a brand of Dominican masculinity, on to Obama himself.[67] His titles as a consultant betray the logic of collapsing an entire region and people: Latin America and the Caribbean with US Latinos. Moreover, the shifting of designated roles indicates that his area of expertise is not clearly defined, making Yeyo a malleable figuration of blackness conjured according to the political agenda or whims of any given moment.

Yeyo's various official positions and questionable behavior also invite the question as to what exactly qualifies him for these positions. His expertise is legitimated by his being the president of his own party, but more so by his own blackness or brownness. He often affirmed that his affinity with Obama was rooted in their shared blackness, playing on the notion that simply being black, rather than being trained, is what qualifies

2.2 Yeyo Vargas at the Pentagon. Video still, LaRisa Terapia, YouTube, April 19, 2012.

one for the position. And even this is debatable, since the audience knows that this is a game of racial impersonation that renders Yeyo's blackness farcical. Trafficking the artificiality of Yeyo's blackness serves as comic relief from the anxieties of audiences facing the emergence of the first black president. Everything from Yeyo's appearance to his antics on the show, his title, his blackness, his party, and its gimmicky theme song cast doubt on his expertise, authority, and qualifications to be a leader.

This is exemplified through ULPO's iconic theme song that plays whenever Yeyo appears on the show, "Este es el partido ULPO!" The acronym, ULPO, is a play on the Spanish phrase *huele-peo*. In Cuba and other parts of the Caribbean, *huele-peo* is a derogatory term used interchangeably with *huele-culo*. A *huele-peo* is a fool who follows someone he ought not to follow. The term is used as an insult or to make fun of someone and is typically translated to mean "ass-kisser." As a black leader, the song undermines Yeyo's authority before the character even enters the stage, mocking him as a follower rather than a leader. Yeyo is perpetually fixed in a position of subordination from the moment he is conjured into the regime of representation, not advising leaders but running after or behind them. He also hinted at the term *huele-peo* not simply as an insult, but also as indexing smell. *Pedo* is the Spanish term for flatulence and *huele* is from the verb *oler*, which means to smell. That Yeyo's entrance always marks the smell of flatulence indexes stereotypes of blackness as smelly. The reference to the smell is encapsulated through the party's slogan: "Respira el cambio" (Breathe the change). Yeyo marks the undesirability of blackness through his smelliness. He marks the stupidity of blackness through his deployment of black speech. And he embodies the exotic traits of blackness as a musician, dancer, and entertainer. This is a black figure of power whose buffoonery neutralizes any potential claim blackness can now have to power and authority. He is not only a parodic figuration of black leadership, but he also positions himself as the leader Obama should aspire to be. Yeyo is the antiblack inside joke that keeps the diasporic identification among a fractured Cuban diasporic imaginary alive.

Yeyo, thus, forms part of the show's larger targeting of the political class. Choteo is being mobilized to critique a black political figure, while this lampooning of the black leader animates and consolidates racist notions of black inadequacy and ineptitude. Yeyo's speech and ideas marked blackness as stupid and deluded. His behavior fixed blackness in stereotypical tropes of black musicality. His theme song marked him as smelly and undesirable. As a stand-in for the political class and for Obama, Yeyo stymies any potential threat that the specter of the first black president of the United States could pose to Miami's Cuban diasporic imaginary.

In this sense, Yeyo's function is twofold. First, he animates the racial scripts that correspond to racial hierarchies in Miami's Cuban diaspora. Second, his shifting roles, combined with the fact that he represents black Caribbeanness and Afro-latinidad, also suggest that Yeyo is a malleable stand-in for various iterations of blackness. He is, therefore, a figure of double impersonation who represents an inferior Afro-Cubanness, while his Afro-Dominicanness is a sign of a broader Caribbean blackness from which Miami's Cuban hegemony has long sought to distance itself. But I also suggest that Yeyo is a stand-in for distinct fantasies of blackness that cater to different demographics of the Cuban enclave.

The Polyvocal Nature of Blackface:
The Negrito in Cuba and Miami

Blackface performances in Miami have rightly been theorized as a "transnational phenomenon" and "a product of multiple contested colonial forces" whose representations of blackness are mediated by "Afro-Caribbean descended representations of blackness . . . as well as the heavy colonial burdens attached to them."[68] As such, blackface performance in this city underscores the limitations of reading blackface through a US national lens and ought to be understood as the result of colonial processes. Minstrel performances in Miami from the nineteenth century onward operated alongside bufo performances and drew from caricatures of blackness from Cuba and Bahamian performance traditions alike. Blackface performances in Miami like the ones on *Esta Noche Tu Night* generate hemispheric doubles, where one figuration of blackness can stand in for another and whose presence on stage animates the multiple and disparate structures of antiblackness that emerge from a shared hemispheric history of enslavement. For Cubans in Miami who grew up with teatro bufo, Yeyo is the symbol of a cultural tradition tethered to ideals of national identity. As Elin Diamond writes of performance, "Each performance marks out a unique temporal space that nevertheless contains traces of other now-absent performances, other now-disappeared scenes. Every performance . . . embeds features of previous performances: gender conventions, racial histories, and aesthetic traditions."[69] As a negrito figure, Yeyo is a surrogate who recalls the negrito figures who preceded him, but the negrito figures that exist for the exile and the post-1990s generations of the Cuban diaspora are not the same. Attending to these differences reveal both the transnational and polytemporal dimensions of hemispheric blackface.

Yeyo Vargas must be understood within the historical tradition of teatro bufo in Cuba—a comic revue style in which blackface was a central feature.[70] Teatro bufo emerged in the 1860s precisely as Cuba sought its independence from Spain and to define its relationship to Africanness and the black slave population.[71] White criollo men used teatro bufo to mock high Spanish culture and to articulate pro-independence views.[72] In her groundbreaking book, performance studies scholar Jill Lane links teatro bufo to burgeoning discourses of mestizaje and racelessness and insists blackface performance was "the expression of *mestizaje* as a national ideology" that defined national identity that was neither white nor African but Cuban.[73] Teatro bufo introduced a series of national types to the stage including the *mulata*, the Spanish *gallego*, *chinos*, and so on, but the negrito was the signature character of the genre.[74] The negrito was initially represented by two archetypes: the *negrito bozal*—an African-born slave—and the *negrito catedrático*—a black professor with comic pretensions of erudition. Yeyo's use of flowery language combined with his aristocratic pretensions are grounded specifically in the negro catedrático archetype. The negrito was "a manifestly racist caricature of black people by white actors" that, over time, stood in for "a national sentiment whose primary attribute was a celebrated racial diversity."[75] Blackness was levied as a device and an imaginative surface upon which white creole dreams of national sovereignty and celebrations of racial fraternity could be articulated. This founding moment underscores the centrality of the negrito to the articulation of a raceless national identity and postracial future.[76] From the era of independence, practices of racial conjuring have constituted the underside of a nationalist fiction that disavowed the centrality of race to the formation of national identity. Like Sambos's performance in the previous chapter, acts of racial conjuring in Cuba were not only central to negotiating the slave past; they also were the instrument for articulating and consolidating the racial scripts of mestizaje.

Exiles from the prerevolutionary era would have grown up with noted bufo theater companies such as la Compañía de Manuel Bolaños, la Compañía de Mario Sordono, and la Compañía de Guillermo Moreno. Negrito figures were popular on television in the 1950s and 1960s.[77] In the 1950s, Enrique Arredondo, for example, was perhaps the most famous negrito star on television programs such as *Sitio Alegre, Mi Familia, El Show de Mediodía,* and the Sunday program *Revista Regalías.* During the prerevolutionary era, teatro bufo thrived amid rampant racial inequality and the structural marginalization of the Afro-Cuban populace. Furthermore, bufo plays also reproduced the racial hierarchies that were endemic to Cuban society at the time. Scholars note that Afro-Cubans were systematically denied employment in theater and were portrayed as stupid, incompetent, deceitful, and hypersexual.[78] Ethnomusicologist Robin Moore explains that blacks generally occupied the lowest position of social stratification in the plays. The negrito is often portrayed as subservient, good at singing and dancing, and at times as a hustler who tries to sleep with a light-skinned mulata.[79] For Miami's Cuban exile generation, Yeyo, the negrito, is thus the symbol of a lost prerevolutionary idyllic world and its attendant racial hierarchies that had benefited Cuba's white elite.

Castro's revolution initially rejected the negrito, but by the 1990s, it celebrated him as a symbol of national culture. When Fidel Castro came to power in 1959, he built on discourses of racelessness promulgated by José Martí to claim the revolution was fulfilling the dream of a country free of racism. Castro's regime took an official antiracist stance and proclaimed the revolution had solved Cuba's "race problem."[80] Castro's regime passed 1,500 pieces of legislation in its first three years that redistributed land, offered free health care, launched public antidiscrimination campaigns, and integrated whites-only spaces of the prerevolutionary period, including beaches, recreational facilities, and private schools.[81] The revolution's radical restructuring of Cuban society massively benefited black Cubans and simultaneously prompted the mass exodus of its white upper class—many of whom resettled in Miami.[82] The revolution's commitment to discourses of racelessness and its antiracist stance also had contradictory effects. Since the revolution claimed to have solved racism in its first three years, the state legislated an official silence on questions of race and racism. Blacks were told overnight that the racism they were experiencing no longer existed, and the regime prohibited black organizing, deeming it unnecessary and antirevolutionary.[83]

While the revolution occasioned the unprecedented ascendance of a black middle class in Cuba, it continued the long history of silencing racial dissent and casting black organizing as dangerous.[84] Blacks continued to navigate a racist culture and popular perceptions of black people as being delinquents, hypersexual, natural athletes, and musicians.[85] But according to the regime, since racial harmony had been achieved, there was no need to address race or racism in a systemic way. Instead, racism was dismissed as purely the expression of isolated, individual prejudice, and the embrace of any racial identity was deemed counter to the national project. The revolution's official stance on racelessness temporarily led to a rejection of teatro bufo, casting the genre as bourgeois entertainment of the prerevolutionary era and the emblem of a divisive racial politics that the revolution had presumably left behind. Castro's regime mandated that art and culture in Cuba operate in service of the revolution. Cuban theater was modeled on Castro's revolutionary impetus and Che Guevara's socialist *hombre nuevo* (new man). Imagined as raceless and classless, the new man quickly replaced the triad of bufo characters.[86] While teatro bufo performances initially continued in the revolution's early phase, despite protests from Afro-Cubans, it was later banned and then revamped under the Castro regime.[87]

For Cubans who arrived in Miami during the 1990s, the negrito was tethered to the decline of the socialist state, the renaissance of Afro-Cuban culture, and the erosion of the gains of racial equality made under the revolution.[88] The revolution's ban on teatro bufo in the 1970s was short-lived, and the negrito slowly reappeared on stage in the 1990s after the fall of the Soviet Union. At first, the negrito appeared clandestinely in nonbufo plays, but a full updated bufo cast replete with Afro-Cuban negrito actors in blackface, a mulata, a North American "Mister Smith," or a general *extranjero* (foreigner) figure eventually re-emerged on stage.[89] While some theater practitioners saw the plays as racist, others viewed the deployment of blackface as a mode of retaining cultural heritage.[90] But theorists insist the negrito's return was tied to the marketability of black cultural forms in the tourist marketplace amid a severe economic crisis. Although Afro-Cubans were sources of comic relief, bufo was also a reservoir of Afro-Cuban musical forms that inadvertently thrust black culture in the national spotlight. Teatro bufo was polysemic with a "multiplicity of meanings" that "represented and perpetuated both patriotism and oppression," racial biases, and alternatives to white Cuban nationalism.[91] During the Special Period, the genre's emphasis on Afro-Cuban culture proved marketable to tourists willing to pay in *divisa* (foreign currency), and the regime declared teatro bufo cultural patrimony.

This celebration of teatro bufo was in keeping with the state's reorientation of the economy toward foreign investment by depenalizing the use of foreign currency and lifting its repression on black religious practices, among other policy changes.[92] This period saw a resurgence of scholarship on race and a renaissance of Afro-Cuban cultural forms, increased tourist demand for Afro-Cuban culture, and the valorization of black culture in Cuba's emergent hip-hop movement and the theater scene.[93] The renewed celebration of teatro bufo displaced the raceless hombre nuevo and reinscribed the negrito as an emblem of national identity. Facing a debilitating crisis, the regime mined blackness on stage in exchange for foreign currency. Furthermore, the elevation of teatro bufo to the status of cultural patrimony in the 1990s amid increased market liberalization and a withering social state coincided with the erosion of the gains of racial equality achieved in the revolution and a stark decline in the material well-being of the Afro-Cuban population.[94] As the cynosure of Cuba's cultural patrimony for new Cubans arriving in Miami after 1990, the negrito represented a failed socialist state, the return of racial inequality, and the accelerated reinsertion of Afro-Cuban cultural forms in capitalist networks of racial trafficking.

Because the negrito is a familiar cultural trope to both the early waves of Cuban exiles and the new Cubans who arrived after the 1990s, Yeyo marks distinct temporal coordinates of the racial imaginaries of home for different factions of the Cuban diaspora in Miami. That these racial pasts differ suggest that the negrito is a polytemporal figure who retains the multiple racial pasts and racial imaginaries of home. He is a vestibule of cultural memory, the heralded icon of cultural patrimony, and the symbol of a national identity that is entangled with discourses of racial denialism. Yeyo's polytemporality is grounded in a capacity to simultaneously represent distinct temporal moments of the nation and iterations of the negrito and be legible enough to unite a divided Cuban diaspora under the auspices of a shared national culture. The polytemporality of Yeyo, a figuration of blackness on *Esta Noche Tu Night* is important because it indicates that acts of racial conjuring can simultaneously speak to different temporal coordinates of the nationalist fiction. He can cater to the discourses of racial fraternity from before and after the revolution and still enable collective identification across different sectors of the Cuban diaspora.

But Yeyo is polyvocal in that this figure is not limited to Cuba; he also stands in for the figurations of blackness from Miami's blackface tradition. From the late nineteenth century to the early twentieth century, Miami's minstrel stage not only served as a crucial domain for defining the racial, sexual, and gendered hierarchies of the city, but its renditions of blackness drew from distinct ethno-racial traditions, culling from the US South and North as well as Caribbean tropes from the Bahamas and Cuba.[95] Minstrel performances featured Bahamian songs like "Nassau Boy" and improvised performances by "Nassau Negro" natives, mining a transnational repertoire of blackness that spoke to the city's Caribbean and US American audiences alike.[96] Black performers in Florida also challenged these tropes, as the famous Bahamian-born black minstrel Bert Williams did. The polyvocal nature of Miami's black caricatures has remained a steady feature of acts of racial conjuring well after the first wave of Cubans arrived. Bufo and *zarzuela* performances were common in Miami, even as blackface waned in other parts of the United States due to the presence of the Cuban enclaves. Actors in blackface appeared in William Shakespeare's *Otelo* in 1974 by the Patronato del Teatro, and in the 1988 play *El Velorio de Papá Montero* staged at the Teatro Martí. The Cuban exile actor Néstor Cabell continued to stage bufo performances in Miami.[97] Whether in music, vaudeville, or Shakespeare, the figurations of blackness on Miami stages speak through the racial codes of blackness and the conventions of traditions of racial impersonation from the two Americas.

Furthermore, Yeyo represented the antileftist negrito of the exilic humor tradition in Miami. Yeyo's deployment on *Esta Noche Tu Night* to critique the Left is part of a tradition of racial impersonation in Miami that was bound up in anti-Castro sentiment. Representations of blackness in the Cuban diaspora operated within a larger ludic landscape defined by antirevolutionary desire for the fall of Castro and nostalgia for Cuba libre. Satirical newspapers like *Zig Zag Libre, Chispa, Cubalegre, La Política Cómica*, and others were all founded by exiles in the 1960s and were ludic sites both of political critique of Castro and communism, and of cultural preservation. In 1964, exiles organized the event Añorada Cuba (Yearning for Cuba) featuring dance, music, and dramatic works from children in Miami. Children also featured in drawing contests for the best political caricatures of revolutionary leaders.[98] The event was divided into different sections, including one, "AfroCuba," featuring a performance of the popular Afro-Cuban lullaby "Drume Negrita" (Sleep my little black baby) by Angelita Luaces. The lyrics distort black speech with malapropisms such as *drume* (instead of *duerme*) as the black woman, a maternal figure, struggles to put the baby *negrita* to sleep. The mother promises the *negrita* a fruit if she goes to sleep, or a whipping from the babalao if she refuses.[99] While Añorada Cuba undoubtedly united different sectors of the exile community, it "kept alive an upper-class version of Cubanness that was characteristic of the previous Republican period."[100] Doing antiblackness on stage was historically part of the expression of a larger antirevolutionary ludic project that simultaneously elevated Cuban whiteness.

In comedy like that of Cuban exile Álvarez Guedes, negritos—African Americans and Afro-Cubans alike—were frequently the butt of the jokes, but Afro-Cubans, the main beneficiaries of the revolution, were typically cast as the voice of anti-Castro critiques. Their migration to Miami, and the fact that many died when Castro's regime sent them to fight in Angola, are often cited as evidence of Castro's failed revolution during comedy routines. Some of Álvarez Guedes's jokes are recycled in popular performance today. Afro-Cuban comedian Conrado Cogle is known for his famous persona Boncó Quiñongo from the television show *Sabadazo* in Cuba and Miami's show *Pellízcame que estoy soñando* (Pinch me, I'm Dreaming) (2008), hosted by the beloved Cuban comedian Carlos Otero. Cogle does not perform in blackface, but his stereotypical portrayals of the negrito as sneaky, criminal, and foolish with a poor command of Spanish are culled directly from the bufo playbook and are perfectly legible to Cuban diasporic audiences. Like other Cuban entertainers who recently arrived in Miami, Cogle must prove his anti-Castro credentials to work in the entertainment industry. And his self-deprecation and lampooning of his own blackness is a crucial device for insertion into the diasporic imaginary and its maintenance of the hegemony of Cuban whiteness.

In Cogle's stand-up routines, he frequently opens by mocking his own dark skin, verifying if the audience can see him since he is so dark-skinned, and offering to smile to help. In some performances, he flaunts his anti-Castro credentials by claiming that Cuba is a Third World country aiming or fighting to be a Fourth World country, and that all Cubans want to leave. At the end of his performance "Boncó y la ciencia negrológica," on AméricaTevé, he culls an anti-Castro joke directly from white Cuban comedian Álvarez Guedes's routine. Boncó explains that when he decided to leave Cuba for the United States, he was warned to be careful because blacks are not worth a thing over there, to which he replies, "I'm not going the US to sell blacks!"[101] In Cuban exilic comedy, blackness has historically been conjured "for symbolic use to criticize the Castro government," and to insist that claims of racism in the United States are exaggerated and made by those who are unwilling to work.[102] In doing antiblackness, Boncó panders to antiblack stereotypes and white Cuban exilic hegemonic discourses about racism in Cuba and the United States, while reinforcing a Miami Cuban tradition of wielding negritos to reject the Cuban revolution and to critique the Left. Like Cogle, Yeyo the negrito speaks through and with the figurations of blackness embedded in the anti-Castro politics of a white Cuban imagination in Miami.

Yeyo, like the zambo/sambo at the Andean fiesta, operates within a prismatic field of signification and, as such, is not just a hemispheric double. He is a constellation of figurations of blackness that houses multivalent racial fantasies circulating in the hemispheric fold. The negrito is a figure of multiple temporalities, a symbol of a prerevolutionary Cuban society and its attendant racial hierarchies, a sign of national patrimony and the failures of the revolution, and a symbol of anti-Castro sentiment. Circulating in the hemispheric fold, he stands in for hemispheric iterations of blackness: an abject black Caribbean identity in Miami, an Afro-Dominicanidad, an anti-Castro Afro-Cubanness, and an inadequate African American president. This polytemporality and polyvocality render the negrito legible to audiences across the national differences of the hemispheric fold and malleable to the needs of his conjurers. Grounded in a shared hemispheric history of slavery and the overlapping transnational registers of antiblackness that it spawned, the negrito is conjured to reinforce a set of racial hierarchies built upon the subordination of blackness despite the proliferation of nationalist discourses of mestizaje in Miami. But Yeyo is not only transcending the tensions within the Cuban diaspora; he is also mediating the symbolic significance of Obama's election, the emergence of a new repeating nationalist fiction in the United States, and the subsequent shifts of the geopolitical relationship between the two Americas.

Doing Antiblackness and the Black Gaze in Miami

Doing antiblackness is a ludic ritual that unites the Cuban diaspora in Miami, enabling them to both critique the Cuban revolution and President Barack Obama. Afro-Cubans were key beneficiaries of and have long been cast as loyal to the revolution.[103] Yeyo's representation of a black leader symbolizes the ascendance of a black middle class in Cuba during the revolutionary years. That Yeyo is the president of a worker's union party suggests he is representative of the Left and of Castro's revolution. Thus, his rendition of an inept black leadership figure who was unsuited for his positions serves as an allegory for the advancement of black figures during the revolution. In the racist visions of the white elite of Cuba's prerevolutionary era, these figures were unworthy of and ill-equipped for their newly acquired status in Cuba's professional sphere. For this demographic, Marrero's doing antiblackness activates racial memory, lampoons Castro's presumed alliance with Afro-Cubans, mocks Miami's Afro-Caribbean immigrant as a figure of social abjection, and lampoons the figure of the black leader as Obama rises to power.

But for the racially diverse, post-1994 demographic, doing antiblackness is both a practice of rejecting US processes of racialization and of integrating into the diasporic fold. While Yeyo is played by the white Cuban immigrant Carlos Marrero, he frequently interacts with Cuban immigrants who, despite how they may individually identify, would possibly read as black or brown. Alexis Valdés, the host of *Esta Noche Tu Night*, reads as brown, *mulato*, or even *jabao* (a very light-skinned black person). My purpose here is not to ascribe racial animus, diagnose black self-hatred, or identify an intentional or even conscious reproduction of antiblackness on the part of an individual performer. Rather, I see doing antiblackness as a set of strategies that enable black and brown performers to engage in forms of diasporic identification as they negotiate the racial politics of a hemispheric city. In their study of Yeyo, Hernández-Reguant and Arroyo contend that Yeyo represents the category of latinidad—a racial category that newly arrived black and brown Spanish-speaking immigrants in Miami frequently reject.[104] Constructs of latinidad privilege Puerto Ricans and Chicanos and racialize them as nonwhite. Since these immigrants overwhelmingly identify according to their nationality or as white on Miami's racial censuses, Hernández-Reguant and Arroyo postulate that Yeyo, the black Dominican, is the incarnation of all the things they are not. Distance from him

2.3 Yeyo Vargas sitting with Alexis Valdés, the host of *Esta Noche Tu Night*. Video still, Roigarm, YouTube, July 18, 2010.

marks a distance from latinidad as a US racial category, and his position as black or Afro-Latino marks a distance from blackness itself. As the embodiment of both blackness and brownness, Yeyo marks Latino as a racialized category that is distanced from whiteness. Hernández-Reguant and Arroyo's assertions are certainly true, as Valdés represents the new brown cosmopolitan subject engaged in nationalist posturing against an impending future of racialization that Yeyo represents.

Doing antiblackness as a form of racial distancing is certainly at work in Valdés's relationship with Yeyo on the show. Throughout their exchanges, Valdés regularly corrected Yeyo's malapropisms, questioned his advice and his relationship with Obama, and directed him when he could not find the camera he was to speak to directly (figure 2.3).[105] This is apparent in the following dialogue, where Yeyo admonishes Obama for eating a hamburger at a restaurant:

VALDÉS: Hamburguesa no tiene de malo. ¿Cuál es el problema (…)?

YEYO: Yo siempre le recomiendo a mi compadre Obama que no viole ese protoloco.

VALDÉS: Protocolo.

YEYO: Exactamente. Y yo le digo que si él quiere pertenecey a la alta hamburguesía, no puede estar comiendo esa vaina. Tiene que comer comida más esquisitosa...

VALDÉS: Sí (...),

YEYO: como de mafongo y mangú.

[VALDÉS: There is nothing wrong with a hamburger. What's the problem (...)?

YEYO: I always advise my *compadre* Obama not to break this proto-loc (*protoloco*).

VALDÉS: Protocol.

YEYO: Exactly. I told him that if he wants to belong to the high ham-bourgeoise, he cannot be eating that stuff. He must eat food that is more exquisitous (*esquisitosa*)...

VALDÉS: Yes (...),

YEYO: like *mofongo* and *mangu*.][106]

In this scene, Yeyo uses malapropisms: *protoloco* instead of protocolo, *hamburguesía* instead of *burguesía* (bourgeoisie). This scene is salient, however, because it articulates his understanding of aristocratic and bourgeois culture. Not only is Yeyo barely able to pronounce the word *bourgeoisie*, but to him, what constitutes the cuisine of the aristocratic class are in fact the Dominican staples of mofongo and mangu. Yeyo is the black man who does not know his place, a fool with comic pretensions to aristocracy, but who knows very little of the aristocratic class. But more importantly, in that scene, Valdés corrects Yeyo's misuse of words, explaining the Spanish word for *protocol* is "protocolo" and not "protoloco." While Yeyo is the black fool, Valdés serves as his guide and expert. For it is Valdés who ultimately teaches Yeyo, directs his behaviors, and corrects his Spanish. In this game of racial play, Valdés is affirmed as the knowledgeable mulato Cuban counterpoint. A spectator and interlocutor to Yeyo's antics, Valdés is the expert who knows intellectual ways of speaking, of being, and who truly understands the political class. Yeyo is a device through which both the white impersonator and the brown mulato host engage with and mock black leadership.

While the white Cuban impersonator Carlos Marrero fixes black sub-ordination by conjuring Yeyo as the figure of the black buffoon, it is Alexis Valdés, the mulato host, who works as Yeyo's instructor and sustains Yeyo's subservience. Valdés, the racially ambiguous brown subject, is a stand-in for the racialized spectator at home, and he also functions as a racial mediator who wields his own brownness to authorize the lampooning of black-ness on the show. This distancing from the tropes of black buffoonery is a rejection of his own social abjection. These practices of racial distancing do not undo the antiblack discourses that Yeyo animates. They leave them intact while allowing racialized immigrants to displace them onto Yeyo and to participate in practices of diasporic identification. Indeed, doing antiblackness sets in motion a cross-racial alliance and consolidates a dias-poric identification between a white and a brown Cuban immigrant. The figure of the brown man colluding with the white male racial imperson-ator in the production of antiblackness on stage establishes a racial frater-nity and affirms a shared national identity that supersedes the problem of racial difference.

This racial distancing is also at work in Yeyo's interaction with Miami's very own Obama look-alike—a black impersonator named Gerardo Puis-seaux. Puisseaux is an Afro-Cuban man of Haitian descent who worked as a car salesman in Miami and garnered media attention for his strikingly similar physical appearance to Obama. He came on the scene in 2008 and worked as a media delegate for Channel 41, with the Spanish-language television channel AméricaTevé. He trailed the Obama campaign when they came to Florida. Puisseaux also appeared on Univisión and other television shows as Obama. While he was not a frequent guest on *Esta Noche Tu Night*, his presence as a black impersonator is important because until his cameo, Yeyo's engagement with Obama was largely hypotheti-cal. Puisseaux's visits to the show as Obama brought the black president to life. As a "real" black man impersonating Obama, Puisseaux functions as the counterpoint to Yeyo's farcical blackness. While Yeyo struggles to speak Spanish correctly, Puisseaux always spoke perfect Spanish with a heavily inflected English accent. Yeyo jokingly took credit for Puisseaux's Spanish, claiming to have taught him how to speak the language. As an Afro-Cuban on the show, his role is to conjure a black American cultural outsider, to affirm the boundaries and cultural differences that divide the black American president and the Cuban American and immigrant audi-ence at home, as well as to register a black gaze.

Puisseaux oscillates between playing along and refusing to accept Yeyo's advice. For instance, in one episode, he bestows formal recognition upon Yeyo as the liaison to all Latin people in the United States and to those in the Dominican Republic. But he refuses to accept Yeyo's foolish recommendations to add a merengue track that plays when someone opens a US passport.[107] While Yeyo is a black fool, Puisseaux as Obama is often represented as levelheaded, sane enough to dismiss Yeyo's antics, but without dismissing Yeyo's position as liaison and mediator for Obama on the show. This black gaze oscillates between recognizing Yeyo's buffoonery and keeping black buffoonery safely at a distance from the actual black person on stage. And yet, any notion that Puisseaux marks a site of black resistance on the show is undermined by his own participation in its antiblackness. For example, in an episode that aired on May 11, 2011, Yeyo enters the show following Valdés's interview with the former mayor of Hialeah, Raúl Martínez. Yeyo tells Martínez he has a surprise for him and welcomes the Obamas to the show. President Obama, played by Puisseaux, enters with his daughter and Michelle Obama. The audience roars with laughter. Alexis Valdés inquires about Obama's daughter, who is played by a white male little person in blackface, dressed in drag as a black girl. Obama explains that she is doing well in school, as the white male drag performer holds a Mickey Mouse toy. Michelle Obama is played by a black woman. The white person in drag sits in her lap as Puisseaux as Obama proceeds to congratulate Martínez on all his work.[108] Obama declares Martínez the lifelong mayor of Hialeah and offers him a certificate. He then instructs his daughter to kiss the former mayor. As the white drag performer approaches Martínez, the audience guffaws. Amid the laughter, Yeyo instructs Michelle Obama not to be shy and to say something. When she opens her mouth to speak to Martínez, her dentures fall out of her mouth. She picks them up from off the floor and hurriedly sits back down. She hides her face in her daughter's arms, embarrassed as the audience laughs at her.

In this scene, Puisseaux serves as an accomplice in the show's mockery of the Obamas, the first black family. In casting a white adult man in blackface to play Obama's daughter, the show trafficked in what Moya Bailey calls misogynoir—anti-black forms of misogyny that pervade representations of black women in the media.[109] The show's lampooning of Michelle Obama is in keeping with racist critiques of her from sectors of the media in Miami.[110] In rendering her as a woman whose teeth are too big for her mouth, it inscribes black female physiognomy as a site of excess. In this scene, black women and girls are grotesque figures who do not conform to the ideals of femininity. That the black girl is played by an adult man reaffirms the tendency to view black girls as adults and to relegate them to the margins of childhood. The two black women simply appear as objects of ridicule and devices of comic relief. The derision of Michelle Obama's physiognomy is a mockery of the notion that a black woman is suited to be the First Lady—the national symbol of ideal womanhood and feminine elegance. And yet, the comedy also simultaneously relies on the mockery of the little person in drag, mobilizing ableist notions that deem little people as perpetual children. Puisseaux participates in the show's antiblack and misogynistic critique of the US political class and its derision of the Obamas, the first black family, as comedic spectacle.

The balsero immigrant may identify with Puisseaux, who is portrayed as knowledgeable and articulate, and simultaneously disidentify with Yeyo on stage. The "real" black man on stage serves as a willing participant, a nonthreatening black presence who sanctions the antiblackness and misogynoir while safely distancing himself from it. Doing antiblackness with Yeyo on stage is thus a social ritual that enables black and white demographics of the Cuban diaspora to distance themselves from the racist tropes of blackness. The performances of both Valdés and Puisseaux reveal how diasporic identification within an exile imaginary requires participation in representations of symbolic domination over blackness. But they also signal the centrality of Yeyo as a device through which varying factors of the Cuban diaspora may identify with one another; access diverging and disparate memories of home; consume the cultural artifacts of home; advance political critiques of the revolution, Castro, and the US political establishment; and distance themselves from US processes of racialization. For racialized subjects, doing antiblackness is a strategy and technique of doing diasporic citizenship and belonging in spaces marked by transnational regimes of Cuban whiteness. Doing antiblackness is at the core of the scene of racial enjoyment that I discuss at the opening of this chapter.

Diasporic Identification in the Hemispheric Fold

Yeyo's black buffoonery is encoded through the sonic tropes of musicality, through speech, and through appearance. As a figuration of blackness, he does multivalent work for Cubans living in the diaspora in Miami. The negrito has long been a figure through which the national romance of mestizaje has been articulated, and today its polyvalent meanings enable a shared identification among distinct factions of the diaspora. In this case, impersonation sets the racial terms of diasporic belonging. However, I am not suggesting that the fissures of Miami's Cuban diaspora are somehow overcome or that the diasporic imaginary is neatly unified through the consumption of Yeyo on stage. I assume diasporic identification to be momentary and contingent. The action of doing antiblackness must always be repeated and reaffirmed through a call and response. Yeyo's call was an action of black buffoonery, and the response was the laughter and applause from the audience. Indeed, Yeyo's buffoonery hailed diasporic audiences into doing antiblackness from the moment he entered the stage. The negrito also mediated the shifting geopolitics between the two Americas, the emergence of the Pink Tide in Latin America, the election of the first black president of the United States, and the overlapping formations of anti-blackness in the hemispheric fold. Doing anti-blackness thus constitutes the expression of a hemispheric sensibility that interpellates enclaves of hemispheric creole whiteness and bolsters the racial abjection of Afro-Caribbeanness.

The acts of racial impersonation that I have analyzed so far in this book illuminate how the figurations of blackness on stage animate and reinforce the systems of racial exclusion that permeate local and diasporic nationalist discourses of mestizaje and colorblindness. Both Yeyo in Miami and the negrito in Sambos's performance in the Andes index how blackface traditions reproduce a set of racial fictions and fantasies that sustain the racial scripts of mestizaje and enable identification across national borders. In the fiesta, the identification transcends the racial differences of the troupe and the national differences in the audience, while in this television show, the identification is forged across the fissures of the diaspora and the distinct Latin American immigrant enclaves in the city. In both chapters, slavery's logics of subjection are at the heart of the scene of racial enjoyment. Racial conjuring animates multiple registers of antiblackness that organize the different racial matrixes of the hemispheric fold. While those examples of hemispheric blackface reinforce antiblackness in scenes of racial enjoyment, in the ones that follow, I assess the ways these dynamics can be disrupted or inverted. Scenes of racial enjoyment are not only where the hierarchies of race and gender are reinforced, but also where racial scripts are critiqued and reworked. I now turn to how some black artists use blackface performance to flip racial scripts and to engage in acts of resistance in the hemispheric fold.

CHAPTER THREE

Flipping the Racial Script

Blackface Performance as Resistance in Colombia

Liliana Angulo's *Mambo negrita* is an installation featuring a series of thir-teen digital photographs of Afro-Colombian women in blackface that was exhibited at the Museo de Arte Moderno de Bogotá in 2006.[1] The artist set up the installation as a triangular labyrinth, in a corner of the museum's third floor. Spectators could only enter and exit the installa-tion through a small door. Upon entry, viewers were greeted by a photo-graph of the artist Liliana Angulo in blackface. She is la negrita, the little black girl or little black woman. Angulo is wearing a bright red-and-white polka-dot headwrap, midriff top, and skirt that match the color and pat-tern of the fabric in the background (figure 3.1). The matching fabric blurs the distinction between the background and foreground so that she ap-pears literally dressed in the wallpaper. Her headwrap is tied in a bun that sits atop her head, barely touching her forehead, while her orange red lip-stick strikes a stark contrast against the black paint on her skin. She leans forward as she looks straight at the camera with her mouth wide open, baring all her teeth. Her midriff top reveals her cleavage and bare stomach and yet, her facial expression and the position of her body are ambiguous. Is she opening her mouth to smile or to shout? Is she charging at the cam-era, or is she standing in defiance?

As we venture further inside the labyrinth, the photographs multi-ply, showing a variety of stereotypical images of black women. Angulo seems to sing in one image, while in another, she poses like a classic pinup girl (figures 3.2–3.4). In the latter pose, she holds her two hands behind her head. Her elbows stick up, her hips lean forward seductively, and the sleeves of her midriff flare at her shoulders and expose her underarm. The other black model is similarly dressed in the wallpaper. Her tight midriff exposes her cleavage and the sides of her stomach, which, like the rest of her body, is painted black. She closes her eyes and purses her lips to offer a kiss. Together, these models smile and pose for the camera in titillating

3.1 The artist Liliana Angulo in blackface, 2006. Courtesy of Liliana Angulo.

fashion, offering playful snapshots of sensuality, pleasure, happiness, and eroticism.

In other images, the black women appear with an array of kitchen and domestic objects: a plunger, a frying pan, and a knife (figures 3.5–3.7). But the portraits do not quite stage the relationship between the black servant and the kitchen objects that one would expect: the models pose with defiant and aggressive gestures.[2] One model holds a frying pan threateningly in the air while she closes her eyes and gnashes her teeth. The other model holds up a plunger with both hands above her right shoulder and lunges aggressively toward the camera. Her lips no longer offer a kiss but are instead slightly parted to reveal her teeth. Her eyes are wide open, and she furrows her brow. Now the first model grips the knife in her left hand, leaning forward, and opens her mouth as if she were shouting in a rage. In these images, their smiles and sensual gestures are all gone, and they now pose as if ready to attack. In juxtaposing the black female body with the objects of domestic labor, these portraits highlight the fraught relationship

3.2–3.4 Two black women models in blackface singing, smiling, and blowing kisses at the camera. Courtesy of Liliana Angulo.

3.5–3.7 Black women models in blackface pose aggressively. One holds a plunger, the other a frying pan and a knife. Courtesy of Liliana Angulo.

between black womanhood, domesticity, and objecthood. By transforming the objects of domestic servitude into weapons, the installation subverts the symbols of black female domesticity. While in some images, the
models seemingly embrace the role of a happy domestic servant or sexualized pinup girl, in others, they stage a refusal to play these roles. In its
move from ambivalence, servitude, and titillation to defiance, the exhibition provides a representation of black womanhood that is not fully complacent or not quite happy to serve.

Liliana Angulo, whose full name is Astrid Liliana Angulo Cortés, is a
black multimedia artist born in Bogotá, Colombia, in 1974. Angulo was
trained as a sculptor at La Universidad Nacional de Colombia in Bogotá
and received an MFA from the University of Illinois in Chicago. Like many
Afro-Colombians from the capital, Angulo is the child of a black migrant
from the Pacific coast. Black communities in Bogotá face the challenge of
being perceived as foreigners or interlopers in a largely white city because,
as I explain, Colombia's triracial configuration has historically designated
Bogotá as a white or mestizo space.[3] She belongs to the city's small artistic scene, sharing company with noted Afro-Bogotán artists such as Wilson Borja, Mercedes Angola, Maguemati Wabgou, and the activist group
Colectivo Aguaturbia, of which Angulo is a member, and their project IRA (Imaginación Radical Afro). These artists all attend to the experience of living in the margins of Bogotá's mostly white metropolitan
space.[4] As a multimedia artist, Angulo has been using sculpture, photography, video installations, and performance art since the 1990s to explore
questions of race, gender, and the representation of Afro-Colombian culture in contemporary art and media. Her work is dedicated to critiquing
stereotypes and valorizing Afro-Colombian traditions and culture from a
black perspective. She is currently one of the curators of the Museo Afro
de Colombia.

Like noted black female artists from the United States such as Adrian
Piper, Carrie Mae Weems, and Kara Walker, Angulo uses the deconstruction of stereotypes to cast a critical light on typical renditions of blackness
and black womanhood. Art critics note her tendency to tackle stereotypes
head on, to present images that oscillate between "ambiguity and viru-
lence," and to generate discomfort among viewers.[5] In her description of
her own work, Angulo states:

> I work on blackness—from my own experience and my environment—
> on contemporary identities and the acts of affirmation that they ex-

press. Within my visual arts process, I have approached the physical characteristics of black people and their representation in images which circulate in the mass media and in historical documents, seeking in many cases to question the stereotypes that weigh on the black body, in contrast with the dominant Western model of beauty. I have also been interested in metaphors related to power that historically connote the skin and the different parts of the body and even in its relationship to space. I approach the black body understood by ancestral traditions as malleable material and in general addressing it as political territory on which different forces act.[6]

Over the span of her thirty-year career, Angulo has engaged blackness in multiple ways. She has sought to interrogate black female iconography in historical archives, affirm and catalog black hair styling practices in black communities, stage public interventions around discourses of antiblackness, and commemorate the history of slavery in Colombia.[7] *Mambo negrita* exemplifies the artist's penchant for the deconstruction of stereotypes of blackness. At first glance, some of the images in the piece may be read as acquiescing to stereotypical representations of black women, but the images, the arrangement of the space, and the use of repetition suggest that Angulo uses blackface as part of a larger artistic gesture of racial confrontation and resistance.

While *Mambo negrita* has been the subject of scholarly consideration in the last decade, when Angulo staged the exhibit it initially received sparse attention in Colombia. This is due, in part, to the fact that *Mambo negrita* debuted before the advent of smart phones and social media, and that art criticism, at the time, was concentrated in small online magazines such as *Esfera Pública* and *Escáner Cultural*. *Mambo negrita* received mixed reviews among art critics on those forums. One article questioned her refusal to use art to offer positive representations of blackness and claimed the piece remained trapped in the social trauma of lived reality, while another praised the piece for its critical position on the social reality of racism.[8] This disagreement only underscores the salience of unpacking the productivity of wielding blackface in artistic gestures of resistance. Whereas Alexis Valdés and Carlos Marrero's conjuring of Yeyo reinscribed racist tropes of black buffoonery, Angulo's installation is an example of how black artists can engage in acts of racial conjuring to humanize the black subject, offer alternative modes of seeing the black body, and disrupt stereotypes. This chapter shifts our focus to resistance as a domain of racial enjoyment, wherein black subjects critically rework the racial scripts of mestizaje and engage with slavery's logics of rebellion in the hemispheric fold. Resistance, as I show here, may be both direct or ambiguous, and the acts of racial conjuring may upend or subvert the stereotypes. As explained in the introduction, I use racial enjoyment in a capacious sense to name the affective range of gratification—pleasure, wonder, fascination—representations of race elicit from spectators. Here I suggest that ambiguity is at the heart of this domain of enjoyment because whatever pleasure or wonder Angulo's stereotypical images of black womanhood may produce for spectators, it is momentary and unstable at best. Hemispheric blackface also entails these moments where black artists conjure blackness to trouble, destabilize, defer, or delay racial gratification and instead, produce discomfort in a scene of racial enjoyment.

Angulo's meditation on racial stereotypes is particularly important because *Mambo negrita* was staged amid Colombia's multicultural turn. In the 1990s and 2000s, Colombia undertook a series of multicultural reforms that recognized and guaranteed the protection of the rights of minority populations in the country's political and juridical spheres.[9] As I detail, these reforms marked a departure from a country historically organized around a politics of mestizaje and colorblindness, which had imagined the nation as culturally homogenous but racially diverse.[10] Like the discourses of mestizaje that I analyze in Cuba, Miami, and Peru, Colombian mestizaje produced structures of racial silence that sidestepped or obscured racial difference. When Colombia's institutional approach to racial difference shifted, the national artistic scene also began to engage with the question of race. Through Angulo's work, we see again how acts of racial conjuring serve as a recourse for (re)defining or troubling racial hierarchies as the nation turns away from colorblindness toward multiculturalism.

In this social and artistic context, Angulo's art addressed the aesthetic regimes of citizenship, whose visual vocabularies had continued to render the black female body a symbol of servitude, domesticity, objecthood, and hypersexuality. This critical engagement with the normalizing and disciplinary instruments of racialization pushed against any pretense of a shallow celebration of racial diversity in Colombian art that a national shift to multiculturalism supposedly portended. Angulo's intervention also rubbed up against Colombia's nationalist fiction of mestizaje. Put simply, with *Mambo negrita*, Angulo staged a reflection on racialization that forced visitors to confront the problem of racial representation, racial difference, and the persistent legacies of colonialism and enslavement that shape the imagination and lives of black women. Although her work has now moved away from the deconstruction of stereotypes, the artistic strategies she deployed here are in keeping with those of earlier pieces like *Negro utópico* that I analyze briefly in this chapter. Her performance in *Mambo negrita* reveals the endurance of racial scripts at this moment of new political articulation, and she operationalizes racial conjuring to both expose and destabilize the mechanisms through which racial power is enacted and inscribed on the female body. *Hemispheric Blackface* traces how slavery's logics permeate all forms of cultural entertainment. This scene of racial enjoyment took place in a museum—a venue of high art—whose social codes of spectatorship are typically more formal than those of the carnival or the television show I analyze in previous chapters. Angulo signals that the racial power of the museum, as a formal institution of high art, resides in the legitimizing imprimatur that it grants upon its art objects including the black female body. Furthermore, her exhibit indexes the roles of museums and high art in trafficking images of blackness for racial enjoyment.

I analyze Angulo's exhibit to begin to discern the ways black artists wield blackface, and impersonation more broadly, to stage a political intervention. I argue that Angulo occupies the position of the happy servant to intervene in stereotypical constructs of the negrita or black womanhood, and in local configurations of race in Colombia. In examining stereotypical constructs of the negrita that fix black women as symbols of domestic servitude and objects of hypersexuality, I ascertain how Angulo uses blackface as an instrument of disruption and subversion. We have already seen how blackface works to fix blackness as a racial stereotype. Here I show how racial impersonation operates in tension with evolving structures of racial silence through processes of inversion. Black artists can weaponize blackface as an instrument of resistance and to destabilize racial scripts, preventing blackness from ever being fully fixed.

Racial Formation, *Mestizaje*, and Multiculturalism in Colombia

In the nineteenth century, Colombia's colonial society was organized around a racially stratified caste system that situated blacks and indigenous people at the lower echelons of society and celebrated whiteness as the symbol of progress and modernity.[11] At the time of independence,

Colombian elites faced the daunting task of seeking to unite this society. Rather than adhere to colonialist paradigms and discourses of scientific racism that deemed racial miscegenation a sign of inferiority, the elites romanticized racial mixture and emphasized cultural homogeneity.[12] But the celebration of racial mixture did not undermine racist ideas about blackness and indigeneity as backward and undesirable; rather, it venerated whiteness and thought mixture would improve the population. Key thinkers in the early twentieth century, for example, believed that racial mixture would produce a "culturally and biologically homogenous people that were stronger than any of their individual roots."[13] Hence, they celebrated the mestizo as the ideal citizen subject destined to leave the indigenous and African elements behind and herald a whiter future for the nation.[14] The resulting veneration of the mestizo was crucial to the crafting of a national identity that disregarded the issue of race.[15]

According to the logic of Colombian mestizaje developed in the early parts of the twentieth century, everyone is mixed but ultimately Colombian.[16] Like the other sites examined in this book, the nationalist fiction superseded the problem of race, even as the reality of racial exclusion persisted. Although an "explicit derogation of blackness" was uncommon in discourses of mestizaje in Colombia after the 1940s, nationalist discourses still emphasized the mixture of European and indigenous people while silencing or excluding blackness.[17] Black Colombians were subsequently erased from popular narratives and representations of national identity.[18] This erasure and exclusion were compounded by two things. Because the state held a legal position of colorblindness, throughout the twentieth century Colombia rarely compiled ethno-racial statistics. But when it did, the population mostly identified as mixed and census takers concluded that black, white, and indigenous people lived in perfect harmony and ethno-racial questions were therefore unimportant.[19] Just as in Peru, the absence of ethno-racial censuses contributed to the invisibility of the Afro-Colombian population and proved an obstacle to both identifying and organizing around their collective needs.

A second factor that contributed to the invisibility and marginalization of Afro-Colombians is a discourse of mestizaje that is defined in profoundly spatial terms. Due to the organization of labor and trade routes during the colonial era, Colombian mestizaje is organized around a discourse of regionalism, and each region is associated with a particular population: Blacks with the coasts, Indians with the Amazon lowlands, and whites and mestizos with Bogotá and the Andean highlands.[20] Peter Wade calls this regionalism a "cultural topography" of race whereby region serves as a language and proxy for race and racial hierarchies.[21] Since the nineteenth century, racial difference in Colombia was encoded in territory: the Andean highlands are seen as a symbol of beauty and industriousness, while the coasts were perceived as a symbol of savageness, laziness, and hypersexuality.[22] In Colombia, racial formation was thus articulated through what Katherine McKittrick identifies as the "*where* of race."[23] As McKittrick reminds us, space is normatively understood as unwavering, secure, as something that "just is" rather than being socially produced.[24] The national discourse of mestizaje imagined and reorganized the national space to naturalize racial hierarchies.[25] Historically, the Colombian government has not had much influence outside of the major cities. Because state power is concentrated in Bogotá, the two coasts have long been isolated and, as a result, receive fewer resources. The unequal distribution of resources inherent to Colombia's cultural topography of race consolidated black erasure and marginalization. James Sanders explains that not only were Afro-Colombians marginalized in national discourse, but their geographic isolation also consolidated their ideological distance from the rest of the national polity.[26] The language of territory occluded the salience of race, disavowed its centrality in the organization and distribution of national resources, and maintained the illusion of national harmony.

Angulo's work intervenes, thus, in a context in which a nationalist discourse of mestizaje had marginalized and rendered blackness invisible and overlooked the reality of racism as a feature of national life. But she also exhibited *Mambo negrita* just as the state was slowly moving away from disavowing the salience of race to recognizing it. Between the 1980s and 2000s, Colombia, like other Latin American countries, undertook a series of multicultural reforms that recognized and guaranteed the protection of the rights of minority populations.[27] Colombia's multicultural shift was a result of the emerging embrace of human and "collective rights" discourse in the global arena, the constitutional crisis of the 1980s and 1990s, and the organizing of Black activist groups, most notably the Proceso de Comunidades Negras de Colombia (PCN).[28] Amid the emergence of a set of international policies that enabled indigenous groups in Latin America to claim their right to territory, Colombia adopted the provisions from the International Labour Organization (ILO) Convention on Indigenous and Tribal People of 1989, using much of its language as the blueprint for crafting its new constitution in 1991.[29]

The country's multicultural turn also coincided with a period of so-ciopolitical instability in the 1980s and early 1990s, when the Colom-bian government faced a crisis of legitimacy due to increased violence among guerrilla groups, the state, and the mobilization of drug cartels. Black and indigenous activist groups used the push for state transforma-tion and constitutional reform to their advantage and lobbied the govern-ment to respond to their demands. As a result, in 1991, Colombia adopted a new constitution that recognized the country as "multicultural" and pluri-ethnic and officially recognized blackness and indigeneity as eth-nic groups.[30] Colombia's multicultural reforms were far more extensive and robust than those I analyze in Peru. At the constitutional level, the multicultural turn in Colombia entailed the adoption of two political re-forms in 1991 and 1993 whereby the state formally recognized the collec-tive property rights of black communities in the Pacific, protected their cultural identity and rights, and recognized blacks in the Pacific as an ethnic group.[31] The state then set up a special commission to address the rights of black citizens, guaranteed black communities the right to col-lective territory and ethnic development, designated two special seats for Afro-Colombians in the House of Representatives, some three hundred positions in the state for Afro-Colombian representation, and ensured the inclusion of the study of Afro-Colombian history and culture in the edu-cation system.[32]

The consensus among scholars, however, is that the multicultural re-forms did not entirely undo or completely move away from the racial de-nialism that typified mestizaje in Colombia.[33] The processes surrounding the production of reforms themselves reproduced Colombia's refusal to en-gage race as a salient category, even as it acknowledged the need to protect minority groups.[34] For example, the National Constitutional Assembly (ANC) overseeing the reforms refused to address the concerns of Black ac-tivists and excluded urban activist groups who had organized explicitly around racism and discrimination because such explicit engagement with race was too divisive.[35] As a political tactic, black groups from rural areas deliberately distanced themselves from urban Black activist groups and consolidated alliances with indigenous groups.[36] Moreover, there were no black people represented in the ANC, so an indigenous person had to speak on behalf of both black and indigenous communities. The new reforms ul-timately defined blackness in ostensibly indigenous terms, claiming a right to land and the possession of a distinct cultural identity. Thus, Colombia's new multicultural citizenship demanded the deracialization of blackness, so blacks could benefit from the reforms.[37] Tianna Paschel argues similarly that the first wave of multicultural reforms did not include the general population but specific subsets, like the black communities on the Pacific coast, even though black organizations largely pushed for policies that catered to the needs of both rural and urban black communities.[38] The ANC, therefore, displaced and excised race from the conversation by embracing the language of ethnicity.[39] As a result, these multicultural reforms only permitted the recognition of certain types of blackness.[40]

In the decade that followed, multicultural reforms did, however, open the door to more explicit and direct engagement with racism in Colombia. The 2005 census, for example, inaugurated the term "afro-colombiano" at the state level, advancing a new definition of blackness rooted in a shared history of enslavement and descent from Africa.[41] After the first reforms, urban Black activists pushed for a more expansive definition of blackness than the state had provided, others successfully sought to increase state recognition of black communities on the Atlantic coasts, and the PCN slowly shifted its discourse of blackness from ethnicity to center antiracism.[42] The mid-1990s and early 2000s saw the emergence of various projects focused on people of African descent in the global arena. The international conference in Durban, South Africa, in 2001 greatly enlivened organizing for black rights in Colombia and in the region.[43]

The renewed global attention to blackness combined with the multicultural turn led to increased interest in notions of racial diversity in Colombian art. State and financial institutions began to sponsor art exhibitions that not only embraced the emergent discourse of national plurality but also attended to representations of blackness in Colombian art and the contributions of Afro-Colombian artists. These exhibits included *Viaje sin mapa: Representaciones Afro en el arte contemporáneo colombiano* (2006) (Journey without a Map: Representations of Blackness in Contemporary Colombian Art), *Velorios y santos vivos: Comunidades negras, afrocolombianas, raizales y palenqueras* (2008) (Wakes and Living Saints: Black, Afro-Colombian, Raizal, and Palenquera communities), and *¡Mandinga Sea! África en Antioquia* (2013) (Mandinga Sea! Africa in Antioquia).[44] Angulo's participation in *Viaje sin mapa*, the first major exhibition that centered blackness in Colombian art, launched her career. Thus, not only did Angulo stage her interventions amid a national transition from racial denialism to racial recognition, she also had to contend with new regimes of multicultural citizenship that set the terms and parameters for the types of performances of blackness that were deemed recognizable and permissible in the eyes of the state. As it did in other contexts within the hemispheric fold, for Angulo in Colombia, blackface would become a recourse for mediating a moment of new political articulation.

Viaje sin mapa: Negro utópico and the Fungibility of Blackness

Viaje sin mapa was curated by the Afro-Colombian artist and professor Julia Mercedes Angola Rossi and a white professor, Raúl Cristancho, from la Universidad Nacional de Bogotá. In addition to exhibiting her art, Angulo worked as an assistant to the curators. The exhibition, which took place in 2006, consisted of a variety of artistic genres, including performance art, installation, videos, and paintings. Thanks to the sponsorship of Colombia's central bank, Banco de La República, the exhibition was shown in Bogotá and in cities with large Afro-Colombian populations, such as Cali, Quibdó, and Cartagena. The exhibition's curators intended to initiate a dialogue about what it meant to be black in the wake of the multicultural reforms.[45] While not all the artists who participated were black, blackness figured in each of their individual works. *Viaje sin mapa* examined the complexity of defining blackness in Colombia as it offered artistic reflections on black phenotype, black cultural practices, the history of slavery, Afro-Colombians' relationship to Africa, and the idea of space or territory. In the exhibit's catalog, Cristancho explains that after the constitutional changes of 1991 and the law of 1993, "es posible pensar el ser afrocolombiano en un sentido integral y de manera dinámica según la necesidad de ir redefiniendo su identidad y su imaginario." (It is possible to think of the Afro-Colombian in a comprehensive sense and a dynamic way in relation to the need to redefine one's identity and imaginary.)[46] While the contributions of Afro-Colombians to Colombian music, folklore, and dance was already well documented, the multicultural turn saw a critical reflection on the invisibility of blackness and Afro-Colombian artists in visual art and the fact that few of them are formally trained.[47] Until then, Colombia's contemporary art scene had seldom engaged with questions of race. Angola notes that when blackness did appear, it was often subject to an exogenous gaze.[48] The exhibition was therefore intended to start a conversation about blackness in artistic practice, to situate blackness within the genealogy of Colombian art, and to make visible a previously marginalized body of work.

An extensive analysis of each of the exhibition's artistic works is beyond the scope of this book, but in works such as Fernando Restrepo's *Las calabazas del sol*, Cristo Hoyo's *Tambucos, ceretas y cafongos*, Lorena Zúniga's *Blanco siniestro*, and Fabio Melecio Palacio's *No todo es igual, no todo tiene la misma significación*, artists explored racial constructs of beauty, experiences of prejudice and discrimination, the impact of Colombia's civil war on black communities, black ritual and religion, and the preservation of Afro-Colombian cultural practices. In keeping with the exhibition's reflection on racial stereotypes and antiblackness, Angulo presented *Objetos para deformar, Negramenta, Un negro es un negro*, and *Negro utópico*, which engage the gendered configurations of antiblack stereotypes and the politics of seeing in relationship to the black body. Prior to *Viaje sin mapa*, Angulo had exhibited different versions of *Negro utópico* since its first public showing in 2001. I focus on the version she presented in *Viaje sin mapa* to not only locate her within the exhibition's larger conversation about blackness, but also because in comparison to the other works she showed at the exhibit, some of the strategies she deploys in this version of *Negro utópico* are somewhat similar to the ones used in *Mambo negrita*, and they demonstrate a general approach to deconstructing stereotypes of blackness amid national celebrations of multiculturalism.

Angulo, for example, uses ambiguity in her presentation of stereotypes to engage in acts of opacity. In *Negro utópico*, the artist offers a series of blackface self-portraits in which she dons a large Afro wig and wears a suit and a tie. In each image, the subject's face is covered with such a thick layer of black paint that her face is virtually unidentifiable. Except for the black gloves, the color and pattern of the clothes are the same as the background, which in this case is yellow tablecloth with a fruit motif (see figure 3.8). The tablecloth is so striking and large that it looks like the wallpaper of a kitchen. Although the title of the series translates as "utopian black man," and at initial glance, the piece seemingly presents the image of a black man doing domestic work, it is actually the artist dressed in drag. The drag performance registers a gender ambiguity that refuses the transparency of the gender binary. Is this a negrita impersonating a black man, or is it a black man performing domestic chores? More importantly, is this an inversion of the gendered and racialized expectations of domestic work?

The ambiguity in *Negro utópico* extends to the presentation of the black body as part object, part human, particularly through hair: in each of the images, the subject dons a wig made of Brillo pads used for cleaning pots, pans, or cooking items, which she also utilized in an earlier piece,

3.8 *Negro utópico* series, 2001–6. Courtesy of Liliana Angulo.

Pelucas doradas (1999). Throughout the series, the subject strikes three sets of poses while holding or employing objects associated with domestic labor — an iron, a broom, a cutting board, and a blender. In the first set, the subject's steel-wool hair is golden, and they wield a knife to scrape slices of banana from a cutting board into a blender.[49] In the second one, the hair has become gigantic, but it is no longer golden. In addition, the subject clutches the broom like a standing mic and poses like a rock star, cocking their head back as if they were singing, and touches their hair with another hand. In the third set, the subject is shown again with the smaller wig as they iron their tie on the ironing board. Each set concludes with the subject completing each action: blending the fruit and drinking from the blender, offering a new pose with the broom, and simply posing with the iron on the ironing board. Even though the figure is seen with household items, some of the gestures do not conform to the expectations of a domestic servant at all. How does one interpret this play between objecthood and subjecthood, the performance of gender ambiguity and racial excess, the use of gestures, and the piece's reference to a constellation of racial stereotypes, including the black domestic servant and the black entertainer, as well as its allusion to the politics of black hair? And why is this piece framed as a utopia?

Laura Levin describes *Negro utópico* as an act of self-camouflage, "a form of art-making" in which "the subject negotiates the terms of their appearance."[50] Furthermore, Levin sees Angulo's use of blackface as "a refusal to embody a transparent racial type."[51] In *Negro utópico* Angulo's refusal of transparency is encoded in the ambiguous gestures, the gender-bending, the deployment of blackface, and the out-of-placeness of the black man in the kitchen. The thickness of the black paint occludes the subject's identity so effectively that it renders the black body opaque. In other words, this is a performance of what Daphne Brooks calls "spectacular opacity" — a cultural phenomenon where marginalized figures wield "gestures and speech, as well as material props and visual technologies . . . to confound and disrupt conventional constructions of the racialized and gendered body."[52] She further explains that spectacular opacity "emerges either as a product of the performer's will, or as visual obstacle erupting as a result of the hostile spectator's epistemological resistance to reading alternative racial and gender representations."[53] The subject's opacity is one of several defamiliarizing strategies that Angulo utilizes, like other black artists, to "contest the dominant imposition of transparency systematically willed on black figures."[54] This is particularly relevant for discerning the implications of her performance of racial excess by way of her use of an overwhelming blackface mask. As Tina Post explains, while blackface on white performers points to the enactment of black skin on stage, because black skin is already present for black performers, blackface on black skin is less about the embodiment of blackness; instead, it is a critical engagement with the "idea of blackness."[55] In *Negro utópico*, the idea of blackness is articulated through the confusing mixture of black stereotypes that are never fully legible. The blackface mask indexes blackness as surplus layer that obscures black subjectivity, but it is also wielded as a defamiliarizing tactic whereby the artist enacts a refusal to comply with the imperatives of gendered and racial legibility that are placed on black bodies.[56] Angulo's artwork deploys and reworks a set of stereotypical racial codes not to reaffirm racist constructs of blackness but to engage in performances of opacity that are themselves acts of refusal.

Angulo also uses impersonation to defamiliarize racial signifiers and to expose the violence of racialization. *Negro utópico*, for example, offers a stunning reflection on the work the black body is made to do in processes of racialization. The paint on the skin, the black gloves, and the wig made of Brillo pads are the accoutrements of a racial assemblage that underscores how parody can make visible processes of racialization—the modes through which corporeal features such as hair and skin are made to function as racial signifiers. In *Negro utópico*, the performance of racial excess indexes how racialization imbues the body with meaning. Moreover, in rendering bodily features like hair as cleaning objects, Angulo illuminates how such processes of racialization, as they emerge from histories of slavery, disciplined and transformed the black body into merchandise or instruments of labor. By staging the literal transformation of the blackened body into an object and having the subject operate in an ambiguous, liminal zone between human and thing, this racial assemblage underscores how processes of racialization have been coterminous with the rendering of black subjects as not quite or not fully human. As theorist Mara Viveros explains, Angulo uses dark humor to exaggerate racist stereotypes and to underscore "the tensions and ambiguities that sustain stereotypes of gender and race, forever linking them to the history of slavery and postcolonial servitude that one often prefers to forget."[57] Indeed, Angulo's engagement with the "thingification" of blackness indexes the violence of racism and histories of slavery wherein "blackness marks simultaneously both the performance of the object and the performance of humanity."[58]

The defamiliarization of the stereotypes extends to Angulo's critical interrogation of the relationship between racialization and space. In our conversations, Angulo has explained that *Negro utópico* was inspired by a racist advertising event she witnessed at a shopping mall where black women were called upon to act as live mannequins to wash a new jeans product that was on sale at a store.[59] She intended *Negro utópico* to be a critical reflection on the naturalization of the black woman as a fixture of domestic space. Angulo presents herself as an opaque negrita in drag, so consumed by the kitchen-tile pattern of their clothes, the tablecloth, and the background that theorist Giraldo describes her as a *mujer negra cocina* (kitchen black woman), the incarnation of the kitchen.[60] This is an act of what I am calling *spatial drag*—a strategy that she also uses in *Mambo negrita*. Spatial drag rejects the presumed distinction between material body and physical space; instead, it redraws and blurs the boundaries between the two. When enacted by racialized bodies, spatial drag exposes how space—and its systems of racial signification—is inscribed onto bodily matter and, concurrently, how the body shifts, reconfigures, consolidates, and reenacts spatial meaning. The subject's blending with the kitchen-tile background captures this process of spatial inscription. As a mujer negra cocina—or perhaps, given the protagonist's gender ambiguity, a *cuerpo cocina* (kitchen body)— they underscore the configuration of the black female body as a literal kitchen fixture and its social disappearance. In *Negro utópico*, the kitchen is shown to be a site of racial and gendered enclosure for the black woman, and this reveals that space is not a passive background but an actor in the production of racial signification, laying the coordinates of racial confinement and obscuring black subjectivity. Moreover, since, as Lane notes, the "kitchen will travel with her when she leaves the room," the meaning of the black female body is never fully dislocated nor unfixed from the space of racial subordination.[61] Spatial drag breaks the illusion of space as a hermetically sealed unit of racial meaning and thus indexes the racial body as bearer, transporter, and ground zero of spatial/racial coordinates.

And yet, gender-bending, as a feature of this performance of opacity, is a strategy of defamiliarization: the figure of the black man in the kitchen disrupts the gendered expectations placed on the black female body and the designation of the kitchen as a space of black female labor. This form of defamiliarization works in two ways. First, it marks a queering of the black female body; it denaturalizes the body's role as a kitchen fixture and troubles the kitchen's power as a disciplinary space of black female domesticity, labor, and commodification. Second, in using drag, *Negro utópico* doubles as a meditation on the racist imperatives placed on black women *and* black men. Angulo may have intended the piece to be a critical reflection on stereotypes of black women, but the title "negro" instead of "negra" and the protagonist of the piece suggests that this is also a reflection on stereotypes of black men. Mara Viveros notes that while much has been said about the sexualization of black women, very little has been written on stereotypes of black men, who are construed in Colombia as Dionysian beings fundamentally interested in the excessive enjoyment of sex, dance, and alcohol.[62] As Viveros explains, in Colombia, the black man represents the subordinated referent through which hegemonic white and mestizo masculinities are constructed. But in *Negro utópico*, none of the typical stereotypes of black masculinity are legible or clear. The spectacle of a black man undertaking tasks associated with black female servants does not conform to conventional gendered and racialized expectations. The setting marks an out-of-placeness: the kitchen does not quite fit with these stereotypes, thus complicating the stereotypical meanings attached to black masculinity. *Negro utópico* evokes the figure of a feminized black man and, through it, the specter of a queer masculinity. Like the machita in the Danza de Caporales, whose flirtatious interplay with the caporala undermines and disrupts the patriarchal and heteronormative scripts of the dance, so the queer negro in Angulo's piece also challenges gendered norms.

This queer masculinity intervenes in gendered conventions that deem kitchen chores the domain of women and represents a refusal to comply with conventional patriarchal mandates that deem completing kitchen chores to be counter to the standards of "manly" behavior. In the piece, the specter of the black queer man displaces the black female body as a fixture of the kitchen and, concurrently, refuses to reproduce conventional stereotypes of the negrito. And yet, unlike the machita figure, whose interaction with the enslaved black bodies works to reproduce the subjugation of blackness at the scene of enjoyment, in Angulo's piece, a queer masculinity's challenge of gendered norms troubles the logics of racial power. For though the presence of multiple stereotypes in *Negro utópico* may initially seem to conjure the fantasies of a racist utopia, the stereotypes of both black men and women are mismatched and rendered strange and illegible. The stereotypes are collapsed through a performance of spectacular opacity that upends the racist and gendered expectations placed on the black male/female body and that undercuts the disciplinary racial power of the space.

Furthermore, the actions of the protagonist in the images are also refusals to fulfill the mandates of a racist utopia that rely on black servitude.

In the last image, the subject's pose subverts the expectations of servitude by serving themselves: they are seen drinking the juice from the blender. For whom exactly are they making the juice? Is this really the mere fulfillment of the duties of the black servant working in the kitchen? Or is this an act of defiance, a reclaiming of ownership over the space and site of racial domination? The spectacular opacity of the poses, gender, and blackface throughout the series enables the piece to disrupt the racist utopia, to subtly mark a wry refusal, and to stage moments of black autonomy. Angulo ultimately transforms the racist utopia of *Negro utópico* into one of those "dark points of possibility that create figurative sites for the reconfiguration of black and female bodies on display."[63] This attempt to render the stereotype the scene of transformation and radical possibility through racial conjuring is at the heart of Angulo's artistic project, introduced in *Negro utópico* and further explored in her interrogation of the stereotypes and racial scripts assigned to black women in *Mambo negrita*.

Defining the *Negrita*

In her artist statement, Angulo explains that *Mambo negrita* is a critical engagement with the iconography of black womanhood and its relationship to objecthood:

> In this work, I am interested in the icons of generic faces that represent black women. These are common souvenirs in the memory of many people because they formed part of the decoration of spaces and objects related to housework; they were present in the domestic spaces of the home, especially the kitchen, and they themselves were constituted as domestic objects. These objects interest me because they represented— without seeing her—a black woman: the faces generally have blue or green eyes, and they correspond to representations of other stereotypes that are simply painted black.... These types of images—generally smiling and placid—reveal the hierarchical place of the woman in colonial hegemony and, in the case of the poor black woman, correspond to a triple segregation that objectifies, exoticizes, and perpetuates stigmatization.[64]

The artist further reveals that the piece offers a multilayered stereotype, as it was meant to examine the iconography of the black female body as it shifts between domestic servitude and rumba: the former refers to "docility and submission" and the latter to "exoticism and sexuality."[65] She also seeks to explore the "normalizing and disciplinary consequences these representations have had on the formation of the identity of women of African descent."[66] This statement is important because it underscores that *Mambo negrita* is a critical reflection on the stereotype of the happy domestic servant and hypersexual negrita who is ever ready to serve, and with the racial and sexual politics of collectionism—the negrita as kitsch—and with a particular racial iconography across popular culture. The piece engages the modes and technologies through which the negrita comes to be imbued with meaning. In preparation for *Mambo negrita*, the artist started a personal collection of negrita images and souvenirs culled from popular culture, local markets in Colombia, and her travels abroad. I incorporate her personal archive here not only to present the iconography of black women in the Colombian imaginary that serve as the exhibit's primary references, but also to examine the disciplinary technologies she mentions and to unpack who the negrita is and the work she has been made to do within regimes of representation.

Negrita is a term of both endearment and racial paternalism. It does affective work in that it functions as the grammar of familial love and sexual desire. For example, it is often used as the nickname for the darkest member of a family or as a term of affection between spouses or lovers.[67] Because it is wielded to convey affection, belonging, intimacy, and familiarity, the *negrita*'s racial and sexual meanings are easily disavowed, and its invocation is presumed to be an act of racial innocence. This presumption of innocence naturalizes the entanglement of black womanhood with sexual desire and endearment. In these quotidian, colloquial expressions of love, the *negrita* serves as an empty canvas upon which fantasies can be projected or even displaced. Angulo's archive poses a challenge to the presumption of innocence that shrouds representations of the negrita because it presents an image world that fixes black womanhood in conditions of servitude and racial fantasy. At the heart of these representations is the fantasy of a negrita that is docile, compliant, obsequious, and nonthreatening.

Angulo's personal collection of negritas includes a set of kitchen souvenirs used for storing cutlery or spices as well as cutouts of the maternal domestic servant Eufrosina, a character from the popular Mexican cartoon Memín Pinguín. As a souvenir, the negrita evokes nostalgia from a past time or place, and as a kitchen object, she represents domesticity and "hominess." That many of the souvenirs are kitchen kitsch is also significant because as kitsch, the negrita is a mass-produced, undifferentiated thing among things: a cheap object signaling bad taste. But the racial and sexual politics of collectionism are also crucial because they are about the fantasy of racial ownership and possession. In examining the relationship between kitsch objects and pleasure, Stephanie Brown writes that "the objects' ostensible purpose is to evoke desire, both to own the object in question and for what the object represents, . . . [and] to enhance one's prestige by displaying the object."[68] Following Brown, negrita kitsch both captures the fraught relationship between blackness and objecthood and it is the ground zero for the enactment of a fantasy of racial and sexual servitude hiding in plain sight. The pleasure lies in the fact that the owner's ideas and fantasies of the racial other are imprinted upon a material object; the racial other is rendered fungible, transformed into merchandise, and instrumentalized for a particular task. Moreover, collecting negrita kitsch can be read as the accumulation of racialized and sexualized property signaling the class aspirations or wealth of its owner. Brown's claim that the object evokes desire is also salient because it suggests that negrita kitsch functions as what Robin Bernstein calls a "scriptive thing": an object that interpellates the owner and prompts a set of meaningful behaviors and actions.[69] These behaviors may be revised or resisted, but the negrita is an object that hails someone to own her, desire her, and make use of her in the kitchen.

Angulo's personal archive also includes images of black women on commercial products such as sugar packets, candy, and cleaning products. An unsettling example is Beso de Negra (Black woman's kiss), a popular chocolate from Colombia that features on its wrapper a dark-skinned woman wearing a head bandanna, a strapless tank top, red lipstick, and earrings, with her hand open as if she were showcasing the chocolate (figure 3.9).[70] Beso de Negra is the Colombian version of a Nestlé chocolate that has long been associated with blackness and antiblack slurs in Europe, which led to its eventual renaming.[71] In 2020, Nestle changed the image of the product's Colombian version and rechristened it Beso de Amor (Love's kiss). The recent change notwithstanding, Beso de Negra exemplifies the logics of symbolic possession as enacted in racial advertising. Racial advertising is the meeting ground for the fungibility of blackness, capitalist production, and racial consumption. As both a stand-in for and an extension of Nestle's chocolate, the black female body is interchangeable with the commodity. Saidiya Hartman explains that the relationship between pleasure and the possession of the enslaved person is made possible by the "replaceability and interchangeability of the commodity" and

3.9 Nestle's chocolate Beso de Negra. *La Republica*, 2020.

the "extensive capacities of property."[72] Fungibility is central to the mechanics of racial advertising because the latter relies on the figurative instrumentalization of the black female body, its divestment of subjectivity, and its conflation with merchandise. This conflation renders the black female body always available for consumption and for distribution within the circuits of racial capitalism. At the same time, Beso de Negra is also about the erotics of racial consumption. In advertising the chocolate as a "kiss" from a black woman, the product offers the consumer a sexual encounter with racial difference. The placement of the scantily clad black woman on the wrapper combined with the promise of the kiss cements black women as a hypersexual and erotic commodity ready to fulfill the (sexual) fantasies of the consumer. The negrita is depicted as sensual, exotic, and voluptuous. As a titillating seductress, she once again interpellates the consumer, invites their desire, and permits their transgression of any cultural taboos around sexual and interracial desire.

Another commodity that appears in Angulo's archive is Límpido (Crystal clear), a detergent produced by the local company JGB and owned

3.10 Límpido, featuring a black woman on the label. Screenshot, Megaseo supermarket website, 2025.

by Clorox. Límpido features the famous black woman "Blanquita" on the label (figure 3.10).[73] Blanquita was a domestic servant played by the Afro-Colombian actress Alicia García who appeared in advertisements for the bleaching product in the 1990s alongside her white mistress. Dressed in a white apron and headwrap, Blanquita cuts the figure of the happy servant in many of the television commercials. She smiles as her white mistress compliments her work and expresses amazement at the whiteness of her recently washed clothes. Blanquita affirmed the power and efficiency of the product and had notable famous ironic quips such as "La ropa queda blanquita, blanquita como yo—(The clothes stay white, white like me).[74] The irony of the phrase and her name—Blanquita translates to "little white girl or woman"—rendered her blackness the butt of the joke. Unlike Beso de Negra, here the black woman is desexualized but docile. She is a happy, naive, and clueless servant. In 2020, Clorox announced plans to change the image due to backlash.[75] Nevertheless, whether as hypersexual or asexual, Beso de Negra and Límpido facilitated and sustained a consumer's fantasy of black female complicity in her own servitude.

Another negrita in Angulo's archive is the cartoon character Negra Nieves, probably the most popular representation of the black female body in Colombia. Created by the cartoonist Consuelo Lago, a rich white woman from El Valle de Cauca, Negra Nieves first appeared in 1968 in *El País*, a newspaper in Cali, and in the decades that followed, she has featured in other popular newspapers across the country including *El Espectador* in 1975, *La Prensa* and *El Colombiano* in 1989, and *Cromos* in 1999. Lago based Negra Nieves on her black domestic servant. Following public backlash in the 1990s from notable black organizations such as the Foundation for the Advancement of the Black Race, she updated the character by referring to her as Nieves and portraying her as a pontificating university student.[76] In the cartoon, Nieves and her companions are drawn against a white background. She has wild, kinky hair and is sometimes accompanied by her hulky boyfriend Hétor, who is characterized as a simpleton. The protagonist's name represents a play on the fairy tale, "Snow White." In the fairy tale, Snow White's domesticity is initially a form of punishment by her jealous stepmother, the queen, but in her relationship with the seven dwarves, Snow White happily cooks and cleans for them. Lagos's conjuring of a negrita as a racialized Snow White represents what Jill Lane describes as "discursive blackface"—"a narrative form of racial impersonation" in that a white woman transforms the traditional fairy tale into a racial fantasy about the consummate happy black domestic servant or the carefree, mischievous black girl.[77]

Nieves is conjured to voice and embody essentialist stereotypes of black womanhood and celebrate regional identity. For example, Nieves's maxims include "bailo luego soy" (I dance, therefore I am).[78] In one of the cartoons (figure 3.11), Nieves is shown dancing with Hétor above a caption that says "Los caleños somos sol y salsa." (We Cali people are sun and salsa).[79] This image presents the stereotype of black people as natural dancers while also associating the city of Cali with enjoyment. As cartoons, Nieves and Hétor render innocuous the violence of racial ventriloquism wherein a white oligarchical woman conjures a black woman to articulate white and mestizo fantasies of blackness. Like the appeals to a national identity or national culture that were made in Miami and Cuba by sympathizers seeking to defend the negrito figures, when Lago faced accusations of racism, she, too, appealed to regional pride. She insisted that Nieves was "not a caricature but a 'Cali-cature,'" who represented the

3.11 Colombian cartoon character Negra Nieves with boyfriend Hétor. Screenshot, Facebook page, Nieves-Consuelo Lago.

¡Los caleños somos sol y salsa!

"typical character from the Cauca valley" and was unafraid "to tell it like it is."[80] The figure of the negrita enables Lago to transgress social mores and escape the strictures of her elite class and racial position, and to imagine an identification with the common people and the region. By describing Nieves as a "Cali-cature," Lago fixes blackness within a spatial configuration of the national imaginary that confines blackness to the coasts. In Negra Nieves the *negrita* is thus conjured as a servant to do discursive work: she serves as a voice of the everyday person, an uninhibited truthteller, and a conduit through which her white conjurer can stage a racial and regionalist fantasy.

In our conversations, Angulo also informed me that *Mambo negrita* is an engagement with representations of the negrita in Colombian folklore and carnival. The polka-dot dress in her exhibit bears an uncanny resem-

3.12 Black woman dressed as *la negrita puloy* at a carnival in Colombia. *My Beautiful City Barranquilla* (blog), March 21, 2011.

blance to the costumes worn to celebrate the Negrita Puloy de Monte-cristo, an emblem of folklore and dance in the Barranquilla carnival (figure 3.12).[81] In the early 2000s, the Colombian government declared the carnival national patrimony, and UNESCO placed it on the list of Intangible Cultural Heritage of Humanity. In her study of the *negrita puloy*, theorist Monica Gontovnik explains that the figure was invented in the 1960s by a family in Barranquilla.[82] An example of hemispheric blackface, the negrita puloy illustrates the ways the negrita is forged in the interconnected yet disparate networks of racial trafficking in the hemispheric fold. The figure was heavily influenced by blackface characters from Cuba's teatro bufo tradition, the famous black maternal figures Mamá Dolores from the Mexican film *El derecho de nacer*, Eufrosina from the Mexican cartoon Memín Pinguín, and the Mammy from the US hit movie *Gone with the Wind*.[83] The term *puloy* is taken from Puloil—a brand of cleaning products used for housework. Today, the negrita puloy is a popular figure in carnival comparsas.[84] She represents the transmutation of the self-sacrificing black maid into the jovial, happy, sexualized black servant.

Played by a white or black performer, the negrita puloy is often seen dancing on stage in a folkloric red polka-dot costume at the carnival. Her status as one of the emblematic figures of the Barranquilla carnival has made her the symbol of enjoyment. Indeed, the famous slogan of the carnival is "quien lo vive es quien lo goza" (anyone who lives it, enjoys it).[85] Like the performances at the Virgen de la Candelaria discussed in chapter 1, the carnival is also where Barranquilla celebrates a regional history of mestizaje. Akin to Sambos's performance that commemorates blackness while simultaneously fixing it within the scripts of black invisibility from Peruvian discourses of mestizaje, performances of blackness via the negrita puloy at the carnival bolster the illusion of racial harmony in the triracial national imaginary, despite the ongoing reality of racial exclusion.[86] The negrita puloy tethers the black female servant to fun, fiesta, and uninhibited abandon, and her presence consolidates the racial scripts of Colombia's nationalist fiction staged at the carnival.

The renditions of black womanhood in Angulo's archive correspond to the material realities of Afro-Colombian women and are tied to the ubiquitous representations of black women as domestic servants in Colombian popular culture. Colombia's racial hierarchies are made explicit in a 2011 feature from the magazine *¡Hola!* on what it described as "the most powerful women in the Valle del Cauca."[87] The article showcased a picture of the millionaire socialite Sonia Zarzur with the white women in her family and their black domestic servants in the background at her lavish mansion. In the foreground of the image, the four white women of the family were dressed in white shirts, blue jeans, and high heels. They are seated on plush white couches and black chairs. They smiled as they looked straight at the camera. A large pool, lush green landscape with trees, vegetation, and stunning mountains loomed in the background. The two black domestic servants wearing aprons, headwraps, and holding trays in their arms stand behind the white women. A mere detail in the background, instead of looking at the camera, the black women face each other. The visual juxtaposition of the unnamed black female servants and members of the white elite family underscores how white female power is articulated through the subordination of black women in Colombia. It also represents the way racial hierarchies organize gender categories, in that the display of white and mestiza power articulates a racial distinction in the scripts of womanhood. Just as the queer performance of the machitas discussed in chapter 1 underscores how gendered performances are levied to reinforce black subjugation, the magazine's celebration of female power fortifies racial scripts of black servitude. While the turn to multiculturalism in Colombia enabled the recognition of racial diversity and opened the door to new understandings of blackness, there undoubtedly remain ongoing struggles around stereotypical representations of blackness in popular culture. Images like this one reveal the racial constraints and conditions placed on personhood and citizenship by animating the scripts of racial power endemic to local discourses of mestizaje. Although this photograph appeared years after Angulo debuted *Mambo negrita*, it remains salient for understanding how black womanhood continues to function as a sign of domesticity and servitude and how racial fantasies in fictional representations of blackness are tied to the lived realities and representations of black women.

The contents of Angulo's archive suggest that *Mambo negrita* is not a response to a singular representation of the negrita; rather, it exposes the negrita to be a constellation of racial and sexual fantasies that oscillate between the domestic, the hypersexual, the jovial, the submissive, and the complacent. The conjuring of the negrita as an object, a scriptive thing, merchandise, a collectible item, kitchen kitsch, a caricature, and a folkloric figure across Angulo's archive underscores the role of images and material culture in reaffirming the fungibility and availability of the black female body in the hemispheric fold. This fungibility combined with the fantasy of black female complacency suggest that these representations and modes of racial conjuring are methods of racial containment. Angulo unearthed the role the negrita is conjured to play in Colombian popular culture. Her engagement with kitsch objects and candy wrappers illuminates the prevalence of blackface in quotidian material culture and its role in sustaining the racial scripts of mestizaje. These racial scripts are disciplinary technologies precisely because they fix the negrita in tropes of racial essentialism. Furthermore, the rendition of the negrita as object—kitsch, souvenir, or candy—not only indexes the logic of blackness as an object among objects, as Fanon so eloquently writes, but it also reenacts and symbolically replicates the power dynamics of racial possession.[88] They domesticate the negrita, render her docile and complicit in her own subordination, and facilitate the fantasy of racial ownership. *Mambo negrita* appropriates these disciplinary technologies to intervene in these representations and in the dynamics of racial power that they reproduce. When wielded by black artists like Angulo, acts of racial conjuring play a crucial rule in interrogating slavery's logics of symbolic possession and carving out spaces of resistance.

Mambo negrita: Resistance in a Scene of Racial Enjoyment

Soon after Angulo's involvement with *Viaje sin mapa*, the Museum of Modern Art of Bogotá invited her to do an installation for the Ninth Art Biennale (November 2006–January 2007). Members of the curatorial committee were María Belén Saez de Ibarra, Bernardo Ortiz, Gustavo Chirolla, and others. The committee announced the biennale's organizing theme to be *Cohabitar* (Cohabit, or Living Side by Side) and that it sought to facilitate a dialog on "coexistence, tolerance, . . . hybridities, [and] the dialectical relationship between different subjects who live together and depend on a space."[89] While the biennale's invitation for artistic reflections on "plurality and alterity" was open-ended, it certainly corresponded to Colombia's multicultural turn. When Angulo arrived at the museum to participate, she noticed the lack of racial diversity among the other artists and the exhibition's limited engagement with questions of race. She decided then to use her piece to reflect on the racial politics of the biennale, practices of tokenization in artistic institutions, and the exigencies the new multicultural imaginary placed on black artists.[90] Angulo envisioned the piece, in part, as a direct response to the ways black artists are tokenized and summoned to act as racial experts, to bear the burden of representation in white and mestizo spaces, and to undertake certain performances of blackness in the service of official celebrations of diversity and multiculturalism. Since the museum goes by the acronym MAMBO, Angulo named the installation *Mambo negrita*.

The artwork's title is therefore a send-up of an elite artistic institution and the fraught relationship between art institutions, blackness, and black art. In this context, it represents a critique of the exploitation of blackness and the invisibility of black art in elite artistic spaces. Angulo's appropriation of the negrita—and all its connotations of endearment, subservience, and innocence—is a self-deprecating reference to the fetishization of blackness and black artists. Wielding this fraught term as a satirical device, Angulo framed her piece as a performance of racial caricature and as a restaging of the fantasy of racial and sexual servitude that imagines the negrita, and by extension, the black artist, blackness, and black art, as property and objects of display. By positioning herself—a black artist—as a negrita, Angulo answers the interpellative call to be the grateful servant ready to perform blackness for the public in tongue-in-cheek fashion.

This self-deprecating tactic seems to be almost a declaration: "¡*Yo seré tu negrita!*" (I will be your negrita).

In this rendering of the negrita, Angulo co-opted the tropes of her personal material archive. She presented a hodgepodge of stereotypes of black women that strings together the dancing, the domestic, the fetishized, the hypersexualized/eroticized, and the exotic black female body. This installation is a subtle mockery of the demands placed on the negrita to act as happy servants or sexualized objects of desire. Even in her self-deprecating embrace of the negrita, what she ultimately performs is a riff of stereotypes of black womanhood. Self-reflective and ironic, *Mambo negrita* pulls together multiple strategies of defamiliarization to trouble the politics of racial and symbolic possession and to destabilize modes of seeing or not seeing the black female body. I contend that at the heart of her intervention is a double-reflective gesture that exposes technologies of racial disciplining and reworks them to resist stereotypical constructs of black womanhood.

First, Angulo wields spatial drag to blur the boundaries between background and foreground in each photograph. The red polka-dot textile of the background is so overwhelming, for instance, that it threatens to consume the protagonist of each photograph. By dressing each model in the wallpaper, Angulo stages the disappearance of the black female body at the scene of domesticity, indexing the kitchen as a site of racial disciplining. Yet, her use of blackface on black skin highlights the protagonist and ensures that the models, and their blackness, are seen. Marked as a type of racial excess, blackness becomes hypervisible in a scene where it is supposed to simply disappear. Blackface is working here to drag the protagonist out of obscurity, to make the subject be seen. These acts of racial conjuring reconfigure blackness in ways that both expose and trouble the role of space in fixing blackness in racial stereotypes. One may read this racial excess as the refusal to fully disappear into the background. An alternative reading might also suggest that it is from this position of being fixed that the black woman registers her refusal to be fully complacent. Both readings are apropos because, ultimately, blackface is working against fixing the black female body in the kitchen.

Furthermore, in registering a refusal and in oscillating between flirtatiousness and aggression, Angulo also challenges the dynamics of black objecthood. Since *Mambo negrita* is, in fact, the imitation of the black woman as an object, these gestures and refusal constitute a moment where the object comes to life. Fred Moten proclaims that "the history of blackness is testament to the fact that objects can and do resist."[91] Angulo's impersonation of the object indexes the fungibility of blackness, its rendering of blackness into an object, commodity, or merchandise at the heart of practices of racial conjuring. And yet, the oscillation of affective registers of the performance and the attempts to make the black subject be seen is an invitation to "reimagine black objecthood as a way toward agency rather than its antithesis."[92]

Black agency is not only enacted through these refusals, but also through the intervention in the relationship between race and space. As described at the beginning of the chapter, the exhibition space was set up as a triangular labyrinth in the corner of the third floor whose walls, ceiling, and floor were covered with the same polka-dot pattern from the photographs (figure 3.13). In mounting a labyrinth that showcases all these racial stereotypes and fantasies of black womanhood, Angulo re-creates a space and scene of racial enjoyment. And yet, the labyrinth is so cloaked in the same fabric and colors that the space lacks clear definition. The overwhelming red-and-white haze ensures that the space swallows and closes in on itself and the spectator. In addition, the artist placed full-length mirrors that hung from the ceiling to the floor between some of the portraits, which amplified the sense of repetition. The full-length mirrors reflected both the spectator and the portraits on the opposite walls of the labyrinth. The reflections seemingly doubled the individual portraits in the space and rendered unclear the sequence and order of the photographs. In the middle of the installation, the spectator encountered a small television showing a video of a faceless black woman dressed in the same polka-dot fabric dancing to Pérez Prado's vibrant Latin hit song "Mambo Jambo!" on a loop. At every turn, the spectator was surrounded by a maze of repeating images and sounds that confronted them not only with stereotypes of a black female body but also with the reflection of their own image. Angulo stated that her intention was to "overwhelm and disappear the house, the private space, and the space of servitude" and to "generate an ambiguous relationship between the deterritorialization of the space and the body."[93] This deterritorialization is an act of dislocation, a meddling with the internal coordinates of a space of racial enjoyment that has typically been made to function as a site of racial confinement and enclosure for black women. It disoriented the spectator in ways that disrupted the feeling of enjoyment. Disruption is how ambiguity becomes a domain of racial enjoyment that makes racial gratification or pleasure unstable and even uncomfortable.

Room B

Covered patio

Height 4.1 m

Height 2.9 m

Room A

1 m

.95 m

2.1 m

1.25 m

.9 m

2.5 m

2.5 m

2.5 m

2.5 m

7.13 m

27.45 m

16.4 m

1.8 m

.74 m

.74 m

7.1 m

1.4 m

3.9 m

1.7 m

8 m

1 m

3.25 m

2.36 m

5.06 m

4.73 m

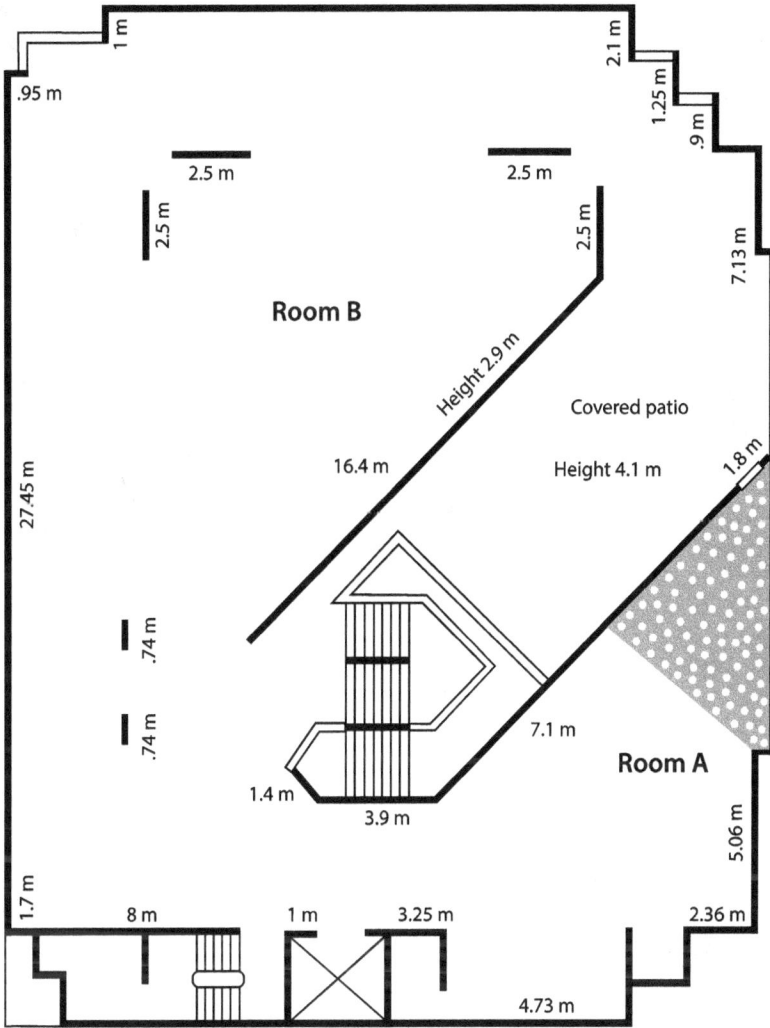

3.13 Drawing of floor plan for the *Mambo negrita* exhibit, Museum of Modern Art of Bogotá, 2006. Courtesy of Liliana Angulo.

Angulo's use of full-length mirrors between the photographs also displayed how hypervisibility works to produce the negrita as archetype (figure 3.14). Yet, she does so not to simply reproduce the stereotype, but to ultimately reverse the gaze and to present an object that looks back. Through the hyperversibility and multiplication of the negritas, she invited the spectators to immerse themselves in a world completely inhabited by these representations. The replication of racialized images may

3.14 Liliana Angulo's photographs displayed with mirrors in the *Mambo negrita* exhibit, 2006. Courtesy of Liliana Angulo.

be understood, in part, as a reflection on the colonial practices of hypervisibility that continue to haunt black people. Within these visual regimes, the enslaved black subject was permanently subjected to both a surveilling gaze and scopic lust.[94] The use of hypervisibility in the exhibit thus symbolically reproduces the predicaments of black women trapped as objects of surveillance and desire in relation to a white and mestizo gaze. Although this specular repetition mirrors the disciplinary practices that have historically constricted the black female body within visual regimes of representation, it does so in ways that force spectators to experience this symbolic entrapment with black women—the objects of the gaze. The spectator not only sees their own reflection but must also confront the images. Angulo thus creates a hall of mirrors where the black female subject literally haunts the spectator who enters. This is the surveilling gaze turned on its head, creating a sensation of a surveilling seer who is almost entrapped by the gaze of the object.

Also, since there is pleasure and power in looking at the other, the mirrors disrupt the pleasures of scopophilia: for to enter the installation is to be both the object of the gaze and the bearer of it.[95] In other words, both the one who looks, and the thing being looked at, are put on display. By blurring the distinction between who is looking and who is being looked at, *Mambo negrita* does not allow the black female body to be fully fixed as the object of the gaze. Thus, the installation creates a kaleidoscopic experience that destabilizes the photographic relationship between seeing and being seen. This is particularly important because within the normative logic of racial spectacle, "black figures [were] there to be looked at, shaped to the demands of desire; they were screens on which audience fantasy could rest."[96] In contrast, through its kaleidoscopic arrangement, Angulo creates a type of "prismatic specularity" whereby the black subject refuses "the static and passive position of traditional racial, visual, and political dynamics [and instead] watches the white audience looking not at an 'authentic' black 'soul' but at an ambivalent fiction that is rooted in white projections."[97] This prismatic specularity creates an unstable visual dynamic defined by the shifting and oscillating positionalities between the seer and seen.

The spectator's experience of shared entrapment, which creates a hyperawareness of oneself and of the racial other, invites a process of self-reflection on one's own positionality and one's own investments and participation in the economies of looking at blackness. *Mambo negrita* asks the spectator to face their own racialization in relation to the racialization of the black female body. For white and mestizo spectators, the experience of shared entrapment forces them to confront their own racial privileges. One must reckon with one's own gaze and the gaze of the other simultaneously. But the prismatic specularity is also important because *Mambo negrita* is not simply about confounding a white and mestizo audience; it is also about registering a black gaze. As Tina Campt so eloquently explains, black artists invert the normal rules of spectatorship and specularity by offering confrontational, oppositional, or interrogating gazes. She explains, a black gaze "disrupts the equation of a gaze with structures of domination by refusing to grant mastery or pleasure to a viewer at the expense of another [and by] refusing to allow its subjects to be consumed by its viewers. A black gaze transforms viewers to witnesses and demands a confrontation."[98] This confrontation is surely at work in the exhibit's call for self-reflection and in its refusal to present a passive black female body available for consumption. For a racialized subject who enters the labyrinth as a spectator, the installation may serve as the staging of what Du Bois refers to as the experience of double consciousness: of both seeing oneself and confronting how one is seen in the eyes of hegemonic culture.[99] In this way, *Mambo negrita* can be experienced as a space

3.15 Headless woman dancing on a television screen as part of *Mambo negrita*. Courtesy of Liliana Angulo.

of solidarity where one identifies with gestures of black rage, or where one confronts the pain and horrors of racialization and of living as a stereotype. Furthermore, in registering a black gaze and bringing the object to life, Angulo creates a site where spectators can bear witness to the double consciousness of the object. This is precisely the transformation of the viewer into a witness that Campt so aptly describes.

While *Mambo negrita* critically engages black objecthood and the fungibility of blackness, as well as the ways in which racial conjuring summons blackness as an empty vessel and dispossessed body, Angulo also subtly affirms black female subjectivity in the piece. The small television at the center of the installation showing a video of a faceless black woman dancing (figure 3.15), along with the installation's title, *Mambo negrita*, evokes the figure of the dancing black female body and its attendant stereotypical association of blackness with musicality. This stereotype constructs black people as naturally musical and as happy-go-lucky, natural entertainers. More significantly, the negrita's face in the video appears completely cut off, so only the body is on display. According to Angulo, the faceless negrita is a mimicry of representations of black women in the work of renowned Colombian painter Ana Mercedes Hoyos, whose paintings frequently document black life and feature black market women from the Palenque de San Basilio. In many of these paintings, black subjects are depicted without a face alongside fruits or other objects from the marketplace. The juxtaposition of the fruit and the faceless black bodies in Hoyos's paintings reaffirms the relationship between black womanhood and objecthood, as the black woman appears as an undifferentiated object, hardly distinct from the basket of fruit.[100]

Facelessness is important because, as theorists Agnes Lugo-Ortiz and Angela Rosenthal note in their examination of portraiture, the face is the primary site of subjectivity.[101] The face was seen as the privileged tool for the visualization of the being and the production of the subject. Within the logic of chattel slavery, "facelessness [became] the means by which the slave is theoretically rendered a non-subject."[102] Angulo's impersonation of a faceless negrita evokes practices of racial effacement in Colombia, pointing to the ways in which contemporary visual regimes obscure the presence of black subjectivity, deny black singularity, and render black women as nonsubjects in the visual field. Yet, Angulo disrupts and destabilizes the negation of black female subjectivity in the video by placing it at the center of the images of different black women in the exhibit. The different faces on the walls and mirrors disrupt the absence of black singularity. The multiplication of diverse black faces surrounding the video registers a difference where facelessness only suggests total homogeneity; it marks a presence where there should be erasure.

The use of Pérez Prado's crossover hit "Mambo Jambo!" as *Mambo negrita*'s theme song is also significant because it is a hemispheric gesture. Mambo is a crossover commercial music genre linking Latin America and the Caribbean to US popular culture. Pérez Prado himself was a migrant figure—moving from Cuba to Mexico to the United States.[103] Due to his commercial success as the Rey del Mambo or the King of Mambo in the 1940s, as well as his constant movement, Pérez Prado became the symbolic figure of a larger pan-metropolitan sound that could be found in global centers like Tokyo, Paris, Mexico City, London, and New York. In placing the negrita archetypes alongside the figure of Pérez Prado and his song, *Mambo negrita* gestures to the transnational reach and circulation of the negrita and her connection to tropes of blackness and latinidad in the hemispheric fold. The faceless black female body covered in black paint dancing to this iconic crossover song is a metaphor for hemispheric blackface wherein a blackface performance is linked — metaphorically or otherwise — to networks of racial trafficking in the hemispheric Americas. And yet, in the installation, the negrita's dancing in the video did not match the song's rhythm: she is off-beat and out-of-sync. The lack of synchronicity between time, sound, and bodily movement constitutes yet another strategy of disruption and resistance. Once again, Angulo reproduces and defamiliarizes the stereotype by offering a negrita who refuses to fully meet the stereotypical demands placed on her. The black female body defies the disciplinary imperatives of temporal and sonic synchronicity and instead registers her agency by moving to her own beat.

Finally, by setting the exhibition to a theme song, Angulo framed the entire installation as a type of fanciful nonsense or as a gimmick of a racial performance. In its citation of visual representational practices, *Mambo negrita* jumbles together portraiture, photography, music videos, advertising, and blackface performance. The exhibition is an artistic reflection that offers a representation of a representation, or a representation of a genre of representation. It is a metaphor for blackface on black skin itself as a type of embodied practice and as a representation of a representation. In this metarepresentation, Angulo uses blackface to disorient, to discomfort, and to completely unfix blackness from regimes of representational entrapment. *Mambo negrita* thus exemplifies a moment where blackface is not being used to reify a stereotype, but is instead appropriated and deployed to critique, resist, and destabilize it from within. Even as the nation shifted from discourses of colorblindness to multiculturalism, acts of impersonation reworked everyday scenes of racial enjoyment to invite the spectator to scratch beneath the surface. Angulo's exhibit exposed the endurance of the racial scripts that relegate black women to the role of the happy servant, despite the new national embrace and recognition of pluriethnicity and racial diversity. Racial impersonation in this artistic work enacts a double objectification that places both the black female body and the ways it has been represented on display. The artist underscores the racial constraints on personhood and on citizenship, even as structures of racial silence have supposedly been dismantled.

In the previous chapters, I underscored how the use of racial impersonation reinforced racial stereotypes of black buffoonery and reproduced subjection as a domain of racial enjoyment. However, in this chapter, I highlight the way it can function to stage an intervention. Both the inversion and reinforcement of constructs of blackness challenge the fiction of

racial harmony and its afterlives. Resistance in the scene of racial enjoyment enables expressions of black agency and acts of spectacular opacity.
Blackface is being wielded here as a disruptive device and belongs to the
piece's larger proposal to reverse modes of looking, to trouble the pleasure of consuming blackness as spectacle. Angulo brings the object to life
to unsettle the configuration of the black woman as an object, to refuse to
be fixed in the position of passivity and stillness, and to ultimately register
black female subjectivity in spaces where it has been denied. Using impersonation, she disappears the space of racial containment and transforms
it into the site of double consciousness, a place of shared entrapment, and
a haunted house. Angulo illuminates the recuperative possibilities of impersonation as she demonstrates that the scripts of racial play can be inverted and rearranged. While I do not argue that impersonation is a space
of black liberation, I am insisting that it can be a site of confrontation
and a tool of critical interrogation. As the nationalist fiction moves away
from colorblindness to multiculturalism, Angulo's piece shows how black
people wield blackface to negotiate a moment of new political articulation. Although *Mambo negrita* offers an example of how blackface can disrupt the enjoyment of racial spectacle, in the next chapter, I ascertain how
blackface may function as a tool of resistance when racial caricatures are
conjured by and for black enjoyment. Whereas this chapter has focused
on the museum, as a domain of high art, I now turn to the politics of racial
enjoyment in popular theater, a domain of "low art" catering to the black
underclass, to discern how slavery's logics are reworked and critically engaged by black publics living in the hemispheric fold.

CHAPTER FOUR

The Postcolonial Below

Roots Theater and Black Enjoyment in Jamaica

When a childhood friend told me that there was a blackface character named Delcita Coldwater who was making waves in Jamaican popular theater, I was shocked. My family and I had always been ardent theatergoers in Kingston. Blackface performance was not a part of contemporary Jamaican theater. Although my middle-class friends were in an uproar about the actress Andrea Wright's use of blackface, I initially did not follow the character. Years later, as I conducted research for this book, I came across a YouTube video of Delcita in the popular play *Di Driva* (The Driver), which debuted at Green Gables Theatre in St. Andrew, Jamaica, to much fanfare in 2008. The comedy was written by the playwright Paul O. Beale and produced by Stages Production, the island's major producer of roots theater—a genre by and for Jamaica's black working class. The video was blurry and the sound quality was poor, but I was so mesmerized by the overwhelming laughter of the audience throughout the play that I rewatched *Di Driva* several times. Delcita was undeniably a hit.

Di Driva tells the story of the marital problems of rich politician Ronnie Jones (played by Donald Thompson) and his wife, former beauty queen Thelma Jones (played by Shermane Wisdom), which center on their struggle to conceive a child. The couple live in a wealthy community in upper St. Andrew. Thelma confides in a family friend, Dr. Susan First (played by Trudy Campbell), about their fertility problems, and the doctor suggests a surrogate as the solution. Dr. First's search for a surrogate leads her to a rural community in the countryside, where she meets Delcita Coldwater (played by Andrea Wright)—the play's lone blackface character. Delcita is a young, dark-skinned, poor woman who is functionally illiterate and struggles to feed her three children. The doctor offers Delcita the job on the condition that she keeps it a secret and does not engage in sexual activity with anyone while working as the surrogate. Delcita agrees and accepts the job. Throughout the play, the audience responds to

Delcita with raucous laughter, but it is in her first meeting with Thelma that I am able to discern the function of this blackface character.

When Dr. First reveals to Thelma that she has found a surrogate, Thelma is ecstatic and insists that Dr. First introduce them right away. But when Thelma and Delcita meet, the audience witnesses Thelma's excitement slowly turn to horror. Dr. First enters the house and calls to Thelma, who then elegantly walks down the stairs. Thelma is a slender, tall, brown woman wearing a tightly fitted green top, white capri pants, and brown sandals. Her long hair is neatly coiled over her back. Dr. First is a dark-skinned woman who wears glasses, a pink button-down shirt, tight khaki pants, pearls, and silver earrings. While all the actors are black, the class difference between Delcita and these two characters is clearly demarcated by language. The middle-class characters, Dr. First and Thelma, speak Standard English, and Thelma's accent especially is associated with an upper-class Jamaican background. They stand together in the center of the stage.[1]

> DR. FIRST: You know? I found the perfect woman to bear your child. [Dr. First squeals and giggles]
>
> THELMA: You have? [The two tightly embrace]
>
> DR. FIRST: And guess what? You are going to love her.
>
> THELMA: So, she's here?
>
> DR. FIRST: Yes, she's here.

The audience is quiet. Thelma nervously straightens her hair and fixes her clothes. Dr. First walks stage right to let Delcita in through the front door. Thelma follows, but Dr. First stops her.

> DR. FIRST: No, no, no. Don't come and kill the surprise, man. Stay right here. Straighten up until I get back.

Dr. First exits stage right, and Thelma quickly cleans the sofa, organizes the table, and adjusts her hair. But as she overhears the conversation between Delcita and Dr. First taking place offstage, her excitement turns to confusion and then horror.

> DR. FIRST: My God! In the name of Jesus! Woman, what are you doing in the cherry tree?

[Thelma looks confused. The audience chuckles.]

DELCITA: Sarry, Maam. Sarry. But de whola a red one deh up a de tap part so das why mi guu up ya suh but me a cuum dung now. (Sorry, ma'am. Sorry. But the red ones were up top, so that is why I went up there but I'm coming down now).[2]

Thelma then freezes and looks mortified. The laughter from the audience is louder now, almost threatening to overpower Delcita, who continues to shout in perfect Jamaican creole from offstage.

DR. FIRST: Come on. Get down. Get down.

DELCITA: Yea yea. Mine from deh suh! Mine from deh suh! Mine mi jump inna yuh 'ead. (Yes, yes. Be careful. Move over. Careful that I don't jump on your head.)[3]

I hear deep belly laughs from some of the spectators as Dr. First convinces Delcita to enter the house.

When Delcita walks through the door, the audience roars with laughter. The sight of her is hilarious. Some patrons bellow "WOOOOIII!" as the audience members laugh and talk among themselves. One shouts, "Lord have mercy!" Another says, "Oh God!" in wonder. Other spectators cackle as Delcita walks obliviously across the stage. In contrast to the other black characters on stage, her face is painted black. Although it is barely perceptible, blackface exaggerates the darkness of her skin and distinguishes her from the other women. It also marks a subtle contrast from the dark skin tone of her hands. Moreover, Delcita looks the part of the country bumpkin who has come to town. She wears a long-sleeved white shirt under an ill-fitting leopard-print gold dress whose hem barely covers the plaid skirt underneath; her black socks almost reach her knees; the bright pink church hat on her head is tossed to the side over a headwrap (figures 4.1 and 4.2).[4] Delcita's body is obscured under this sartorial excess, but the audience can see that she has moppy hair and rotting teeth. When Delcita enters with three large suitcases, she stomps heavily across the stage. Thelma's disdain for Delcita is palpable. Mouth agape, Thelma stares her up and down and walks from stage left to right to stand as far away from her as possible. Audience members continue laughing heartily. Meanwhile, Dr. First moves toward Thelma, encouraging her to step forward so she can introduce her to Delcita, who puts down her suitcases and

4.1 Delcita in *Di Driva*. Screenshot, BLA Productions, YouTube, April 3, 2022.

4.2 Delcita standing with Dr. First and Thelma. Screenshot, BLA Productions, YouTube, April 3, 2022.

smiles at Thelma. The audience is quiet again. Standing between the two women, Dr. First proudly introduces them.

DR. FIRST: Delcita, I would like you to meet Miss Thelma Jones. Miss Thelma Jones, this is Delcita. This is the young lady I was telling you about.

Upon being introduced, Delcita quickly realizes the horror on Thelma's face. Speaking in a high-pitched screeching voice, she confronts Thelma's scornful gaze.

DELCITA: A wah? A wah yuh a look paaan mi so fah? Look ere! Mi a tumbadi yuh nuh? Me a nuh duppy! (What is it? Why are you looking at me like that? Listen! I am somebody, you know! I am not a ghost!)

The squeals and cackles from the patrons are so loud that Delcita pauses before saying:

DELCITA: Di doctor cum fe mi urrly urrly dis mawning an wi neva get fi tap a road. An mi waan pee pee and me a DEAD fi dee dee. (The doctor came for me early, early this morning and we didn't stop [along the way]. And I want to pee. And I am DYING to defecate.)

The audience is now dying with laughter, as Thelma stands there speechless. Dr First whispers, "Bathroom, Thelma. She wants to use the bathroom." Thelma points to the staircase behind Delcita.

DELCITA: Where? Which part?

DR. FIRST: Up! Up! Up!

Delcita turns around and asks, "Round here?" and then exits up the stairs.

What is the function of Delcita and her blackface performance in this play? How might we interpret the tensions in her first meeting with her upper-class employer? How do we make sense of the audience's raucous laughter and enjoyment of the blackface character on stage? They did not receive Delcita with disdain but with delight. I find this scene compelling not only because it invites critical reflection on the politics of black performers in blackface and on the role of blackface in mediating the tensions of race and class, but also because in this scene Delcita, the blackface character, serves a dual function. She is the caricature of Jamaica's black underclass. Her use of Jamaican creole and her clothes, rotten teeth, loudness, and naivety are the presumed signs of poverty, poor hygiene, and illiteracy. Juxtaposed with Thelma Jones, who represents brown, upper-class feminine beauty, Delcita is the metonymic figure of a black working-class identity who must navigate the social prejudices of her upper-class counterparts. Yet Delcita's emphatic assertion of personhood when she declares "I am somebody!" represents a confrontation, a demand for respect, a gesture of defiance. In the play, racial impersonation seemingly marks a racial and class stereotype, but it is also levied in an act of black working-class affirmation. How does this duality and parody complicate the meaning of this blackface performance?

My investment in unpacking the function of the blackface character and the audience's enjoyment of her is driven, in part, by the fact that blackface performance is virtually non-existent in contemporary Jamaican theater. While blackface performances were common in Jamaica in the colonial era, its history is not widely known today among members of the public. The appearance of blackface on stage in Jamaica's postcolonial moment is surprising and unusual, but it is also an opportunity to consider the implications of conjuring a colonial signifier in relation to the racial politics of Jamaica's postcolonial condition. Furthermore, the conjuring of the colonial sign and its infusion with a dual meaning is complicated by the fact that Delcita is conjured for a black working-class audience and is a popular character from roots theater, a black comedic genre. Jamaican roots theater is a debased and denigrated theatrical form that emerged in the 1970s, the decade after the nation gained independence. Ralph Holness, who is considered the pioneer of the genre, is widely credited for naming it "roots" theater to capture its orientation toward the "grassroots" or ordinary experiences of Jamaicans from the lower echelons of society.[5]

Roots theater has been understudied because it is widely dismissed as a bastardized theatrical form.[6] Known for its vulgarity, explicit language, ribald treatments of sex and sexuality, and the affirmation of Jamaican creole, roots theater uses farce to center the cultural practices and quotidian experiences of Jamaica's black masses and the black underclass. Its characters are members of a local community: the country bumpkin who comes to town, the shopkeeper, the bad boy or gangster, the police officer, the driver, the helper, the ghetto girl, the street vendor, and other figures of Jamaica's working class. Conjured for black working-class enjoyment, Delcita is the representation of a marginalized demographic and a dismissed theatrical genre operating beneath the social order. As such, through Delcita, I analyze the complexities of the revival of a colonial signifier, the conjuring of blackface caricatures for black enjoyment, the dismissal of black working-class popular theatrical genres, and the ludic as a place of black working-class resistance and affirmation in Jamaica's postcolonial moment.

In this book, I have sought to map the different domains of an economy of racial enjoyment operating beneath the nationalist fictions of colorblindness and their afterlives that circulate in the hemispheric fold. The previous chapters illuminate an economy of racial enjoyment wherein blackface serves as a tool for the dynamics of either black subjugation or black resistance. But I end this book with an analysis of Delcita and roots theater to also illuminate black enjoyment as another ludic domain that is too easily and frequently dismissed as a sign of self-hatred. I argue that racial enjoyment can be an arena of struggle in which black people in the hemispheric fold participate and stake their own claims, not only as objects to be consumed or lampooned but also as critical actors, consumers, and willful participants. This is important because my purpose throughout this book has not been to frame blackface as good or bad, liberatory or oppressive; rather, in the context of black delight, *Hemispheric Blackface* attends to the paradoxes, contradictions, and ambiguities of the economy of racial enjoyment. Now that I have analyzed the domains of subjection and resistance, I consider their copresence in relation to the contradictions of black enjoyment.

Here I attend to the dualities of Delcita, a figuration of blackness conjured for the black underclass, and map the complexities of a space that I am calling *the postcolonial below*. Unlike teatro bufo, whose renditions of blackness have often been wielded to articulate white creole aspirations and celebrate Cuban national identity, the postcolonial below is a counter-ideological formation that challenges the official racial scripts of the postcolonial nation-state, and it does so while operating *below* the formal and institutional structures of postcolonial resistance. It is grounded in Douglas Jones's idea of the "black below," which he describes as "the conceptual and physical spaces of a ludic, boisterous sociality where Black people refuse to center white supremacist oppression, but celebrate themselves through laughter, tears, and sexuality with little to no qualms about how others will register their delights."[7] I imagine the postcolonial below as adjacent to his black below in that it is similarly constituted by those spaces of black working-class sociality that center the black underclass; celebrate denigrated cultural practices, values, worldviews, and vernacular forms; and do not receive institutional recognition or validation in a post-colonial context. I extend this construction to consider the implications of black enjoyment in an economy of racial enjoyment that has long been organized to consolidate white supremacy. As I argue ultimately in this chapter, the postcolonial below critically engages *abject pleasures*—those forbidden delights that disturb the order of economies of racial enjoyment in hemispheric blackface.

The postcolonial below also differs from Jones's black below in that it considers how the space of black ludic sociality mediates or intervenes in fictions of racial harmony and the contradictions of a creole society. The postcolonial, as used here, belongs to an intellectual tradition of theorizing the Caribbean as a set of Western neocolonies whose societies have been defined by modalities of hybridity, creoleness, and mestizaje that do not always fit neatly within the subaltern studies canon.[8] "The Caribbean postcolonial"—as Shalini Puri calls it—is often relegated to the margins of postcolonial studies, which focuses heavily on East/West and North/South relations.[9] Scholars in Caribbean studies like Mimi Sheller, for example, have sought to complicate the role of culture and representation in negotiating these distinct modalities of creoleness and the exclusionary regimes of citizenship they have produced. She uses "citizenship from below," for example, to theorize how those who have been excluded from regimes of citizenship remake it in extradiscursive fashion by placing emphasis on embodiment, corporeality, sexuality, and race.[10] I turn to theater because in Jamaica performances on stage were crucial to fighting the implementation of colonial rule, engaging in anticolonial struggle, and articulating national identity. The postcolonial below thus lives in a space of triangulation between the theoretical touchstones of Jones's black below and Caribbean postcolonial scholars like Sheller who focus on mapping the myriad quotidian ways in which black people redefine citizenship and trouble nationalist discourses of multiracial harmony. The particularities of Jamaica's postcolonial condition are crucial for understanding its racial politics.

Moreover, the goal of this book is to assess the work of racial conjuring in relation to different modalities of nationalist fictions of color-blindness and their afterlives in the hemispheric fold. In keeping with the conceptual organization of this book, Jamaica invites critical reflection about how the repeating nationalist fiction operates, even in a country where black people constitute the majority. Blackface poses a challenge to nationalist discourses of colorblindness because it makes visible the persistence of antiblackness in the postcolonial context, where definitions of national identity erase or silence the function of race. Through the postcolonial below, I thus attend to the rejected and discarded cultural practices where the racial scripts of creole nationalism and its concomitant celebrations of racial mixture are reworked and subverted.

Hemispheric blackface also points to how African diasporic communities use acts of racial conjuring to carve out their place within economies of racial enjoyment and to marshal the figurations of blackness circulating in the fold for their own devices. In centering the black gaze, I take seriously Jones's call to move beyond simply reading black performers in blackface as trickster figures seeking to confound a white or nonblack audience.[11] Until recently, this approach predominated studies of black minstrel performers and is similar to the one I take in my analysis of Angulo's rendition of the negrita in chapter 3.[12] Delcita is different in that she is a device conjured by and for the black working class to articulate a counternarrative and to critique the social order. Moreover, while I contend that here blackface is a technique of postcolonial resistance, in keeping with my analysis of Angulo as a black artist using blackface, I neither suggest that blackface performance is somehow free from logics of antiblackness, nor do I advance any claims of self-hatred among black publics. Like Jones and others, I, too, presume that black working-class publics are sophisticated critical audiences who are aware of how antiblack and classist tropes are utilized in their own marginalization and, nevertheless, rework them for their own pleasures and enjoyment. This differs from the use of blackface that I have discussed so far, wherein conjuring blackness has been directed primarily at white creole and mestizo enjoyment or consumption. In my theorization of Delcita and the postcolonial below, I also consider the contradictions and limitations of blackface as an instrument of social and racial affirmation for black people in a black-majority space where the history of US blackface minstrelsy is either not widely known or is not necessarily a primary referent for the local population. In the process, I unpack the messiness of black enjoyment of blackface figures, the circulation of debased racial humor in black spaces, and the function of black pleasures within the economy of enjoyment I trace in the Americas.

The Invention of Delcita

Jamaican playwright Paul O. Beale created the character of Delcita Cold-water in 1991. Beale is one of the most important playwrights in roots theater and was crucial to the development of the genre. He was born in 1962 and first began writing poetry and short stories as a teenager. He came from humble beginnings. In his teens, he briefly abandoned his interest in poetry when he was forced to drop out of school and work as a bus conductor. Beale returned to school soon after and graduated with a certificate in agriculture. He migrated from Manchester, a rural parish in Jamaica, to Kingston in 1986. He maintained his passion for theater while working as a teacher, warehouse supervisor, and in various odd jobs in the 1980s. He finally got his big break in theater when he worked with the legendary Ralph Holness on the play *Unda Mi Nose* (1987), which catapulted him to fame in the entertainment industry. Throughout an illustrious career that ended with his death in 2019, Beale created many popular Jamaican characters for theater and television, making an indelible mark on roots theater and Jamaican entertainment.[13] He wrote more than three hundred television episodes, forty-three stage plays, five short films, several radio dramas, and television commercials as well as poetry and books. Notable hit plays include *Granny Rule* (2004), *Xtortionistz* (2010), *The Plumber* (2010), *Ova Mi Dead Body* (2011), *and Di Politicians* (2012). His comedy series *Me an' mi Kru, Joint Tenants*, and *EnTRAPreneur* aired on the local television station CVM TV. He was known for his raw comedic style and his portrayal of everyday working-class characters from Jamaica's cultural life. Near the end of his career, he turned to writing children's stories.

Although Beale is widely respected in local theater circles and recognized as, perhaps, the most prolific writer of roots plays, upon his untimely death those who knew him well claimed he was disappointed not to have received national recognition for his work.[14] This could be due to widespread social prejudice that renders roots theater an undervalued, second-rate cultural industry and a lesser theatrical genre in comparison with respected "high" art forms like Jamaican dance theater. The paradoxes of Beale's fame speak to the reality for artists working in the postcolonial below. Roots theater, for example, has its own circuits of authorization and legitimation that span local and international marketplaces, but artists frequently lament the public perception of their accolades and recognition within these circuits. Some practitioners also reject the term *roots theater* and insist it is simply Jamaican comedy. Overall, success in roots theater typically offers cultural workers less social and professional currency as they ascend to mainstream and more respected venues of Jamaican entertainment.[15]

Nevertheless, one of Beale's most notable contributions is his creation of Delcita, his most famous character, for Jamaican theater. The character first appeared in a play titled *Police and Baton* (1991) as a sidekick to the character Handicap, and, in the 1990s, she was featured in two of Beale's most notable films, *Stamma 1* and *Stamma 2*. Delcita has also appeared in other Beale plays, including *Granny Rule* (2004), *Money Worries* (2010), *Di Politicians* (2012), *University of Delcita* (2013), and others. In the fictional biography *Delcita Coldwater Volume One* (2016), Beale tells us that she was born and raised in a rural community in Manchester and that her mother, Icilda Coldwater, was abusive, while her father was a womanizer. Delcita is determined to leave the countryside to make a life in Kingston. Beale explains in the text that he envisioned the character as a "representative of the masses" who "speaks her mind," shows determination, and is street smart, ambitious, intelligent, and confident.[16] Furthermore, he did not want to depict a figure from Jamaica's inner city or urban poor; he imagined a rural character. In many of the plays, she is represented as the country bumpkin who comes to town and ends up working for upper-class families, either as a secretary, domestic worker, surrogate, or live-in nurse. Delcita is a representative of rural black womanhood who offers witty one-liners and metes out advice, in the process bringing to the fore the politics of urban/rural migration, formations of antiblackness, and the racial, gendered, and class contours of structural inequality in postcolonial Jamaica.

Andrea Wright and her blackface rendition of Delcita is so iconic that people often forget that Delcita existed before her. Over the years, Delcita has been played by three different actresses: Tamika Reid, Andrea Wright, and Ann McKenzie. Originally hailing from a rural district in Clarendon, Wright modeled the character's speech and mode of dress on the women from her childhood community. She first worked with Beale in 1989 and appeared as Delcita in the 1990s. She continued to play the character in noted plays such as *Granny Rules* (2004), *Di Driva* (2008), *Ova Mi Dead Body* (2010), and *Court House Drama* (2012), and she reprised the role even after a professional dispute with Beale in 2015. Within the roots theater scene, Wright is lauded for her portrayal of the character, and her performances have won her notable local awards such as the

Gleaner's Youthlink Actress of the Year in 2012. Local and international advertisements and press coverage of roots plays have referred to her as "the Caribbean foremost female playwright, actress and comedienne" and the "Jamaican Queen of Comedy."[17] I focus on Wright's interpretation of Delcita not only because hers is iconic, but also because, unlike the other actresses, she is the only one to black up and incorporate rotten teeth into her performance. This explicitly made the distortion of phenotypical features of blackness central to her rendition of black rural womanhood, and it was the only one to cause public controversy. This suggests that the public perceived her performance as different from the other renditions.[18]

When I returned home to Jamaica during graduate school, my black, educated, middle-class friends were scandalized by Delcita's use of blackface. I heard members of the public call in to local radio talk shows to decry her deployment of the form, claiming it perpetuated negative stereotypes of black people as loud and ignorant. Wright defended her use of blackface, claiming that "it is a way to make people laugh," and that its historical usage did not concern her because it is not at the forefront of most people's minds.[19] The backlash was so intense that years later, when I contacted the actress to do an interview, she politely declined.[20] In more recent years, Wright has played Delcita without her distinctive blackface makeup in noted plays such as *Border Patrol* (2015) and *Honeymoon* (2019), in short videos on social media, and in a few livestreamed plays. For my purposes here, I limit my analysis to the plays in which she blacks up simply because it was the period in which she received the backlash. I neither suggest that Wright stopped engaging in forms of blackface when she stopped blacking up, nor that Delcita ceases to be part of the postcolonial below thereafter. But I do think the implications and politics of representing black caricatures shift according to how one chooses to embody and represent blackness, and that these types of representations also shape how black audiences receive the caricatures.

Reviving the Colonial Sign: Blackface in Jamaican Theater

Although Wright invoked collective amnesia of the history of blackface performance, I argue that she is, in fact, signifying on a colonial sign and on larger black working-class countercultural aesthetic forms. Blackface performance for white planter audiences appears in Jamaican theater in the decade leading up to the mid-1840s, and it constitutes one of the earliest representations of blackness on the Jamaican stage.[21] After a twenty-year hiatus, the sporadic arrival of notable US minstrel troupes, such as the Original Georgia Minstrels (1869), the Christy Minstrels (1872), and Edwin Browne's Minstrel and Novelty Company (1884) to the Caribbean had a lasting impact on indigenous comedic theater well into the 1950s.[22] This is evidenced through the notable hit song "Big Big Sambo Gyal" by the Cudjoe Minstrels, which remains a popular folk song on the island even today, and through the minstrel format of the iconic Jamaican comedic duo Bim and Bam, whose work in the 1930s is considered a precursor to contemporary roots theater.[23] In the recent scholarship on blackface performance in colonial Jamaica, scholars Chinua Thelwell and Kellen Hoxworth note that it was in fact central to the formation of a transoceanic, imperial British empire and the incorporation of Jamaica's white planter class into its attendant networks of Anglo-white supremacy.[24] My intention is not to parse out the nuances of blackface performances in distinct colonial epochs, as is the remit of other scholarly work. However, this history is important to note because, despite Wright's reliance on collective amnesia or ignorance of the history of blackface performance, it did play a crucial role in systems of racial stratification and in imperial formations of white supremacy during Jamaica's colonial era.[25] Hemispheric blackface signals to these forgotten histories of performance traditions in the Americas and of conjuring blackness to consolidate structures of white supremacy that emerged from British colonial rule and US cultural imperialism in the Caribbean.

But Wright's revival of this racial device is also important because it marks the postcolonial below as the space for discarded, forgotten colonial signs and denigrated, rejected forms. The postcolonial below is the venue for the recycling and reworking of the detritus of a colonial past wherein a black marginalized subject like Delcita can wield the colonial signifier of Anglo-white supremacy to firmly assert her humanity and declare, "I am somebody!" Here I use the term *blackface* in its broadest sense to denote an act of racial conjuring that stages a caricature of blackness. Indeed, blacking up is one facet of her larger embodiment of a racial caricature, as Wright places black strips on her teeth to signal they have rotted away and her hair is typically unkempt. Yet her aesthetic rendition of blackface is extremely subtle. The layer of dark paint on her face is often so thin that it is barely perceptible, rendering her face slightly darker than the rest of her arms and body. This subtle reworking of the remains of a colonial signifier transforms blackface into shine, an understated gloss punctuating a black body that showcases various gradations of color and tone.[26]

While Wright's act of racial conjuring is a nod to the past that highlights the colonial burdens attached to blackface and black skin, she is also signifying on larger contemporary aesthetic practices of Jamaica's black working-class and dancehall culture. Dancehall music and culture emerged out of the political violence in Jamaica of the 1970s and 1980s, the island's failed experiment with economic structural adjustment programs, the explosion of the informal economy, and the exacerbation of the class/status hierarchy in the country.[27] Like hip-hop or reggaeton, its adherents are mostly inner-city and working-class citizens. Known for its talk-over style on digital "riddims," dancehall emerged after the heyday of reggae music and is known for its celebrations of guns, sex, and *bling bling* aesthetics. Although Jamaican dancehall music stars like Beenie Man, Sean Paul, Spice, and Vybz Kartel receive critical acclaim internationally, in Jamaica, dancehall continues to be seen as "low culture." Jamaican roots theater is considered a companion to dancehall culture and is a space of cultural preservation for the black working class. Little wonder, then, that dancehall as musical form and cultural practice figures so strongly in many of the plays.[28] Wright is drawing from its aesthetic forms.

Wright's act of racial conjuring lives within quotidian registers of racial play associated with the larger aesthetic practices of Jamaica's black working class, like skin-bleaching. Frequently dismissed by Jamaica's middle and upper class as a sign of self-hatred, skin-bleaching by black working-class women in dancehall culture entails the transformation of black skin for fashion, style, and to make the individual be seen.[29] I do not deem it a sign of self-hate because that presumes one can gauge racial self-esteem by "the degree to which the black body is left 'natural.'"[30] I see Wright's play with different gradations of skin tone as adapting the colonial sign to the subterranean aesthetic counterculture expressions of the black underclass. Within this cultural ethos, black skin operates as merely a canvas upon which one engages in forms of self-making that are ephemeral, transient, and subject to change. These cultural spaces value individual creativity and the capacity to fashion one's image to stand out in the visual field over conforming to the dictates of racial uplift decided by the middle class.

Natasha Barnes explains that skin-bleaching is a contradictory representational practice and beauty ritual. The women who engage in it see it as "'following fashion' (i.e., indulging in hair and cosmetic choices that are provisional and hence subject to change)."[31] She likens this reworking of the racial body to the people who work on black hair, treating it as a "raw material that is constantly processed by cultural practices" and invested with meaning and value by black people across the diaspora.[32] For example, though straightening black hair is "imbricated in racist semiotics," it is also part of the "contextualized alternative expressive modes" black people in the Black Atlantic take up to appropriate the styles of the dominant culture and reinscribe upon them a set of oppositional meanings.[33] Barnes further likens this to Robin D. G. Kelley's analysis of Malcolm X's usage of the conk hairstyle in the 1940s, which is not merely a mimicry of or desire for whiteness, but the articulation of an urban black stylishness circulating in the Black Atlantic.[34] Wright's reworking of black skin is very much in keeping with the ethos of a subterranean oppositional culture that plays with skin tone. She therefore revived and thrust the colonial sign into larger black working-class repertoires that use the transformation of the racial body to articulate a black, urban, working-class sensibility, fashion, and style.[35]

Wright's use of blackface also operates within larger aesthetic practices among the black working class wherein they rework the black body to respond to how they are visualized in Jamaica. In her analysis of the introduction of the videolight in dancehall culture in the 2000s, Krista Thompson emphasizes the centrality of skin-bleaching in negotiating a cultural status of unvisibility that renders black people in the dancehall both hypervisible and unseen in society.[36] She explains, "Skin bleachers lighten the surfaces of their bodies to appear on video and in the video light" and to "be representable, registered, and recognized."[37] Skin-bleaching is one of several drastic body-altering practices black people engage in to be registered in visual regimes. Skin is thus transformed into a surface that registers the effect of light reflecting on and off surfaces and as a representational space for figuring black subjects. Thompson builds on Paul Gilroy's assertion that black diasporic subjects are produced differently through visual means and that black urban cultures engage in shared performances of visibility that are about staging the very process of being seen and represented.[38]

Bearing this in mind, Wright's deployment of blackface is an inversion of skin-bleaching that also engages how blackness is seen and not seen in the visual field. Her play on the darkness of black skin is salient because the history of visual technologies such as photography and film is plagued by the failure to capture blackness and render it fully legible in the field of vision.[39] While Wright does not fully obscure black subjectivity the way Angulo does in *Negro utópico*, this inversion of skin-bleaching is a gesture of darkening the representational screen where blackness figures. In using blackface, Wright subtly amplifies the very darkness that visual technologies have obscured, overlooked, rendered opaque or invisible, perhaps playing on the notion of blackness as too dark to be seen. Whereas skin-bleaching has been theorized as troubling the presumed naturalness and stability of blackness in dancehall culture, Wright's act of racial conjuring is not a disruption of the naturalness of the racial category.[40] Rather, it is a steadfast evocation and affirmation of blackness, a punctuation of dark skin that has not been readily captured in the visual field. Blackness appears here as surplus, a racial excess that a black working-class subject levies to talk back to those in positions of authority.

Delcita's act of racial conjuring signifies both on a colonial sign and on black working-class vocabularies of racial play that critically interrogate how blackness is brought into being—what types of blackness are seen, affirmed, and ignored in the visual field. Thus, my metaphorical usage of blackface as colonial detritus refers to the racial residues of a colonial past that the postcolonial nation has presumably overcome, the historical and continued status of blackness itself as waste and as sign of racial abjection, and the symbol of a discarded black comedic tradition in the postcolonial context. Furthermore, it also denotes a radical transformation of the colonial signifier and its reinsertion into the contemporary repertoire of black working-class forms of racial play, whose modes of reworking the black body are themselves the subject of social reproach and disdain. Hemispheric blackface is at once the space of forgotten histories of encounter and the site for diffuse repertoires of racial play whose affiliations with established performance traditions of impersonation of yesteryear are loose and tenuous. Nevertheless, that Delcita's act of racial conjuring is lightly tethered to colonial and contemporary structures of social abjection is crucial to its functioning within a larger counterspace operating beneath the social order. In this sense, her reworking of the racial body to conjure a figuration of rural black womanhood also shows how the postcolonial below functions as a space for challenging the racial scripts of creole nationalism.

Creole Nationalism in Jamaica

Jamaica's discourse of creole nationalism was consolidated between the 1940s and cemented after independence in 1962 through its national motto "Out of Many, One People."[41] Although over 90 percent of the Jamaican population is black, the motto suggests a multicultural, multira-cial society. In his critique of the national motto, theorist Rex Nettleford explains that the "many" refers to Jamaica's predominantly white upper class, which includes Sephardic Jews, Lebanese Syrians, whites of Anglo-Saxon and Nordic stock, descendants of Indian and Chinese indentured laborers, and some "high-brown" Jamaicans understood as "functional whites."[42] Nettleford also contends that the imagination of Jamaica as a creole culture occludes the fact that the national elite idealizes European culture, "puts everything European in a place of eminence and things of indigenous (that is native born and native bred) or African origin in a lesser place."[43] Creole nationalism emerged as the nationalist intelligent-sia's response to the historical realities of decolonial struggle and black na-tionalist organizing, such as Garveyism and Rastafarianism in the 1920s and 1930s, which was popular among the working class. "Out of Many, One People" was a nationalist maxim that sought to stymie the race and class mobilizations of the times and to counter burgeoning ideologies of black liberation. Deborah Thomas defines it as "an aspirational slogan that nevertheless reproduces colonial social hierarchies by parenthesiz-ing blackness, thus pushing out the possibility of a hegemonic blackness within the public sphere."[44] Furthermore, creole nationalism is based on classical European nationalism, which centered history, emphasized the sharing of a common culture, and obscured the entanglement of race and class. In the postcolonial societies across the Anglophone Caribbean that adopted the precepts of classical European nationalism, race was sub-sumed within the national question.[45] Subsequently, in the Jamaican con-text, the elite erased race by emphasizing that one's "Jamaicanness" was what was most important. Despite its emphasis on multiracialism and universalism, creole nationalism re-entrenched colonial values and hier-archies of race, color, and class, leading to what Aaron Kamugisha calls "the coloniality of citizenship."[46] Fantasies of a united multiracial polity silenced alternative imaginations of the nation that centered around black liberation and wielded the romance of a national identity to erase and deny hierarchies of race altogether.

Creole nationalism also enabled the intellectual elite to position them-selves as the arbiters of cultural taste and as guardians of the lower classes, and to develop a set of racial scripts.[47] While they were Eurocentric in their outlook, the elite still sought to distinguish the new nation from Britain and the United States. They elaborated a set of cultural policies to define national culture at the time of independence. They legitimated and recuperated African-derived cultural practices and "folk culture," which had been repressed under colonial rule, and redeployed them as raw material to produce a national cultural identity. They privileged the speech patterns, food, rituals, music, and dance forms from the rural peasantry over those of their urban counterparts.[48] The mining of black folk cultural forms, however, did not substantially alter the material conditions or social positions of black people, nor did it signify a departure from colonial imaginations of "progress" and development. Moreover, the embrace of folk blackness into the new regimes of citizenship was always conditional on its modeling of a "tamed blackness" that rejected black political organizing and "mirrored the values of the creole professional middle classes."[49]

Thus, the racial scripts of creole nationalism were centered around an urban blackness/rural blackness dyad, which wielded the politics of respectability to enact forms of social differentiation. As I have written elsewhere, the politics of respectability is a value complex that organized colonial society, the post-emancipation period, and the formation of the postcolonial nation-state in Jamaica.[50] Oriented toward the "bourgeois valuations of family, Standard English, [and] decorum," respectability emphasizes "the cultivation of education, thrift, industry, self-sufficiency via land ownership, moderate Christian living, community uplift, the constitution of family through legal marriage and related gendered expectations, and leadership by the educated middle classes."[51] The politics of respectability served as an anchor for an exclusionary nationalism that centered heteronormativity and masculinity, privileged the interests of the brown middle class, and simultaneously excluded poor blacks, women, and queer citizens.[52] The parenthesizing of blackness that inheres in the creole nationalist formula and in its formation of national culture therefore operates according to a set of gendered and sexual heteropatriarchal logics. These logics have been reconsolidated through what M. Jacqui Alexander calls *heteropatriarchal recolonization*, which "operates through the consolidation of certain psychic economies and racial hierarchies as well as within various material and ideological processes, initiated by the state both inside and beyond the law."[53] Respectability sets the terms for the incorporation of blackness into the national imaginary, determines who is constructed as the ideal citizen, and organizes the racial scripts of creole nationalism.

These racial scripts have also led to the veneration of the "browning" as Jamaica's ideal citizen and as the face of creole multiracial harmony. In the Caribbean, the categories of black and white are elastic concepts that signify various ways of being and belonging. As in other regions, racial categories are constructed by and through a set of social relations, gestures, and actions that can shift and transform cultural meanings that are mapped onto race. In the case of Jamaica, "brownings" were historically the descendants of free colored persons who were the offspring of white planters and slave concubines. Brownness, as Donette Francis writes, "maps a plantation legacy of interracial intimacies between white men and black women and often carries a certain privilege—and, in many cases, an access to property, as one way of accruing generational wealth."[54] In addition, it represents a category of social whiteness that relies on performances of respectability—adjusting modes of speaking, dress, and mastering European (British) customs—and distancing from the black majority.[55] As Sylvia Wynter notes, in the Caribbean, one can simply behave in a way to prove one is not a nigger.[56]

Jamaica's brown class consists of civil servants, lawyers, and journalists, and they are an intellectual and educated group who have either ascended or been born into social whiteness. As functional whites, brownings also represent the racial and social standard of beauty and desirability. Valued over their black counterparts, brownings are typically featured on billboards, in local advertisements, and, until recently, as beauty queens in Jamaica.[57] As feminist theorist Patricia Mohammed indicates, the brown woman has emerged as the ideal of feminine beauty in the Caribbean: "The mixed or mulatto woman disrupted the notions of a Victorian purity of the white woman, and the idea of the 'hot constitution'd' black female sexuality."[58] While brownness is indeed the ideal outside of dancehall culture, its value is not explicitly named because racial problems are typically seen as an issue of the colonial past. Instead, what was once plainly named in the language of race has now been displaced onto class, language, or even space.[59] Like Latin American discourses of mestizaje, Jamaica's discourse of creole nationalism silences race and celebrates a mixed-raced subject while simultaneously producing a system of racial, cultural, and social value that keeps antiblackness in place. These racial scripts are crucial in *Di Driva* because Thelma and her husband Ronnie represents the brown class and the political elite.

Delcita poses a challenge to discourses of creole nationalism in that her act of racial impersonation contests the erasure of race in those discourses and in imaginations of folk blackness within the nation. Like Angulo's performance, blackface on black skin is a performance of racial excess that defamiliarizes blackness. By this, I mean it denaturalizes black skin, emphasizing it as a corporeal layer that does a particular type of work on stage and therefore makes blackness hypervisible. In rendering the blackness of a rural countrywoman hypervisible, impersonation exposes the imbrication of race and class in Delcita's structural marginalization. Rejecting the creole nationalist erasure of racial difference and its privileging of class, her character theatricalizes the entanglement of race and class, wherein working-class identity is coded as a sign of blackness and vice versa in Jamaica. Moreover, the use of racial layering on Delcita's face indexes how Jamaica's racial economy assigns social value to color. I have already discussed the phenomenon of skin-bleaching among Jamaica's lower classes and what it represents for racial ideology in Jamaica. Scholars also describe it as a mode of "buying racial capital," which indexes the role that bodily resources (skin tone, facial features, etc.) and whiteness play in determining one's status and social hierarchies.[60] But in the case of Delcita, the use of blackface signifies a rejection of the racial logics of creole nationalism that demand people aspire to brownness or whiteness. Instead, she reclaims blackness—the devalued symbol of Jamaica's color hierarchy—and metaphorically wields it as a surrogate prop in performances of black working-class affirmation.

As shown in her confrontation with Thelma, she confronts the scornful gaze of the brown elite and asks, "What? Why are you looking at me like that? I am somebody! I am not a ghost."[61] Here, Delcita presents the ghost, an icon of paleness, as the opposite signifier to blackface to affirm a marginalized social positionality. In invoking the figure of the ghost, Delcita names and refuses constructs of the black working-class subject as a figure that is not seen, that haunts, that lingers, that evokes fear, that represents an (un)dead subjectivity. In this sense, blackface is also doing temporal work. As the colonial signifier of a bygone era, blackface emphasizes the temporal place of the country bumpkin as the sign of a premodern blackness in the nation—a blackness that is the past. The proclamation, "I am not a ghost," therefore refuses the temporal place of the country bumpkin and of a premodern blackness and instead marks a black presence and blackness as the present. Through her acts of defiance, Delcita rejects the designated "tameness" of a folk blackness and its place as non-threatening raw material within creole nationalism. She both humanizes and co-opts the trope of the benign country woman to refuse the demands of a domesticated, assimilated blackness in the national imaginary and to upend the racial scripts and temporal logics of creole nationalism.

Furthermore, Delcita's deployment of the Jamaican creole term *duppy* is also salient because of its association with African-derived epistemologies and folk knowledge. The word *duppy* is not merely a direct translation of the English term *ghost*. The duppy is somewhat similar to the "jumbie" figure of the islands of the Eastern Caribbean. Jessica Swanston Baker describes the "jumbie" as a dead figure representing folk knowledge that is rejected and denounced "in a context of Christian respectability."[62] Within Jamaican folk knowledge, the duppy may be a good figure, like a departed loved one or relative who visits in dreams to offer advice, or a bad apparition seeking to do harm. The duppy is a restless soul who does not leave willingly. Black Jamaican folk traditions prescribe a set of tricks or rituals for family members to deter the return of the duppy of a recently departed loved one. As a child, I learned that if I were to encounter a duppy, I should either swear, wear my clothes inside out, or eat salt to chase the apparition away.[63] The "duppy" is also deployed in popular insults like "yuh favah duppy" (you look like a duppy), signaling unattractiveness. Delcita's proclamation that she is not a duppy, the symbol of undesirability, the figuration to be cast away or warded off, in her confrontation with Thelma is a clear acknowledgment of which cosmologies are valued or discarded. These tactics are emblematic of larger counter-ideological formations of the postcolonial below that contest the racial scripts of creole nationalism.

Roots Theater and the Postcolonial Below

Indeed, creole nationalism has always had to contend with the competing vision of poor Jamaicans who have long embraced an explicitly racialized imagination of liberation in their fight against class depravation and racism.[64] Rastafarianism, rudie, and the grassroots mobilizations of the 1960s became central cultural references that challenged the fictions of multiracial harmony, contested middle-class sensibilities, and marked the reassertion of black nationalism at the time of independence.[65] Examples of Jamaican grassroots mobilizations in the 1960s that challenged the fiction of multiracial harmony include the Henry Rebellion, the Coral Gardens and anti-Chinese Disturbances, and the reprisal of the People's National Party (PNP).[66] As Deborah Thomas insists, creole nationalism must also contend with the emergence of "modern blackness"—a modified form of black nationalism—in the 1990s.[67] Modern blackness is marked by the election of P. J. Patterson in 1992, whose rule was accompanied by the persistent recasting of blackness in the public imagination through cultural programs and other public projects.[68] A rejoinder to the creole multiracial slogan, "modern blackness" is "a bracketed blackness that continually deconstructs the creole nationalist motto by calling attention to the relations of power that are often erased within the creole formulation."[69] Modern blackness did not undo the racial scripts of creole nationalism, but it represents a moment of new political articulation. Delcita emerges well after its emergence. Scholars also propose reputation, slackness, and ghetto feminisms as counter-ideological formations that operate in tension with the politics of respectability by critiquing patriarchy and affirming women's erotic autonomy, sexual agency, and fulfillment in the public domain.[70] In addition, dancehall remains one of the most heavily theorized counter-formations of the urban underclass where the gendered and sexual scripts of heteropatriarchal recolonization and the politics of respectability are challenged and subverted.[71] These spaces and counter-ideological formations all form part of the postcolonial below because they are the nuclei for the subcultural practices, cultural movements, and lifestyles of those challenging and living below the social order.

The postcolonial below refers to the meeting grounds, the practices, and temporal regimes where Jamaica's black underclass articulates competing visions of liberation, rejects the racial scripts of creole nationalism, and celebrates their own cultural practices. The "below" in the postcolonial below points to the spatial dimensions of creole nationalism and its geographical class divisions. The postcolonial below is downtown—the neighborhoods below uptown—and the rural communities on the outskirts of the urban cities. It consists of those living below the poverty line: the underclass living in or around the gullies, near the waste, muck, and grime of the city. The below simultaneously refers to those who are looked down upon, whose way of life is beneath those of the "civilized" upper classes. It is the space of the downlow, where nonnormative expressions of gender and sexuality thrive, and where folks dare to straddle, transgress, and push against the borders of heteronormativity. It is the space of abjection operating on the borders of modern blackness. The below consists of those who operate under and outside the regimes of citizenship—the bodies that are overlooked and not seen. The postcolonial below, thus, names the social and political undercurrents flowing beneath and in a different direction from the surface current.

Roots theater marks the postcolonial below as a submerged space operating beneath and outside traditional mechanisms of anticolonial struggle. This is particularly the case for roots theater, whose malignment is partly due to the function of theater in Jamaica as a site for negotiating the colonial past and in defining national identity. During the colonial era, theater served as an instrument for transplanting English cultural values onto British colonies. In the 1700s, European and North American companies toured the British West Indies bringing Shakespeare, opera, and theater forms from the metropoles to the white settler planters in the island.[72] It was the space where homesick white settlers and planters in Jamaica kept abreast of the cultural tastes of the metropole, and theatergoing was considered the performance of a civilized subject.[73] Theater scholars and practitioners have noted that this colonial past led to the veneration of theater from the metropoles as the standard of "legitimate theater" and was an obstacle to the development of an indigenous theater.[74] Furthermore, theater was a site of racial segregation that excluded enslaved Africans from the stage.[75] Blackface performance was one of the few early representations of blackness in Jamaican theater. The theater was the space for the articulation of colonial whiteness and the implementation of the racial stratification of citizenship, but it was also a battleground for self-determination, the fight for dignity, and the validation of local culture.

As an anticolonial space that embraces the ordinary man, roots theater emerges out of the long-standing fight for the establishment of an indigenous, Caribbean theater. Yet the genre does not quite share the nationalist impetus of other anticolonial theatrical projects, such as the major pageant *Jamaica Triumphant* of the 1930s or even of the establishment of prestigious companies such as National Dance Theatre Company (NDTC) in the 1960s, whose efforts to establish an indigenous theater—though groundbreaking—have, at times, been given to celebrations of creole multiracial nationalism.[76] Roots theater is not generally beholden to the race and class politics of creole nationalism. And though it is certainly tethered to histories of black theater that emerged out of performance practices of enslaved Africans during colonization and the elocution contests that Marcus Garvey organized in the 1920s and 1930s, the genre is politically promiscuous and does not neatly reflect a pan-Africanist, black radical sensibility. Roots theater is a site of black popular sociality that revels in the informal. Indeed, it is borne out of the informal Tea Parties in local neighborhoods in the 1940s and 1950s, or what Rex Nettleford calls "Yard Theatre," which includes informal Rasta groundings, revival gatherings, pocomania meetings, and other organic encounters among communities.[77] Roots theater rejects the conventions of traditional theater in its breaking of the fourth wall and instead maintains the intimate feel of communal gatherings. The plays are high-tempo affairs and entail frequent interactions between audience members with the characters on stage: as the plot unfolds, the audience typically shouts commentary. This intimacy between characters and audiences consolidates its function as a cultural form that expresses a subordinate social life. The plays are fundamentally grounded in "the experiences, pleasures, memories, traditions, local hopes and local aspirations, local tragedies and local scenarios that are the everyday practices and everyday experiences of ordinary folks."[78] The postcolonial below is the space of the colloquial, the organic, and the familiar.

And while the postcolonial below is an offshoot of institutional mechanisms of anticolonialism, it tends to operate on the margins of institutions. Roots theater certainly benefited from the fight for an institutionalized Caribbean theater, which included the development of Jamaican pantomime by Greta Fowler's Little Theatre Movement (LTM), the establishment of the Department of Extra Mural Studies at the University of the West Indies, and the Edna Manley School of Visual and Performing Arts. But the genre simply has not been granted the institutional legitimacy and recognition afforded to them.[79] Furthermore, roots theater celebrates and is embedded in the folk. It emerges from the work of theater stalwarts Louise Bennett and Ranny Williams, whose folk tales and Anancy stories were crucial to the reclamation of Jamaican creole and black folk culture.[80] But unlike these two influential figures, some roots performers may not have the validation of a classical, traditional education in theater. For example, though some formally trained actors perform in roots plays, roots theater is the province of mostly working-class thespians like Keith "Shebada" Ramsey who may or may not be classically trained in theater.

The marginalization of roots theater is also due, in part, to its reimagination of the theatrical space. Roots theater embraces the small theater as a vital institutional cog in the historical development of Caribbean comedy. The establishment of the Barn—the small theater—in 1965, for example, occasioned the launch of the careers of comedic stalwarts such as Oliver Samuels, Fae Ellington, Voiler "Maffie" Johnson, and Glenn "Titus" Campbell, and it enabled a local black comedic tradition to flourish.[81] Ralph Holness's establishment of roots theater was deeply tied to the success of the small-theater business in the 1970s. Stages Productions has certainly staged roots plays in small-theater venues such as Green Gables

Theatre and Pantry Playhouse, but it has generally expanded the theatrical space to include the unheralded everyday venues of the black popular working class. They have often sought to break the urban/rural divide that has rendered theater the province of the urban city, opting instead to cater to rural communities without traditional theater houses in the island. In the 2000s, the hit roots play *Bashment Granny*, for example, was staged in popular venues such as Mass Camp in Kingston and even in open fields in rural communities in May Pen, Clarendon, while the play *Ova Mi Dead Body* (2011) was staged at Colonel Cove in Morant Bay, St. Thomas. This is partly due to the unrivaled popularity of roots plays, whose audiences are often too large for a small-theater venue. One showing of *Bashment Granny*, for instance, had thousands of attendees. In this manner, the postcolonial below opts for the less decorous and rarefied places and, therefore, insists on the reconfiguration and reimagination of the theatrical and decolonial space.

That roots theater has so reconfigured and expanded the theatrical space is a response to the social prejudices that undervalue the form. Indeed, as the companion to dancehall culture, whose relationship to a global capitalist economy has always been ambiguous, roots theater has found ways to establish its own networks of authorization. This is in keeping with what David Scott explains as "the increasing moral, social, and economic autonomy of the popular classes, an expansion of their ability to insert themselves in the global economy in ways (whether legal or illegal) that circumvent or bypass the middle-class-controlled state and the capitalist-controlled economy."[82] Stages Production has recently announced plans to build new theater houses in the island and to release DVDs of its plays. It frequently stages its plays for diasporic communities in London, New York, Florida, and in several parts of the eastern Caribbean. In this sense, roots theater shares kinship with the chitlin circuit, a crucial site of African American performance that was historically the subject of reproach from the black middle class and that was widely dismissed as a second-class entertainment network in the United States. Just as the chitlin circuit affirmed black performance and cultural forms by establishing safe performance venues for art forms produced by and for African Americans, so, too, does roots theater operate as its own theatrical enterprise with its own standards, categories, aesthetics, and marketplaces.[83]

In the past, some practitioners have heralded the recent expansion of the genre as proof of roots theater's ascension to the mainstream and its legitimacy as a comedic genre that ought to be undifferentiated from any other Jamaican art form. But the growth of these networks demonstrates that the postcolonial below has established its own marketplaces and circuits of authorization, not that it has somehow overcome the social prejudices that dismiss it as a form of "low" art.[84] While the postcolonial below operates as the underside of the culturally dominant, I do not propose that it somehow exists outside cultural hegemony. The postcolonial below, and the other black popular cultural forms it houses, is always capable of being expropriated and assimilated into the mainstream. Cultural hegemony is never about pure victory or total domination, anyway.[85] That certain figures, characters, or even theatrical spaces may be swallowed up by the mainstream is a reflection of the ongoing negotiation of the relations of cultural power, not evidence that roots theater has ceased to function as a counterpoint to elite cultural forms. The genre remains a fundamentally black working space where those on the margin of society "discover and play with the identifications of (them)selves," how they are imagined and "represented not only to the audiences out there who do not get the message, but also to themselves for the first time."[86] Indeed, roots theater is a site of awareness where the black underclass critically engages how they are perceived, how they see themselves, and how they interact with their own marginalization. This awareness is at the heart of my reading of Delcita as a fixture of the postcolonial below who both embodies stereotypes of blackness and serves as a voice of resistance for the black working class.

The Complexity and Contradictions of Racial Impersonation

Impersonation is a means through which those living in the postcolonial below confront and undermine the social and racial prejudices of the upper class. In the play *Di Driva*, all the characters trade insults, engaging in roasting and social ribbing. Some of the language used to describe Delcita, however, emphasizes and fixes her place within Jamaica's social, class, raced, and gendered hierarchies. She is described as "the bottom of the barrel," "a mad woman" who lacks a good "education level."[87] In addition, Delcita's appearance is frequently the subject of ridicule. The audience infer that she is dirty when the middle-class characters either stand at a distance from her or immediately sanitize any furniture she has touched or used. Her rural background is invoked to imply that she is the symbol of backwardness, a subject lagging behind the progress, development, and modernity associated with the big city and the nation. Beale's intentional casting of Delcita as the representative of the masses means that she is a figure through which the social, racial, and class prejudices of the nation are conjured and amplified on stage. At the same time, Delcita is a device through which these social prejudices are challenged and renegotiated. For example, in the scene I discuss earlier, once Delcita leaves the room, Thelma chastises Dr. First for having chosen Delcita as a surrogate, citing her improper conduct and lack of education. Dr. First defends her choice and asks Thelma if she should have chosen instead a "Beyoncé" or a "Lisa Hannah" (a former Miss Jamaica World) who could potentially sleep with Ronnie (Thelma's husband). The dialogue thus exemplifies the class prejudices of Miss Jones and Dr. First, as their justification for choosing Delcita relies on the presumption that she is so undesirable she will not pose a threat to the Jones' marriage. But while her upper-class counterparts intend to use Delcita to produce borders of desire, she has other plans.

When Delcita returns to the stage, both Thelma and Dr. First explain the terms of her stay in the house, such as eating "right" and exercising. But Delcita quickly turns the tables on them and insists on setting her own conditions. She tells Thelma to warn her husband not to sexually harass her and threatens to stab him for any unwanted advances; demands that she have her own room, television, and the costs of her telephone calls covered; explains her meal preferences are chicken back and dumpling (staples of the poor); and demands to know when she will receive her first payment. When Thelma refuses to pay her upfront and relays that she will compensate her after the birth of the child, Delcita grabs her bags and leaves. While Dr. First presumes Delcita's class background and appearance would render her a nonobject of desire, Delcita immediately exposes the manifest desirability of working-class black women to upper-class men who claim otherwise. She also names and demands they preemptively address the reality of sexual violence that domestic workers experience and readily invokes the threat of violence as a method of self-defense. Her assertiveness in outlining a series of conditions for her employment is significant because she refuses to accept a position of complete subordination to her employers. Her walking away affirms a willingness to stand up for herself, to negotiate on her own terms, and to reject any form of exploitation. In the postcolonial below, the blackface mask operates as a screen through which the working class seeks to upend the dynamics of class and racial power, to address the realities of their own experiences, and to rework the terms of their interactions with the brown elite.

Indeed, Delcita is the figure through which the black working poor "talks back" to authority. In some instances, she names the social prejudices and exclusionary practices of the ruling class. For example, in the play, when Thelma's husband Ronnie Jones speaks in Standard English to Dr. First, imploring her "to extricate this imbecile [Delcita] from within [his] domain post haste," Delcita mocks his attempts to be verbose. She declares he is speaking nonsense because he thinks she will be unable to understand him. Delcita names the weaponizing of Standard English as an exclusionary practice by the ruling class toward working-class Jamaicans who do not speak English. She also facetiously responds to Ronnie Jones's insult that she is the bottom of the barrel, claiming: "Mr. Jones, as much as me look suh, even ef dem pack me up inna de laas bottom a one barrel, me wodn't waan yuh pan tap a me!" (As much as I look like this, if they packed me in the last bottom of a barrel, I would not want you on top of me!)."[88] In rejecting Mr. Jones, Delcita demonstrates an awareness of her own socially constructed abjection, and she establishes and remakes the borders of desire on her own terms by rendering him undesirable, even in the eyes of the least desirable subject. Similarly, in the play *Xtortionistz*, when the wife Mavis, who is African American, warns Delcita that she will not allow her to disrespect her "a third time," Delcita threatens violence and mockingly responds in an American accent that "if there's a third, you gone fly like a bird."[89] Rejecting the role of an obsequious servant, Delcita exhibits fearlessness. Irreverent and headstrong, this blackface character occupies a position of racial abjection to resist, dismantle, and undermine relations of power. In talking back, impersonation enables the black working-class subject to both register an awareness of how she is seen and to enact a black oppositional gaze.

While Delcita's act of impersonation entails at times wielding her own abjection to stage an oppositional gaze, at other times, it represents a takeover of the stereotypical trope of the black country bumpkin to strategically undo its meaning. Although the blackface character of Delcita frequently panders to the stereotype of the countrywoman, it simultaneously doubles as a wise, irreverent, and perceptive figure. For example, in the play *Money Worries* (2010), Delcita is portrayed as an ignorant, barely educated secretary of a lawyer, Mr. Valentine Case (played by Sheldon Shepherd), whose private practice is in financial trouble. Not only does Delcita turn away potential clients, but she also insists on offering them terrible legal advice. Whenever potential clients take umbrage at her advice, for instance, she simply yells "Yuh Mooma!" (Your Mama!) and slams down the phone. Delcita is therefore the unruly fool who actively sabotages Valentine's business.[90] Although Delcita is barely educated, she is the first to recognize that Valentine has been swindled by a crook when she discovers irregularities in his financial records. The crook, who turns out to be Delcita's unscrupulous boyfriend, Trevor, ultimately pins his crime on Delcita.

Her wisdom and insight are also affirmed in the play *Xtortionistz*, in which Delcita is hired as a nurse to work for an elderly woman. The woman's daughter-in-law, Mavis, has a criminal past that she has kept from her husband, the elderly woman's son. In the play, Delcita quickly discovers Mavis has been stealing money from her husband and using it for various fraudulent activities. Delcita refuses to keep Mavis's secret. When Mavis's identity is revealed and she threatens to kill the two upper-class characters, Delcita turns up with the police to save them. Delcita, the blackface character, is portrayed as clever and more perceptive than her upper-class counterparts. Her wit and guile persistently enable her to outsmart her employers. At the end of *Di Driva*, Delcita and her working-class boyfriend Driva (played by Keith "Shebada" Ramsey) blackmail Mr. Jones to renegotiate the terms of the payment and earn millions of dollars to keep the surrogacy a secret. Delcita gives birth to six children, but it is ultimately Driva, not Mr. Jones, who is their biological father. The children, however, will still earn the social benefits of bearing Mr. Jones's family name. The figure of the country bumpkin is thus revamped as an empowered hero who, along with the other working-class protagonists of the play, reworks her situation to her own benefit. The postcolonial below becomes the place of black working-class subterfuge and triumph.

Impersonation is a device through which the black underclass questions and rejects social norms and articulates its own social order. In *Money Worries* (2010), when Valentine says Delcita is sexy and the theater audience acts surprised, Delcita questions everybody's surprise and declares "beauty in the eyes of the beholder."[91] And, in one scene in the play *Miss Elsayda* (2014), Delcita holds a mirror and, upon looking at her reflection, emphatically declares "Dis a mi pension! when mi look mi si beauty!" (This is my pension. When I look, I see beauty!").[92] Through the use of the mirror, Delcita stages an oppositional black gaze that articulates a counternarrative of black female beauty. A similar conversation takes place in *Di Driva* when the upper-class brown wife Thelma seduces Delcita's boyfriend Driva. Thelma asks Driva if he has a girlfriend and, without naming Delcita, he exclaims "One beautiful girl! Shi did enta Miss World one time and dem sen ar back home cuz a grudge. De Judge dem say fi har beauty, dem cyan understan it. It nah av no security code!" (One beautiful girl! She entered Miss World once and they sent her back home because of a grudge. The judges said they couldn't understand her beauty. It didn't have a security code).[93] Rejecting conventional notions of beauty, Driva insists that Delcita is beautiful and that her disqualification from the standards of beauty are the result of personal grievances or "grudges" on the judges' part. One may understand the statement as insinuating that Delcita's beauty is so far-fetched it is incomprehensible, but Driva's affirmation of Delcita's beauty suggests that the incomprehensibility refers to the limitations of the judges who rely on gatekeeping ("a security code") to consolidate their definitions of beauty, which are, in fact, designed to keep certain people out. Blackface may render Delcita a caricature of blackness, but she is the figure through which the characters affirm black beauty and the desirability of a black countrywoman and, concurrently, dismiss the gendered and racial standards of the ruling class. Within the postcolonial below, the black popular working class celebrates, prioritizes, and centers its own norms, social standards, and codes with no regard or interest in the elite's approval.

Thus far, I argue that the postcolonial below is the place where the black working class invokes the detritus of the colonial past to engage in practices of social questioning, working-class affirmation, resistance, and "talking back" to figures of authority. It is where the black underclass revises the stereotypical tropes invented by the ruling class to mock them and rework them for their own affirmation. It is also the place to register awareness and to enact an oppositional gaze to how the black working class is seen. While Delcita is a center through which all these acts of resistance take place, she is not merely an oppositional figure; she also represents a debased humor that does not always counter social norms. Because the postcolonial below operates below the social order and centers a black working-class ethos, it is also a space in which black publics reject socially accepted boundaries of what should or should not be humorous and who ought to find pleasure in a particular set of racial tropes. Delcita, for example, often serves as the mouthpiece of patriarchy and misogyny, frequently meting out advice to women in the plays. In *Money Worries* (2010), when a potential client in an abusive common-law relationship calls the office for legal help, Delcita informs her that according to the law, she has not been in her domestic partnership long enough to receive any benefits if she were to leave her partner. As such, Delcita advises her to stay in the relationship and to simply close her eyes when she receives the blows from her husband. In this case, Delcita acts as an oblivious mouthpiece of patriarchal violence. She refuses affinity with the woman on the phone and displays a lack of solidarity and empathy. The callousness of Delcita's advice and disidentification not only portrays her as ignorant but also underscores a debased humor that finds pleasure and humor in domestic violence and physical abuse.

Moreover, while Delcita's character revises the figure of the country bumpkin, these revisions do not constitute a complete abandonment of the stereotype. Delcita oscillates between two functions: the embodiment of a black stereotype and an instrument of black resistance. When Delcita is hired as a nurse in *Xtortionistz*, upon meeting her upper-class employers, she presumes they are the patients, offensively comments on their looks, and attempts to inject them with medication. Luckily, the doctor who supervises her intervenes. When the couple questions her qualifications, Delcita assures them that she is certified, but that it is the first time she is treating someone. Throughout the play, she refuses to follow the doctor's orders and instead administers home remedies or serves antibiotics with prohibited beverages. In these instances, Delcita is portrayed not only as irreverent but also as a simpleton who is unqualified for the position. Her ignorance is also on display in the play *University of Delcita* (2013), where she appears for a job interview uninvited and justifies her presence by explaining that she simply missed the first call. In another play, the audience laughs at the fact that Delcita did not go to high school because she fell asleep during the common entrance exam.[94] Although it operates alongside her boisterous social critiques, the stereotype of the country bumpkin is, at times, still the butt of the joke. The postcolonial below, then, is also the place where one hits below the belt. It revels in deviant pleasures and savage, uncouth takedowns. It thrives in irreverence for authority figures and the social boundaries of humor itself. More importantly, it is a space that exposes the paradoxes of black enjoyment.

Black Enjoyment: Abject Pleasures of the Underside

Aside from a figure of resistance, Delcita represents a comical take on black working-class identity that black publics enjoy. Put simply, black people find Delcita funny. I want to highlight here the black enjoyment of blackface tropes because it is too often overlooked and undertheorized. The messiness of black enjoyment of antiblack tropes does not undermine my claim that Delcita is a figure of black working-class resistance. Rather, I am suggesting that the postcolonial below is a ludic space where black publics also find pleasure and enjoyment in tropes of blackness that were not meant for their delight. Finding pleasure where your pleasure is presumably denied or foreclosed is, in fact, an affront to the social order.

Black enjoyment is a trojan horse crashing a ludic terrain that has been ordered to reproduce the dynamics of racial power that fix blackness as objects of ridicule, conjured for the whims and delight of a dominant class. Because black popular culture is a "contradictory space," and a site of "strategic contestation," black enjoyment of blackface tropes in the postcolonial below is not the tell-tale sign of self-hatred or ignorance, but a contradictory strategy of social defiance, a radical refusal to be beholden to the terms of a ludic racial order that either renders black enjoyment absent or can only imagine its presence as complicity or sanctioning of antiblackness.[95] Black enjoyment is the carving out of an alternate ludic space within the symbolic terrain of racial enjoyment where black people set their own terms of enjoyment and refuse to seek the validation or approval from those in the majoritarian culture. It is an expression of radical disregard where black people set, define, and uphold their own ludic racial order. Black complicity is not at stake in Delcita's performances, because the embodiment of the stereotypes coexists with the figure's critical reworking of tropes of antiblackness. It is precisely this unstable game that challenges any easy fixing of Delcita as the mere mouthpiece of antiblackness conjured to be consumed by the dominant class. While in the previous chapters I write about racial conjuring as the locus of enjoyment for white and mestizo publics and, in the case of Yeyo in Miami, a vital instrument of diasporic belonging, here I imagine this domain of racial enjoyment as inherently contradictory and paradoxical. It relies on disidentification, abject pleasures, and radical disregard.

As I mention earlier, I take my cues from Douglas Jones's groundbreaking essay on black minstrels in the post–Reconstruction era in the United States, in which he critiques scholarly tendencies to view blackface characters played by African American actors as trickster figures. Jones instead theorizes black enjoyment of black minstrel characters.[96] Because Jones does not critically engage the internal fissures that exist within black working class audiences in his conceptualization of the black below, blackness seemingly remains an undifferentiated category. Black spectators' identification with one another and with the figuration of blackness on stage in the space of black sociality is presumably stable, complete, and totally naturalized. Furthermore, Jones does not attend to the fact that black people routinely reproduce antiblackness in spaces of black sociality—whether in a family unit or among ourselves. In my view, for black enjoyment to surpass the facile reproduction of antiblackness, the figuration of blackness needs to somehow enable a space of critical reworking of the racist trope itself. In my rendering of the postcolonial below, I diverge from him in that I see disidentification as central to the production of black enjoyment. Further, I find it necessary to trouble the "black" in black enjoyment, to nuance the process of identification, and to rethink the terms of black enjoyment.

Delcita's oscillation between the fool and the voice of black resistance, for example, means blackface does not function as the sign of a stable or fixed racial ontology, and blackness is never inhabited as only the object of ridicule. The dialectic of black wittiness and black ignorance at the heart of her performance ensures that black publics can persistently engage in acts of disidentification with her rendition of blackness on stage. Theorist José Muñoz defines disidentification as a survival strategy, where one neither fully assimilates nor completely opposes the dominant structure, but where one remakes and rewrites a dominant script.[97] Disidentification is a hermeneutic, a process where one reworks a stereotype for one's own needs, and the spectators themselves engage in a type of disidentification as they consume this practice. In Delcita's performance, blackface represents a constellation of different ideas of blackness, and its multiple valences enable a type of distancing wherein a black spectator can see the black character on stage as *not me* and *not not me*. The "not me" refers to the aspects of blackness that the black spectator can discard and reject as the mere figment of an antiblack fantasy. The "not not me" refers to the other aspects of blackness that are close enough to the realities of their own experiences to make an identification possible. But since Delcita's rendition of blackness on stage is never stable enough for them to see it as a complete or full reflection of themselves or to be understood as an exact reflection of *me*, black identification with her is always incomplete.

As an affront to the social order, black enjoyment is reliant upon shared laughter as an act of identification with the other black people in the audience and the safety of operating within a space of black sociality. The "black" in black enjoyment is a space of plurality that houses multiple positionalities within Jamaica's black underclass who live on the island

and in the diaspora. It emerges from shared experiences of enslavement and colonization and the remarginalization of poor black Jamaicans under the creole and brown class after independence. In my view, the "black" in black enjoyment refers to those whose cultural forms and modes of being are routinely reviled, who rub up against the politics of respectability and who refuse assimilation into the standards and moral codes of a creole order that would never affirm them anyway. Laughing at the character on stage is the instrument of communal bonding, the gesture of recognition forged through seeing the images of themselves on stage, the consolidation of a black sociality. Black enjoyment does not somehow mean that black discomfort with the renditions of blackness on stage is never in the room. Black enjoyment is fragile and momentary. The interactive nature of roots plays means that the characters (and actors) on stage must always contend with the approval or reproach of the black spectators in the seats. Laughter as the signal of enjoyment can quickly turn to disapproval. I imagine black enjoyment as produced through that organic, dynamic interchange that is facilitated through the breaking of the fourth wall in roots theater. Black enjoyment thus exists in the fraught affective space between black discomfort and black complicity, and the borders must always be constantly reinforced for black delight to thrive. And it is precisely within those moments of ludic reconstruction, disidentification, and radical disregard that a black working-class sociality is forged.

Furthermore, this domain of racial enjoyment houses a libidinal economy built on abject pleasures. Theorists define the abject as an "in-between, ambiguous [. . .] intermediary entity" that "threatens the constitution of the subject who is invested in the myth of wholeness or completeness."[98] Abjection is a process through which one attempts to "circumscribe and radically differentiate something" or someone that, "although deemed repulsively *other* is paradoxically, at some fundamental level, an undifferentiable part of the whole."[99] The abject is "the condition/position of that which is deemed loathsome and the process by which the appraisal is made."[100] The constitution of the whole or the subject requires the continual jettisoning of the abject. The process of abjection "confirms but also repeatedly determines the status of that which disturbs identity, system, order and does not respect borders, positions, rules."[101] The postcolonial below—its practices, spaces, and the black, queer, and deviant subjects that inhabit it—are loathsome to the dominant order, continuously jettisoned from the national body to shore up the constitution of the ideal citizen subject. Although the figure of Delcita may certainly exemplify a performer using abjection to "expand the pantheon of available contestatory subjectivities while augmenting possible approaches to politicized aesthetics," contestation is only one aspect of the ambiguous dynamic that is operative within this libidinal economy.[102]

Abject pleasures are not only the delights of these abject subjects living on the margins of a postcolonial society, but they are also the joys deemed counter to the ideals of respectability and racial uplift. I imagine abject pleasures as those amusements that are, by nature, too ambiguous, contradictory, or paradoxical to be embraced as merely subversive acts of resistance. Black enjoyment, in the context of Delcita's performance, thus represents a libidinal economy built on mordant pleasures that are rejected, dispelled, and cast away as signs of ignorance and self-loathing because they are shameful to the social order. In their study of abject comedy, theorists Maggie Hennefield and Nicholas Sammond explain that classic comedy theory typically views laughter as the instrument for regulating social relations of power.[103] They suggest that laughter either works as a "social corrective" that derides behavior that is out of step with modern life or it functions in recuperative fashion—as in the carnivalesque—wherein grotesque, reviled, and dejected bodies "revolt against their own exclusion."[104] I imagine the laughter that Delcita elicits in roots theater as belonging to this abject comedy because it is neither recuperative nor a social corrective. Instead, I insist that in the context of black enjoyment, laughter defies the "familiar paradigms between a disciplinary trap and a subversive escape."[105] Thus, laughter is not the sign of a momentary suspension of social norms or collective catharsis. Rather it is the expression of a domain of racial enjoyment that is itself an abject ludic space residing in the interstices between subjection and resistance.

By signaling the postcolonial below as adjacent to the black below, I am seeking to map a libidinal economy of black insouciance that is not delimited to a singular nation-state but is part of disperse and interconnected diasporic circuits of black enjoyment in the hemispheric fold. Hemispheric blackface is also the site for these libidinal economies forged by communities across the African diaspora, wherein black people free themselves from the quest for legitimacy and validation from the majoritarian sphere and simply center themselves. The postcolonial below that houses abject pleasures thus lives next door to the performances of ratchetry found on Black Twitter. Andre Brock Jr. positions being ratchet as "(uber) performative authenticity—as 'bout it,' 'real' and 'doing the most,'" while L. H. Stallings claims it entails "performances of the failure to be respectable, uplifting, and a credit to the race."[106] The postcolonial below is also parallel to the chitlin circuit, or what Rashida McMahon eloquently calls "the Black Circuit." She describes the Black Circuit as a performance enclave where African Americans look "inwards for merits of success and acknowledgement rather than outwards" by creating a theater world for African Americans "whose interests have been devalued and marginalized, even by other Black Americans."[107] While I acknowledge the chitlin circuit here, I limit my engagement with it so as not to reproduce the very hegemony of US blackface minstrelsy that this book seeks to contest. My point is to emphasize the postcolonial below as a node in a diasporic circuit composed of black ludic spaces in which black people do not fight for a seat at the proverbial table, but instead build our own.[108] To think of this abject ludic space in diasporic terms is to underscore the limitations of the nation for wrestling with a set of strategies and approaches wielded by black people living in the hemispheric fold. Delcita not only enables me to trace the entanglement of nationalist fiction with this ludic circuit, but the mapping of this domain of racial enjoyment also signals the potential for black people to use racial conjuring to set their own terms.

I conclude this book with Delcita and the paradoxes of black enjoyment to underscore how black people carve out their own ludic circuits, reimagine the figurations of blackness circulating in their midst to affirm themselves, intervene in economies of racial enjoyment, carve out spaces of solidarity, and identify with one another. Because hemispheric blackface can help us discern how black people negotiate both the endurance of slavery's logics and nationalist celebrations of colorblindness and multiculturalism, I end with this instance of radical disregard to emphasize the ways black people can use racial conjuring to chart their own social order. The goal of this book is to map the different domains of racial enjoyment—subjection, resistance, and abject pleasures—that operate in tension with the different modalities of repeating nationalist fictions and their afterlives circulating in the hemispheric fold. Challenging easy theoretical dichotomies of subjection and resistance, I imagine acts of racial conjuring and the domains of racial enjoyment they produce as being ludic sites of ambiguities, paradoxes, and radical possibility.

Hemispheric Blackface
and Its Afterlives

Hemispheric Blackface illuminates how acts of racial impersonation mediate repeating nationalist fictions circulating in the hemispheric Americas. Throughout I examine acts of racial conjuring in the hemispheric fold to critically reimagine the Americas, to decenter the US blackface minstrel tradition, and to retheorize economies of racial enjoyment in the twentieth and twenty-first centuries. By decentering US blackface minstrelsy, we can better see how the Americas are, in fact, defined by repeating nationalist fictions that have obscured or silenced structures of racial inequality. This approach therefore allows me to do two things: First, it enables me to track the ongoing power and prevalence of these fictions and their afterlives in an era defined by the presumed end of myths of racial democracy. I mark the points of convergence and disjuncture of these enduring nationalist fictions across the hemispheric fold. Second, I map domains of racial enjoyment to not only underscore how conjuring blackness permeates everyday life, but also to discern how people critically engage the ongoing power of these fictions in cultural entertainment. Examining racial impersonation is important because, amid the shifts away from nationalist fictions of colorblindness, conjuring blackness can help negotiate the ongoing advancements, reversals, and struggles in racial equality that have characterized the twentieth century. Throughout this book, I examine the persistence of the racial scripts in each nation to insist that acts of racial impersonation illuminate the racial constraints placed on blackness as the nation reconfigures its national story. And this is the case whether they reinforce or trouble the racial scripts of mestizaje and colorblindness that they have put on display.

I take a hemispheric approach to argue that neither the nation nor the US blackface minstrel tradition, by themselves, are adequate theoretical references for discerning the work of racial impersonation in spaces that have been organized around myths of racial democracy. Rather, I argue that, in the Americas, slavery has produced both nationalist fictions of racial democracy that disavowed its legacies of racial exclusion and economies of racial enjoyment grounded in the symbolic possession of blackness. In centering slavery, rather than the nation or a single performance tradition, we can better track how its logics of possession, domination, mastery, and resistance permeate everyday life and economies of racial enjoyment. Hemispheric blackface is thus defined by that tension between a nationalist fiction and the reconfigurations and negotiations of racial power that take place in the ludic domain. By thinking with and across national silos, we can attend to the different modalities of these repeating nationalist fictions that define the Americas and the role of racial enjoyment in mediating their afterlives.

Each chapter illuminates a domain of racial enjoyment in the hemispheric fold and a different version of the repeating national fiction. These domains are part of a whole structure and system of ludic cultural forms. Thus, together, the domains of racial enjoyment that I present necessarily encompass a heterogeneity of ludic objects and a wide range of cultural practices. I track everyday scenes of racial enjoyment in a performance at a carnival, on a TV show, at a multimedia art exhibit at a museum, and in a theater performance. I also reference cartoons, candy wrappers, advertisements, and kitsch objects to map an economy of racial enjoyment that encompasses the visual, the kinetic, the theatrical, the material, and the performative. This move illustrates how scenes of racial enjoyment permeate all our cultural realms. They are monetized, circulated, and consumed across a range of cultural marketplaces. Depending on the cultural mode, they have different global reach and, as is the case with Yeyo on *Esta Noche Tu Night* in chapter 2, for example, the TV show enabled forms of identification across disparate demographics in the hemispheric fold. The processes of identification that I describe in these distinct ludic forms could also be applied to social media as another ludic domain through which slavery's logics make themselves present in our everyday lives.

While racial enjoyment is the mode through which we negotiate the advancements and reversals of racial equality today, the goal of this book is not to make inherent claims that blackface is good or bad, or oppressive or liberatory. Moreover, I do not make any value judgments about the inherent nature of all blackface performance or the individual nations themselves. Other examples in each country could very well be marshaled to make the opposite arguments I have made. Instead, the scenes that I analyze in each chapter present different dimensions of racial enjoyment that span scenes of subjection, resistance, ambiguity, and abject pleasures. In chapter 1 on racial impersonation in Puno, Peru, I present a scene of subjection to underscore how racial impersonation works to fix and sustain the racial script of black disappearance as the nation moves toward recognition of its black population. Beginning the chapter with a scene of slavery demonstrates that the racial scripts of mestizaje emerge from the nation's relationship to its slave past. Reproducing slavery's logics of symbolic possession is a ludic recourse that mediates the turn to multiculturalism and the evolution of Peru's nationalist fiction of mestizaje in the twenty-first century. Racial conjuring thus works to fix blackness amid changes to the national story.

Because the history of slavery is shared, fixing blackness not only serves to reinforce the racial scripts of the national story, but it also enables an identification among publics living in different parts of the Americas. In chapter 2, conjuring Yeyo in Miami negotiates the geopolitical tensions and changes between the two Americas as Barack Obama, the first black president of the United States, rises to power. It also consolidates a hemispheric creole whiteness in the city made up of different factions of Latin American and Caribbean white immigrants who negotiated the turn to the left in Latin America and the Caribbean in the first decade of the twenty-first century. The ludic is a crucial domain through which disparate publics identify with each other and enforce dynamics of racial subjection in a scene of racial enjoyment. Doing "antiblackness" enables distinct demographics of the Cuban diaspora and of Latin American and Caribbean immigrant communities to integrate into the hemispheric fold. This underscores how critical the hemispheric approach is for understanding how summoning slavery's logics serves to navigate the shifts in racial formations of the twenty-first century.

While the first half of the book focuses on acts of racial conjuring that reinforce the dynamics of black subjugation in relation to the nationalist fiction of colorblindness, the second half examines acts of racial conjuring by black people to illuminate black resistance and black enjoyment as two other domains of a larger economy of racial enjoyment. In my analysis of the multimedia piece by the Afro-Colombian artist Liliana Angulo, I highlight how she enacts the racial scripts of blackness to confront, destabilize, and humanize the negrita as a figuration of blackness. Amid the turn to multiculturalism, this act of racial conjuring exposes the ongoing power of the racial scripts of mestizaje within the new nation. When wielded by black people, racial conjuring can be a ludic recourse of confrontation that exposes the endurance of the very racial scripts of mestizaje that the new multicultural state was to leave behind.

But in emphasizing the dimensions of resistance within this economy of racial enjoyment, I do not suggest that when black people engage in racial conjuring they merely do so to subvert a white gaze or to humanize the stereotype. In the final chapter of the book, I aim to nuance the very economy of enjoyment that the previous chapters illuminate by emphasizing the place of black enjoyment of blackface tropes. I theorize black enjoyment in the Jamaican context as an example of "abject pleasures," those pleasures that disturb the order of economies of racial enjoyment. As a reflective moment in this book, the chapter uses black enjoyment to resist the impetus to characterize racial impersonation as positive or negative. Such dualities do not capture the ambiguities, paradoxes, and complexities of black participation in economies of racial enjoyment. Hence, hemispheric blackface presents a complex and contradictory economy of racial enjoyment in today's world, where lives of black people look decidedly different from those of the nineteenth and twentieth centuries. In my theorization of black enjoyment, I refuse to see black people solely in positions of subjection but, rather, as actors negotiating and disturbing practices of racial conjuring that were not meant for their pleasure. The second part of the book thus maps the ludic practices of African diasporic communities living in the hemispheric fold. It shows that hemispheric blackface is also about how black people conjure blackness for their own devices and critically engage nationalist structures of racial silence and their afterlives. At its heart, this book is a critical engagement with an economy of racial enjoyment in the hemispheric fold wherein actors conjure blackness to map out hierarchies of racial power as the nationalist fictions in their midst evolve or remain the same.

Throughout the book, I define *hemispheric blackface* as not only the acts of impersonation that mediate nationalist fictions and their afterlives but also as a prismatic field of signification forged by a shared history of slavery. Hemispheric blackface is a space of encounter of performative idioms and of forgotten performance histories. It is a network of racial trafficking that spawned figurations of blackness and their racial doubles in the Americas. It is the ludic circuits wherein African diasporic communities use acts of racial conjuring to confront and subvert the racial order, to marshal the figurations of blackness circulating in the fold for their own devices, to revel in abject pleasures, and to critically reshape an economy of racial enjoyment organized around their exploitation and exclusion. Hemispheric blackface is a system that engages structures of antiblackness and white supremacy across national borders and that mediates the geopolitical relationships between the two Americas. Throughout *Hemispheric Blackface*, I show not only what black people must navigate in the afterlives of slavery but also how they must negotiate the afterlives of racial silence.

Continuing the Study of Racial Impersonation in the Americas

This book's staging of the hemispheric fold is necessarily incomplete, because the fold is perhaps incommensurable, especially to those of us living within its frame. In this book, I use blackface performance and nationalist fictions to critically reimagine the Americas. Each of these twin conceptual nodes of hemispheric blackface offer the potential for future research. In using repeating nationalist fictions to reimagine the Americas, I move away from traditional disciplinary and geographic paradigms. I include the Anglophone Caribbean because studies of racial democracy and color-blindness have been so heavily tilted to Spanish- and Portuguese-speaking countries in Latin America and the Caribbean. By placing the Anglophone Caribbean in conversation with its Latin American counterparts, I hope to broaden the geographical scope for critical engagement with discourses of postracialism as a central legacy of slavery in the Americas. While studies of blackface performance in Latin America have engaged its relationship to the discourse of mestizaje, there is still very little research on blackface in the Anglophone Caribbean beyond those that track the influence of US minstrelsy.[1] Future study could focus more closely on the role of impersonation in the racial politics of the nations in the Anglophone Caribbean. Newer research could also take a geographical approach and survey blackface performance and discourses of postracialism in other parts of the Americas. While I did not include Canada or Mexico, for example, scholarship suggests that racial impersonation also negotiates other modalities of the repeating nationalist fictions in these sites.[2] There is also very little research about impersonating blackness in the nations of Central America and its implications for the relationship between blackness and indigeneity.[3] Alas, no single study can do it all. My theorization of the hemispheric fold is an invitation for further critical conversation about different modalities of postracialism, their afterlives, and differing constellations of antiblackness.

This book examines blackface performance in moments of new political articulation, but it stops short of engaging the politics of the COVID-19 pandemic, its reconfiguration of the public sphere, and the renewed attention to racial protest that took place. While my chapter on Miami focuses heavily on impersonation during Obama's first and second terms, attitudes, fractures, and differences among the Cuban diaspora in Miami were undoubtedly impacted by life under the Trump administration, whose politics toward Cuba moved away from the emphasis on cultural exchange under Obama. Since the election of Joe Biden, Miami's landscape has continued to change as it welcomes new Cuban arrivals. This is due, in part, to the fact that Cuba is experiencing its worst economic crisis since the Special Period and to the fact that the Biden administration launched a new humanitarian parole program in 2023 that offers a pathway to life in the United States for Cubans, Haitians, Nicaraguans, and Venezuelans who have a US sponsor and who pass a background check. These structural conditions and policies render the transition from life in Cuba to life in the United States much easier for these new arrivals. Future study could consider the implications of these geopolitical shifts and policies for the comedy scene, constructions of Cuban whiteness, and current attitudes toward the embargo.

Finally, this book's examination of racial impersonation sought to contribute to ongoing conversations about blackface as a global form in ways that did not center the US blackface minstrel tradition.[4] At various times in the book, I note moments of encounter between US blackface minstrelsy and other traditions of impersonation, but I generally look to strike the delicate balance of acknowledging its presence without rendering its reach the master narrative for all the acts of racial conjuring in this book. This gesture is an invitation to treat the US blackface minstrel tradition as just one of many others, rather than as a defining feature of all blackface performance in the region. Future study could offer further attention to what traditions of racial conjuring existed in Latin America and the Caribbean prior to the travel of US minstrel performers to the region. Much of the historical work has focused on teatro bufo, but new research would need to map the emergence and evolution of other blackface traditions in different parts of the Americas.[5] The dearth of such necessary historical research has only served to consolidate the hegemony of the US blackface minstrel tradition in studies of impersonation in the region.[6]

Such new work would considerably reshape how one understands impersonation today and the circulation of blackface tropes across the hemisphere. During the times that I have lived in different parts of Latin America, negrita archetypes were a staple of cleaning products, food items, candy wrappers, souvenir shops, and kitchen kitsch. Yet when I researched the negrita figures of Angulo's archive, I found very little critical work on impersonation and material culture focused specifically on Latin America. Tracking the movement of racial objects, their evolution, and their consumption across the Americas would only deepen the examination of the economy of racial enjoyment that this book sought to map. Furthermore, material culture is typically a domain where caricatures of blackness from cartoons and comic books come to life. While cartoon characters like Memín Pinguín in Mexico or Negra Nieves in Colombia have received some critical attention here and elsewhere, future research dedicated to theorizing the nexus of race, cartoons, and material culture in Latin America would benefit any future study of impersonation and economies of racial enjoyment in the region.

I was unable to examine racial conjuring in digital and virtual spheres. Nevertheless, the figurations of blackness that are conjured in GIFs, memes, and on TikTok certainly have a transnational life and circulate in the hemispheric fold. Our reliance on them on social media platforms and text messages render them a staple of our daily conversations and interactions. Now, more than ever, blackface functions as a shared practice across the Americas and the globe. Our reliance on the virtual further emphasizes that the nation proves inadequate for wrestling with the politics of race when the "local is a leaky contingent construction" and national borders are nothing but a membrane.[7] Given that the COVID-19 pandemic has further entrenched the virtual as the primary mode of interaction for so many in the world, new studies of blackface performance would have to offer a deeper reflection on the racial politics of impersonation in an increasingly online world.

In this book, I analyze impersonation to critique the politics of racial enjoyment in the hemispheric fold. Given the incompleteness of this archive, it is my hope that others will seek to track the figurations of blackness conjured in our midst, to unpack their meaning, and to unearth their relationship to the future evolutions of the repeating nationalist fictions circulating in the fold. The goal of tracking these distinct domains of racial enjoyment is to open the door to a set of future conversations, about what it means not only to conjure blackness but also to make legible the figurations of blackness across national and linguistic differences in the Americas.

Introduction: Scenes of Racial Enjoyment in the Hemispheric Fold

1   Lane, *Blackface Cuba.*
2   Nadege Greene, "A Miami Theater Group Has a Change of Heart over Blackface," The World from PRX, June 25, 2018, https://www.pri.org /stories/2018-06-25/miami-theater-group-has-change-heart-over-blackface. For the video clip and further coverage, see also Brenda Medina, "The Miami Parody Features an Artist in Blackface and the Audience 'Loves It,'" *Miami Herald,* June 1, 2018, https://www.miamiherald.com/ news/local/article211404909.html.
3   Whitten and Torres, *Blackness in Latin America and the Caribbean*; De la Fuente and Andrews, *Afro-Latin American Studies*; Appelbaum et al., *Race and Nation in Modern Latin America*; Hernández, *Racial Subordination in Latin America*; Nascimento and Nascimento, "Apresentação."
4   See De la Fuente, *Nation for All*; Hernández, *Racial Subordination in Latin America*; Geler, *Andares negros, caminos blancos.* Black thinkers in Latin America such as Abdias do Nascimento, Manuel Zapata Olivella, Alberto Arredondo, and others were vocal critics of myths of racial democracy. For example, see Nascimento, *O negro revoltado*; Robaina, *El negro en Cuba*; Carbonell, *Crítica cómo surgió la cultural nacional.*
5   As I explain in chapter 2, the Pink Tide referred to the emergence of a bloc of leftist leaders in Latin America in the early 2000s. The policies of some of these leaders marked the advancement of racial equality and shifts in state policies toward race. Affirmative action policies in Brazil were implemented during Lula da Silva's first term, and the election of Evo Morales, Bolivia's first indigenous president, occasioned the protection and expansion of indigenous rights as well as the development of a new constitution that defined Bolivia as a plurinational state. For more, see Crabtree, "Indigenous Empowerment in Bolivia." On Brazil, see Júnior, Daflon, and Campos, "Lula's Approach to Affirmative Action and Race."
6   Lane, "Problems of Framing," 127.
7   On the origins of US minstrelsy, see Lhamon, *Jump Jim Crow*; Smith, *Creolization of American Culture*; Cockrell, *Demons of Disorder.* US blackface minstrelsy evolved to adapt to the emergence of new cultural forms from television to animation. See the introduction in Johnson, *Burnt Cork.* See also Chude-Sokei, "Uncanny History of Minstrels and Machines."

8   See Jones, *Staging Habla de Negros*; Stevens, *Inventions of the Skin*, chap. 3; Carr, "Material/Blackness"; Ndiaye, *Scripts of Blackness*. Hoxworth, *Trans-oceanic Blackface*; Francisco Covarrubias first performed in blackface on Cuban stages in 1812, some thirty years before the first American minstrel shows. See Thomas, *Cuban Zarzuela*, 82, 83. Rine Leal's two-volume study *La selva oscura* (1975) and *La selva oscura: De los bufos a la neocolonia* (1982) offer the most extensive examination of teatro bufo. For blackface in Bolivia and Peru, see Roper, "Blackface at the Andean Fiesta" and chapter 1 of this book. On La Fiesta de Blancos y Negros in Pasto, Colombia, see David Jáuregui Sarmiento, "¿Conoces la historia del Carnaval de blancos y negros?" *Señal Colombia*, December 29, 2021, https://www.senalcolombia.tv /cultura/historia-carnaval-negros-y-blancos.

9   For black-on-black performance, see Chude-Sokei, *Last " Darky."* On blackface in the Anglo-Atlantic world, see Nowatski, *Representing African Americans*. On blackface in the Iberian world, see Fernández de la Reguera Tayá, *Cuba y Catalunya*. For blackface in the British empire, see Hoxworth, *Transoceanic Blackface*.

10   Cole, "American Ghetto Parties." For an early history of using impersonations of blackness to articulate Western modernity, see Ndiaye, *Scripts of Blackness*; Carr, "Material Blackness"; Jones, *Staging Habla de Negros*. On how colonial blackface shaped understandings of the national, see Lane, "Problems of Framing," 115.

11   For the turn away from the nation in blackface studies, see especially Thelwell, *Exporting Jim Crow*; Hoxworth, *Transoceanic Blackface*; Witmann, "Empire of Culture"; Cole and Davis, "Routes of Blackface." All show the transnational reach of US minstrelsy and the limitations of the nation for wrestling with the form. Hoxworth, especially, debunks the notion that blackface was a distinctly US American phenomenon. He charts a transoceanic history of blackface performance across the British empire.

12   On blackface performance troupes in Río de la Plata, see Andrews, "Remembering Africa, Inventing Uruguay." On teatro bufo, see Leal, *Teatro Bufo Siglo XIX*. On "Diplo," see Rivero, *Tuning Out Blackness*. On Memín Pinguín and the role of Mexican *historietas* in national cultural formation, see Rubenstein, *Bad Language, Naked Ladies*.

13   For discursive blackface, see Lane, *Blackface Cuba*; on digital blackface, see Madeline Howard, "What Is Digital Blackface? Experts Explain Why the Social Media Practice Is Problematic," *Women's Health Magazine*, February 11, 2022, https://www.womenshealthmag.com/life/a33278412/digital -blackface/. See also John Blake, "What's 'Digital Blackface'? And Why Is It Wrong When White People Use It?" CNN, March 26, 2023, https:// www.cnn.com/2023/03/26/us/digital-blackface-social-media-explainer -blake-cec/index.html; Jason Parham, "TikTok and the Evolution of Digi-

tal Blackface," *Wired*, August 4, 2020, https://www.wired.com/story
/tiktok-evolution-digital-blackface/.

14   On blackface as a floating signifier, see Cole, "American Ghetto Parties." On
blackface as form, see Yang, *Peculiar Afterlife of Slavery*. On blackface as lingua franca and racial idiom, see Ochieng' Nyong'o, *Amalgamation Waltz*. See
also Lott, *Love and Theft*. On blackface as a transnational language of race,
see Chude-Sokei, *Last "Darky."*

15   Lane, "Hemispheric America in Deep Time."

16   Hartman, *Scenes of Subjection*; Roach, *Cities of the Dead*.

17   Lott, *Love and Theft*.

18   Carpio, *Laughing Fit to Kill*.

19   For more on blackface as shine, see Post, "Williams, Walker, and Shine."

20   Taylor, *Archive and the Repertoire*; Hall, "Cultural Studies and Its Theoretical
Legacies."

21   The term *blackface* has been used in social media discussions of controversial television characters who black up, such as "El Negro Mama" in Peru
and Colombia's Soldado Micolta. The Peruvian Newspaper *El Comercio*
traced the history of blackface to the Elizabethan stage and US blackface
minstrelsy in its discussion of El Negro Mama. See Luis del Campo, "Blackface y brownface: del Otelo al Negro Mama . . . ," *El Comercio*, August 8,
2020, https://elcomercio.pe/luces/blackface-y-brownface-de-otelo-al
-negro-mama-el-origen-de-la-mala-costumbre-que-se-niega-a-morir
-vania-torres-noticia/. In coverage of *el soldado micolta*, writers used the
term blackface to describe the racial impersonation. See Rodriguez Garavito's "La controversia sobre el soldado micolta y su salida . . . ," accessed July
15, 2024, Dejusticia, https://www.dejusticia.org/column/adios-soldado
-micolta/; see also Radio Ambulante's podcast "No soy tu chiste," 48:02, accessed July 15, 2024, https://radioambulante.org/audio/no-soy-tu-chiste.
For *corcho quemado*, see Denise Braz, "Corcho Quemado | ¿Qué Es El Black-
face? Revisando La Educación Racista Que Supimos Conseguir," *Página/12
Web*, July 6, 2018, https://www.paginat2.com.ar/126215-corcho-quemado.
In Spanish it is referred to as *pintarse de negro, corcho quemado* (burnt cork),
cara negra (blackface), and *tiznarse el rostro* (painted face). For *cara negra*, see
Lane and Godoy-Anativia, "Dossier." For *tiznarse el rostro*, see Adamovksy,
"Los Negros, la primera comparsa."

22   Lane, *Blackface Cuba*; Rivero, *Tuning Out Blackness*.

23   I am thinking here about the circulation of bufo tropes and US blackface
minstrel tropes in the region. For work on the circulation of the bufo tropes
in the Caribbean, see Rivero, *Tuning Out Blackness*. In the 1860s, Cuba's teatro bufo performance tradition—a comic revue style for which blackface
was a central feature—produced the figure of the "negro catedrático." Rivero explains that bufo comedies first appeared on Puerto Rican stages in
1873 in local plays *Los negros catedráticos, Un negro bueno*, and *Los Negros espir-*

itistas, written by Cuban scriptwriter Francisco Fernández. The teatro bufo characters also appeared on stages in New York in the early 1920s as Cuban artists traveled to and from the United States. For the travel of blackface from Cuba to the United States, see López, *Unbecoming Blackness*; and Laguna, *Diversión*. For circulation of US blackface minstrel archetypes in Latin America, see Karush, "Blackness in Argentina"; and Derby, *Dictator's Seduction*. Chinua Thelwell has also generously shared with me archival information of the travel of a minstrel, Frank Hussey, from the minstrel troupe the Sable Brothers, who traveled the world in the 1840s, including Brazil, Peru, and other parts of South America.

24 Implemented under colonial rule, the casta system was a hierarchical system that classified racial groups and racial mixture and determined one's social and socioeconomic status; see Rosenblat, *La población indígena de América*. See also Katzew, *Casta Paintings*.

25 Weheliye, *Habeas Viscus*, 4. On the casta system, see Rosenblat, *La población indígena de América*.

26 Here I riff on Antonio Benitez-Rojo's concept of the repeating island, which suggests that within the disorder of the Caribbean there emerges an island of paradoxes that repeats itself; Benitez-Rojo, *Repeating Island*.

27 Múnera, *Fronteras imaginadas*; Mosquera, Pardo, and Hoffman, *Afrodescendientes en las Américas*; Alberto and Hoffnung-Garskof, "'Racial Democracy' and Racial Inclusion."

28 See Ingenieros, "Las razas inferiores"; Bunge, *Nuestra América*; De Friedemann and Arocha, *De sol a sol*.

29 See Kutzinski, *Sugar's Secrets*; Hernández, *Racial Subordination in Latin America*; De la Fuente and Andrews, *Afro-Latin American Studies*.

30 Rama, *Lettered City*. See also Lane, *Blackface Cuba*, 4.

31 Martí, *Nuestra América*, 16 (translation from Lane, *Blackface Cuba*, 2005, 4). Lane insists that Martí's casting of this mestizo autóctono in the place of a native is, in fact, the conjuring of a false originary figure who erases the violence of colonial contact. Martí invents this figure to serve as an "original" American protagonist in his mestizo America; Lane, *Blackface Cuba*, 5.

32 Martí, *Nuestra América*, 24 (translation from Lane, *Blackface Cuba*, 5).

33 Ortíz, *Martí y las razas*, 30.

34 Alberto and Hoffnung-Garskif, "'Racial Democracy' and Racial Inclusion."

35 Freyre popularized the term "racial democracy" in *The Masters and the Slaves*. While Freyre acknowledged the violence of slavery in Brazil, he ultimately saw interracial mixture of enslaved African women with white colonial masters, the childrearing of white children by enslaved people, and all the social interactions between black and white people during slavery to have created an organic social inclusion that softened racial divisions and social hierarchies. For more on Freyre, see Alberto and Hoffnung-Garskof,

"'Racial Democracy' and Racial Inclusion," 274. See also Benzanquen de Araújo, *Guerra y paz*; Ribeiro, *O povo Brasileiro*.

36   Freyre, *Masters and the Slaves*. Many Brazilian scholars have critiqued Freyre's paradigms by highlighting the persistence of systemic racial inequality in Brazil despite celebrations of racial miscegenation; see Araújo, *Guerra y paz*; Ortiz, *Cultura brasileira e identidade nacional*.

37   Throughout the nineteenth and early twentieth centuries, thinkers adjudicated different values to racial miscegenation that involved blackness and indigeneity, but generally they all venerated whiteness. See Ingenieros, "Las razas inferiores"; Bunge, *Nuestra América*; Saco, *Colección de papeles científicos*; Romero, *Estudos sobre a poesia popular*.

38   Paschel, *Becoming Black Political Subjects*, 29. Paschel also notes that while influential thinkers such as Colombian president Laureano Gómez (1950–1953) saw racial mixture as a sign of degeneracy, over time other thinkers, such as the Colombian writer Luis López de Mesa, concluded that racial miscegenation was in fact the solution to overcoming the country's black and indigenous elements. Despite their differences, both López de Mesa and Gómez believed in the moral, aesthetic, and intellectual superiority of Europeans.

39   Vasconcelos, *Cosmic Race*, 30.

40   Stepan, *The Hour of Eugenics*; Saco, *Colección de papeles científicos*; Ortiz, "José Antonio Saco y sus ideas"; Geler, *Andares negros, caminos blancos*; Figueras, *Cuba y su evolución colonial*.

41   Hernández, *Racial Subordination in Latin America*.

42   De la Fuente and Andrews, "Making of a Field."

43   Ledgister, *Only West Indians*, 25.

44   Williams, *Historical Background of Race Relations*.

45   Williams, *Historical Background of Race Relations*.

46   Quoted in Nettleford, *Mirror Mirror*, 23.

47   Thomas, "Democratizing Dance"; Thomas, *Modern Blackness*.

48   Although Maziki Thame argues against the notion of nonracialism, she eloquently underscores how creole nationalism was in fact the articulation of a brown nationalism; see Thame, "Racial Hierarchy."

49   Nettleford, *Caribbean Cultural Identity*, 4.

50   For more on race in Trinidad and Tobago, see Crosson, "Race, Nation, and Diaspora," 419. See also Welcome, "To Be Black Is to . . ."

51   See Welcome, "To Be Black Is to . . ."

52   Hintzen, "Creoleness and Nationalism in Guyanese."

53   Jackson, *Creole Indigeneity*. For a nuanced critique of the limitations of the settler-colonial framework and its erasure of antiblackness as coconstitutive of indigenous dispossession, see Cordis, "Forging Relational Difference."

54   López, *Unbecoming Blackness*.

55   Hay, *I've Been Black*; Aja, *Miami's Forgotten Cubans*.

56   Aja, *Miami's Forgotten Cubans*.

57   On creole whiteness, see Francis and Harris, "Introduction."

58   See Sommer, *Foundational Fictions*.

59   Lowe, *Intimacies of Four Continents*, 11.

60   See Telles, *Pigmentocracies*.

61   Hernández, *Racial Innocence*, 1, 7.

62   Hooker, "Indigenous Inclusion/Black Exclusion."

63   Paschel, *Becoming Black Political Subjects*.

64   See Telles, *Pigmentocracies*. See also "Americas Barometer 2010," Ethnicity
      Module of the Project on Ethnicity and Race in Latin America (PERLA),
      Latin American Public Opinion Project of Vanderbilt University.

65   Hale, *Más que un indio*, 35.

66   For indio permitido, see Hale, *Más que un indio*.

67   Berlant and Ngai, "Comedy Has Issues," 233.

68   Berlant and Ngai, "Comedy Has Issues," 235.

69   Merriam-Webster.com Dictionary, s.v. "scene," accessed August 20, 2024,
      https://www.merriam-webster.com/dictionary/scene.

70   Thomas, *Modern Blackness*, 11, 12.

71   Teatro Trail, "Friends of Trail Theatre and Sala Catarsis/Amigos de Teatro
      Trail y Sala Catarsis," Facebook, edited May 5, 2021, https://www.facebook
      .com/notes/648624872469165/. See also Nadege Green, "Afro-Latinos Say
      Miami Blackface Play Is Part of Bigger Problem with Racism in Latino
      Communities," PBS, May 29, 2018, https://news.wgcu.org/2018-05-29
      /afro-latinos-say-miami-blackface-play-is-part-of-bigger-problem-with
      -racism-in-latino-communities.

1. Blackface and Racial Scripts at the Andean Fiesta: Staging the Slave Past in the Andes

1   Wright, *Café con leche*.

2   It may be an intermediate racial form determined by hair texture; see
     Golash-Boza, "Does Whitening Happen?"

3   The founders of the troupe Sambos Illimani took the name "Illimani" from
     the mountain in La Paz, Bolivia, to affirm the dance's Bolivian origins.

4   The PachaMama is Mother Earth and is a revered feminine deity in indige-
     nous traditions.

5   On the Baile de los Negritos, see Sánchez-Patsy, "País de caporales." For
     analyses of negrito dances in Peru, see Bigenho, "El baile de los negritos";
     and Feldman, *Black Rhythms of Peru*.

6   Maidana Rodríguez, *La danza de los caporales*.

7   Since I was unable to reproduce images from the 2013 dance that I describe
     here with good resolution quality, I have instead shown an image from a 2020
     performance. You can find a video of the original performance in 2013 here:

MycandelariaPuno, "Caporales con Sentimiento y Devoción 2013," YouTube video, 7:07, March 3, 2013, https://www.youtube.com/watch?v=5qjYIuR ErSg. The still image featured here is taken from a video of the performance in 2020. See Samiger Studios, "A. F. Sambos con sentimiento y devoción porteño—danzas con trajes de luces (Candelaria 2020)," YouTube video, 7:55, February 12, 2020, https://www.youtube.com/watch?v=gPmwBlR 8kMs&ab_channel=SamigerStudios.

8   This mask tends to be of the Achachis character of the Afro-Andean dance La Morenada. The Achachis is an old man representing wisdom whose mask features oversized lips, a mole on his nose, and a large pipe in his mouth.

9   Also, members of Sambos Illimani limit their use of blackface in their performances to very few occasions. The directors of Sambos Illimani explained to me that the Fiesta de la Virgen de la Candelaria is only one of two special occasions of their yearly performance calendar in which they don blackface. They also incorporate it in the "Inauguración de traje" (inauguration of the costume)—an event where they formally present their new costume for the year to the public.

10   Cánepa Koch, *Máscara, transformación e identidad*; Cánepa Koch, *Identidades representadas.*

11   Cánepa Koch, *Identidades representadas.*

12   Bakhtin, *Rabelais and His World*; Stam, *Subversive Pleasures*; Goldstein, *Laughter Out of Place*; Guss, *The Festive State.*

13   Poole, "Accommodation and Resistance"; Rockefeller, "'There Is a Culture Here.'" Theorists assert that historically folkloric performances functioned to affirm and create a sense of national identity. See Mendoza-Walker, "Contesting Identities"; and Abercrombie, "La fiesta del carnaval postcolonial." Others underscore that indigenous people, as members of a marginalized group, use performance to contest hegemonic images that wider society imposes upon them. See, for instance, Cánepa Koch, *Identidades representadas.*

14   Member of Sambos Illimani, personal communication, Fiesta de la Virgen de la Candelaria, Puno, Peru, 2013.

15   Bowser, *African Slave in Colonial Peru.*

16   Enslaved black people arrived with a Spanish expedition as early as 1529, and the Spanish later purchased slaves to replace the dwindling indigenous labor force. In the sixteenth century, many enslaved blacks had already acquired European languages and customs, having lived as slaves in Spain or Portugal or having been born as slaves elsewhere. See Bowser, *African Slave in Colonial Peru*, 4; and Feldman, *Black Rhythms of Peru*, 2.

17   Afro-Peruvians also inhabited a space much closer to whites than their indigenous counterparts during the colonial period; see Feldman, *Black Rhythms of Peru*. In fact, blacks acted both as agents of liberation and repression in the Tupac Amaru rebellion—the largest indigenous revolt in the eighteenth century. They were deeply embedded in Peruvian coastal

culture, and in some cities they even constituted a majority of the populace during the colonial era; see Walker, *Tupac Amaru Rebellion*.

18 Feldman, *Black Rhythms of Peru*, 3.

19 Peru ended its participation in the slave trade in 1812, and slavery was fully abolished through two decrees by President Ramon Castilla in 1854 and 1855. Black invisibility gradually happened through decreased presence in the national census. Blacks constituted almost half of Lima's population in 1790. In 1884, blacks accounted for just 18 percent of the population, and by 1908 the black population was listed at a mere 1 percent. While some Afro-Peruvians identified as criollo rather than black in the census, theorists contend that black erasure was due to state attempts to downplay, if not outright erase, its black population. See Golash-Boza, *Yo Soy Negro*; and Cuche, *Poder blanco y resistencia negra*.

20 De la Cadena, "Silent Racism," 143.

21 After Peru's loss to Chile in the War of the Pacific (1879–1884), the creole elite largely blamed Peru's defeat on the backwardness of the indigenous populace, and the Ministry of Education and Health implemented a set of educational reforms with the explicit aim "to civilize the countryside and improve their lives by incorporating [Indians and mestizos] into the national community" (De la Cadena, "Are Mestizos Hybrids?," 271). Between 1900 and 1929, the state increased its investment in rural education by 16.5 percent; see Golash-Boza, *Yo Soy Negro*.

22 De la Cadena, "Are Mestizos Hybrids?"

23 Golash-Boza, *Yo Soy Negro*, 64.

24 De la Cadena, "Silent Racism."

25 Quoted in Feldman, "Strategies of the Black Pacific," 42.

26 For more on the impact of the absence of racial census, CONAPA, and the work of Afro-Peruvian NGOs, see Feldman, "Strategies of the Black Pacific," 43.

27 Hernández, *Racial Subordination*.

28 "Saga Falabella: Acusan spot publicitario de racista y tienda responde," *El Popular.pe*, September 7, 2018, https://www.elpopular.pe/actualidad-policiales /2018-09-07-saga-falabella-acusan-spot-publicitario-racista-tienda-respond e-foto-video.

29 See *Minority Rights Group*, "Afro-Peruvians," accessed May 25, 2023, https:// minorityrights.org/minorities/afro-peruvians/.

30 Becerra, "Stereotypes of Afro-Peruvians."

31 Becerra, "Stereotypes of Afro-Peruvians"; Feldman, "Strategies of the Black Pacific."

32 See Paschel, "Rethinking Black Mobilization," 253.

33 Feldman, *Black Rhythms of Peru*.

34 Moore, *Nationalizing Blackness*.

35 Feldman, *Black Rhythms of Peru*, 126.

36 Sue and Golash-Boza, "More Than 'a Hidden Race,'" 78.

37 De la Cadena, "Silent Racism"; Greene, "Entre lo Indio."

38 Frisancho, *Negros en el altiplano puneño.*

39 Greene, "Entre lo Indio."

40 Greene, "Entre lo Indio," 46; Cuche, *Poder blanco y resistencia negra*, 21, 22.

41 Bowser, *African Slave in Colonial Peru*, 14 (Bowser's translation). El *galli-nazo* is a black bird with a red beak known to live in the Peruvian coasts and is never seen in the highlands.

42 Golash-Boza, *Yo Soy Negro*. See also Rahier and Dougé Prosper, "Afro-descendants, the Multicultural Turn."

43 After the turn to multiculturalism, a group of fourteen Afro-Peruvian activist organizations produced the document "The Platform of Afro-Peruvian Communities," outlining a set of demands for the Peruvian state to address the needs of the Afro-Peruvian population. The state largely dismissed these requests and offered symbolic gestures in their place. It passed Law #28761 in 2006 that designated June 4—the birthday of noted Afro-Peruvian icon and folklorist Nicomedes Santa Cruz—as Afro-Peruvian Culture Day, and President Alan García also offered a formal apology for slavery through Resolution 010-2009; see Greene, "Todos Somos Iguales." At the time of writing, while the constitution grants provisions to its indigenous population that protects their rights to identity and autonomy, there is no equivalent basic law in Peru for the black populace. This privileging of indigeneity was also apparent in the establishment of INDEPA (The National Institute for the Development for Andean, Amazonian, and Afro-Peruvian Peoples) that was run by Elaine Karp, wife of President Toledo. The *A* in INDEPA did not, in fact, initially refer to Afro-Peruvians and at the outset was only meant to represent Andeans and Amazonians. Afro-Peruvians protested, and while they were ultimately included in the name of the institute, INDEPA has largely failed to prioritize the needs of the Afro-Peruvian populace. See Greene, "Todos Somos Iguales"; and Rahier, "Multicultural Turn."

44 See Hobsbawm, "Introduction," 1.

45 Salas-Carreño, *Representación de la esclavitud*, 110.

46 The cargoyuq may be the administrator or mayordomo of the dance troupe or may be a foreman in the dance.

47 In her description of the baile de los negritos from Lucanas, Ayacucho that is danced in Lima's Fiesta de la Virgen de Cocharcas, theorist Michelle Bigenho explains that the dance is composed of a team of four negritos accompanied by a harp, violin, drum, and a percussion instrument called a *chinchichi*. They are led by a cargoyuq who gives each of them a whip, bell, hat, handkerchief, and a poncho with colorful belts that represents their enslavement; Bigenho, "El baile de los negritos."

48 Rosa Alarco states, however, that "los negritos de Huánuco" has very little to do with actual black practices and really draws from Spanish, Arab, and

indigenous influences. This may well be a white or mestizo fantasy about blackness; Alarco, *Los negritos de Huánuco.*

49 Feldman, "Strategies of the Black Pacific." The use of bells on their feet comes from a Spanish dance known as the *baile de cascabel* or the dance of the shepherds. Given that Peru had a historically large black population, some scholars contend that when they were forced to dance in the nativity scenes at Christmas blacks incorporated the whip in the dance as a reference to their enslavement. See, for example, Tompkins, "Musical Traditions."

50 Trouillot, *Silencing the Past*, 15.

51 Wirtz, *Performing Afro-Cuba*, 4.

52 Brewer-García, "Imagined Transformations"; Kaplan, *Rise of the Black Magus.*

53 In indigenous performance traditions, it was common to imitate foreigners or people from other ethnic groups; see Cánepa Koch, *Máscara, transformación e identidad*; Poole, "Accommodation and Resistance."

54 Manuel Rigoberto Paredes, quoted in Sánchez-Patsy, "País de caporales."

55 Sánchez-Patsy, "País de caporales."

56 Sánchez, "Identidades sonoras," 85.

57 Paredes, quoted in Sánchez, "Identidades sonoras," 85 (my translation).

58 Templeman, "We Are People of the Yungas"; Jorge Godinez-Quinteros, "De encuentros, festivales y competencias [Thai]," *La Patria*, December 27, 2015, https://impresa.lapatria.bo/noticia/243263/de-encuentros-festivales-y -competencias-la-danza-del-caporal-sigue-presente; Jorge Godinez-Quinteros, "Del ritmo afro-boliviano de Saya a la danza estilizada de los caporales," *Oruro: Alta Tierra de los Uros* (blog), July 2017, https://altatierradelosurus.blogspot .com/2017/07/del-ritmo-afro-boliviano-y-de-la-saya.html.

59 Maidana Rodríguez, *La danza de los caporales.*

60 The confusion about the relationship between the Tundique rhythm and the Saya was propagated by the band Los K'jarkas, whose *lambada* song "Llorando se fue" (1982) made the caporal rhythm a hit. The band mistakenly referred to the rhythm of the Danza de Caporales as the Saya.

61 Coral, member of Mocusabol, personal communication, La Paz, Bolivia, 2017.

62 Sánchez, "Identidades sonoras."

63 "Negritos Pagador: Con traje afrocubano," *La Patria*, February 9, 2013, http://www.lapatriaenlinea.com/?nota=134638.

64 The New Song Movement is an era of cultural revolution in Latin America in the 1960s that saw the politicization of music, art, and popular culture; see Hutchinson et al., *Chile Reader.*

65 Sánchez-Patsy, "País de caporales."

66 Dennis Luizaga, "Viceministerio analiza prohibir la danza tundiki," *La Razón*, July 9, 2014.

67 "El Estado Plurinacional de Bolivia prohíbe el Tundique," People of African Descent, March 7, 2016, https://afrodescendant.wordpress.com/2016/03 /07/el-estado-plurinacional-de-bolivia-prohibe-el-tundiki/.

68 Martínez Melanchi, "Artist Perspectives."

69 Sigl and Mendoza Salazar, *No se baila así.*

70 David Mendoza Salazar, "La saya, el tundiqui y los caporales," *Suplemento Carnaval de Oruro: Presencia Diario Boliviano*, Feb. 1995.

71 Sigl and Mendoza Salazar, *No se baila así.*

72 Sánchez-Patsy, "País de caporales"; Sigl and Mendoza Salazar, *No se baila así.*

73 Sigl and Mendoza Salazar, *No se baila así.*

74 Sigl and Mendoza Salazar, *No se baila así*, 60.

75 When the member of Urus de Gran Poder debuted their new dance, spectators were so convinced that they were Argentinian gauchos that they referred to them as *gauchos troyeros*. Alejandro Cañaviri-Estrada, personal communication, La Paz, Bolivia, February 3, 2018; Sánchez-Patsy, "País de caporales." The term *troyeros* refers to someone who is very successful or has major public impact.

76 Sigl and Mendoza Salazar, *No se baila así.*

77 There are ongoing campaigns on social media and elsewhere that seek to defend and affirm the Bolivian origins of the Danza de Caporales and to denounce Peru's plagiarism. Bolivian cultural practitioner and radio host Napoleón Gómez has several publications and pamphlets regarding the Bolivian origins of the dance, including two editions of "Caporales 100% Boliviano"; see Gómez and Pinto López, *Caporales 100% boliviano*. Gómez has been one of the vocal figures contesting proclamations that the dance emerged from Peru. There are several Facebook groups affirming the Bolivian origins of the dance and accusing Peruvians of engaging in cultural plagiarism, including one named Caporales 100% Boliviano and another called Perú Capital Folclórica del Mundo, which calls the caporal a source of Peruvian pride. Caporales 100% Boliviano, https://www.facebook.com/Caporaldebolivia/?locale=es_LA; Perú Capital Folclórica del Mundo, https://www.facebook.com/Capital FolcloricadelMundo/posts/231576207175356?comment_id=1711303619 083893&comment_tracking=%7B%22tn%22%3A%22R%22%7D.

78 Apaza-Noa, personal communication, Lima, Peru, 2017.

79 For an example of Afro-Peruvian feminist critique of Blanco Varela, see Monica Carrillo, "Sobre la fragilidad blanca y la boca de sandía: A propósito del poema 'Muchachita negra' de Blanca Varela," Webblog Afronegroblack, August 30, 2020. See also Leonardo-Loayza, "Doblemente subalternizada"; Leonardo-Loayza traces the hemispheric network that shaped associations of black women with watermelons in Varela's work. He emphasizes the influence of US minstrel representations from films such as *Watermelon Man* (1970) and the famous children's song "Negrito sandía" (Little black watermelon boy) by Mexican singer Francisco Gabilondo Soler, also known as Cri-Cri. I am grateful to Olga Rodríguez-Ulloa for alerting me to this controversy and for all her feedback on this chapter.

80   Miguel Becerra does not specify the exact arrival of minstrel troupes to Peru, even though he contends US minstrel "darky" archetypes heavily influenced representations of black characters in Peru. He offers Boquellanta drawn by Hernán Bartra in the Peruvian newspaper *La Última Hora* in 1952 and 1954 as an example. Becerra is, however, correct in his assertion that US minstrel performances took place in Peru. According to a news article published in Kimberley, South Africa, in the newspaper *Diamond News* on October 24, 1883, the writer describes one blackface minstrel named Frank Hussey who performed with the professional minstrel troupe Sable Brothers as early as 1848. According to the paper, Hussey toured the globe. The paper states, "He succeeded in obtaining an engagement in a minstrel troupe known as the Sable Brothers in 1848; but in order to gratify his desire to visit foreign climes he shipped on a sailing vessel called the America… With the assistance of the men on board he organized a minstrel troupe and gave a series of performances in the various ports visited, in the Western Islands, Rio Janeiro [*sic*], Chili [*sic*], Peru, etc." Given that US minstrel troupes performed all over the region in the 1800s, landing in Argentina, Mexico, Cuba, Dominican Republic, and elsewhere, it is not surprising that Peru would have also been a destination for US minstrel performers. I am grateful to Chinua Thelwell for generously sharing with me this archival information on minstrel performers in South Africa.

81   Roach, *Cities of the Dead*.

82   Hartman, *Scenes of Subjection*, 21.

2. Doing Antiblackness in the Hemispheric Fold: Blackface Performance in Miami in the Age of Obama

1   This episode aired on MegaTv on June 19, 2009: MegaTv, "ESTA NOCHE TU NIGHT 06 19 2009 GRUPO ORO SOLIDO," YouTube video, June 26, 2009, 12:27, https://www.youtube.com/watch?v=GpK2prp-DS4.

2   Cuba en Miami, "Entrevista exclusiva con el humorista cubano Carlos Marrero (Pillin)," YouTube video, January 26, 2018, 37:21, https://www.youtube .com/watch?v=wOXjyXC4RmQ.

3   Still image of Yeyo Vargas. Carlos Marrero, "El día del trabajo con Yeyo Vargas," YouTube, YouTube video, May 7, 2013, 9:23, https://www.youtube .com/watch?app=desktop&v=Vl9oVbMphKk&t=179s.

4   José Pérez, MegaTv, personal communication, Miami, January 2020.

5   Nevertheless, on September 21, 2009, *Esta Noche Tu Night* was the most popular show among adult viewers as young as twenty-four years old when it featured the Puerto Rican star Olga Tañonso. For more, see Ayala Ben-Yehuda, "Prime Time for Latin Programming," *Billboard*, October 24, 2009, 25.

6   The *paquete semanal* is a weekly package that includes Hollywood block-

busters, television shows like *Game of Thrones*, music, sports contests, cartoons, and video compilations. It also includes cultural products from Cubans in Miami such as talk shows, YouTube videos, and content for and by Cubans on the island: songs by local musicians, classified ads, etc. For more on the *paquete*, see Laguna, *Diversión*.

7   For Jossianna Arroyo's theorization of Caribbean mediascape, see Arroyo, *Caribe 2.0*, 4.

8   For an example of this, see the discussion of Yeyo Vargas in Laguna, *Diversión*.

9   Portes and Stepick, *City on the Edge*; Nijman, *Miami*; Francis and Harris, "Introduction."

10 Cassanello and Murphee, "Epic of Greater Florida," 5; Francis and Harris, "Introduction," 3; see also Shell-Weiss, *Coming to Miami*. For more on the *balseros*, see Henken, "Balseros, Boteros, and El Bombo."

11 Francis and Harris, "Introduction," 1.

12 For the idea of the contact zone, see Pratt, "Arts of the Contact Zone."

13 Portes and Stepick, *City on the Edge*, 8. Generational diversity among the Cuban diaspora in Miami today would complicate the antiassimilationist paradigms that Portes and Stepick present in their text.

14 For a detailed breakdown of migration per decade before and after the Castro revolution and well into the 2000s, see Duany, *Blurred Borders*. The first wave of Cuban arrivals after the revolution was from January 1959 to October 1962, following the overthrow of Batista; 215,000 Cubans arrived in Miami. The "freedom flights" from 1965 to 1973 brought over 300,000 refugees to the United States. From May 1973 to April 1980, a smaller number of Cubans arrived due to the cancelation of airlifts from Cuba to Miami. The Mariel boatlift in 1980 brought around 165,000 Cubans. Scholars have rightly critiqued and debunked the stigmatization of the Marielito population as criminal by underscoring the vagueness of the Cuban state's definitions of the category of criminality, which could apply to any act of perceived dissidence. Others have noted the number of "common criminals" who migrated to Miami to be a mere 2 percent. For more see Portes and Stepick, *City on the Edge*. See also Jorge Duany, "El éxodo del Mariel, 35 años después," *El Nuevo Herald*, October 26, 2015, https://www.elnuevoherald.com/opinion-es/opin-col-blogs/opinion-sobre-cuba/article41497911.html. Between 2000 and 2010, however, more Cubans arrived in the United States than in any other past decade. For details of Cuban migration, see Portes and Stepick, *City on the Edge*; Croucher, *Imagining Miami*; Aja, *Miami's Forgotten Cubans*.

15 These prerevolutionary hierarchies were grounded in the history of slavery in Cuba, the *régimen de castas*, and a plantation economy that denied enslaved Africans and their descendants the social and economic mobility afforded to property-owning Spaniards and white Cubans after independence. See Andrews, *Afro-Latin America*. Before the first wave of migration

to Miami, the Cuban elite already had strong social and economic networks in the United States. Many were educated in elite US universities and even owned businesses in the United States.

16   López, *Unbecoming Blackness*; Gosin, *Racial Politics of Division*.

17   Aja, *Miami's Forgotten Cubans*. See also Brown and López, *Mapping the Latino Population*.

18   Laguna, *Diversión*, 46.

19   For more on Jim Crow violence against blacks and Jews, housing segregation, and racial zoning in Miami, see Nijman, *Miami*; Mohl, "Whitening Miami." For a history of blackness in Miami, see Dunn, *Black Miami in the Twentieth Century*.

20   In the racial unrest in response to policy brutality in Miami in 1980, for example, one of the accused officers was a white Cuban; see Manning, "Fire This Time."

21   For more on the English-only campaigns in Miami, see Laguna, *Diversion*; see also Portes and Stepick, *City on the Edge*.

22   Aja, *Miami's Forgotten Cubans*.

23   Mirta Ojito's publication in the New York Times, "Best of Friends, Worlds Apart," in 2000, chronicled the story of an Afro-Cuban and a white Cuban who were best friends in Cuba but who had opposite experiences upon their arrival to the United States. While the white Cuban seamlessly integrated into Miami, his black counterpart faced discrimination from police, in housing, and in other spheres. See also Aja, *Miami's Forgotten Cubans*; Hay, *I've Been Black in Two Countries*.

24   Aja, *Miami's Forgotten Cubans*.

25   Francis and Harris, "Introduction," 7.

26   Since the 1990s, blacks have received a disproportionately smaller portion of remittances than their white counterparts because they generally have fewer relatives abroad. Afro-Cubans thus have had less access to hard currency. This has ensured that economic stability in Cuba operates along racial lines, with white Cubans having far more economic power in comparison with their Afro-Cuban counterparts. See De la Fuente, " New Afro-Cuban Cultural Movement," 715; see also Blue, "Erosion of Racial Equality."

27   Nicaraguans in Miami occupy perhaps a more complicated position in the Cuban imaginary because, prior to their arrival to the city, Cubans were very much in solidarity with Nicaraguans seeking to flee the Sandinista communist regime. But these sentiments perhaps were forgotten when Nicaraguans arrived. Albert Laguna, phone call, August 2022.

28   For more on the Haitian experience in Miami, see Manning, "Fire This Time"; Pierre, "Growing Up Haitian in Black Miami."

29   Yúdice, *Expediency of Culture*.

30   Hernández-Reguant and Arroyo, "Brownface of Latinidad."

31   Aja, *Miami's Forgotten Cubans*.

32   López, *Unbecoming Blackness*, 156.

33   López, *Unbecoming Blackness*, 155. See also Gosin, *Racial Politics of Division*.

34   Aja, *Miami's Forgotten Cubans*.

35   Laguna, *Diversión*, 20; See also Jorge Duany, "¿Nueva crisis de balseros?," *El Nuevo Día*, November 12, 2014, https://www.elnuevodia.com/opinion /punto-de-vista/nueva-crisis-de-balseros/.

36   Duany, "¿Nueva crisis de balseros?" See also Duany, *Blurred Borders*.

37   Eckstein, *Immigrant Divide*.

38   Laguna, "Before the Thaw."

39   For more on these diasporic tensions, see Laguna, "Before the Thaw," 154, 155.

40   For more on the audiences who consume blackface caricatures on television in South Florida, see chapter 4 of Laguna, *Diversión*.

41   Joe Klein, "The Fresh Face," *Time* magazine, October 15, 2006.

42   Lusane, *Black History of the White House*. For more on the discourse of postracialism under Obama, see Cobb, *Substance of Hope*.

43   For more on the increase in racist rhetoric and hate crimes, see Lusane, *Black History of the White House*; see also Teslar and Sears, *Obama's Race*.

44   On the Pink Tide, see Larry Rohter's famous article published in the *New York Times* on March 1, 2005, "With New Chief, Uruguay Veers Left in a Latin Pattern," https://www.nytimes.com/2005/03/01/world/americas /with-new-chief-uruguay-veers-left-in-a-latin-pattern.html?_r=0.

45   Macarena Gómez-Barris offers an exemplary overview and critical engagement of the Pink Tide in Latin America and the role of art and social movements in its aftermath; see Gómez-Barris, *Beyond the Pink Tide*, 19.

46   Laguna, *Diversión*, 126. See also Portes and Puhrmann, "Bifurcated Enclave."

47   When famous Cuban salsa group Los Van Van performed in Miami in 1999, they were greeted by vociferous protests. For a long time, sectors of Cubans in Miami viewed artists who came to the United States but chose to return to Cuba as supporters of Castro and the revolution or agents of the state. See Mireya Navarra, "Famed Cuban Band Is Set to Perform in Miami, and the Overtone Is One of Strain," *New York Times*, October 9, 1999. See also Manny García, Jordan Levin, and Peter Whoriskey, "The Band Plays On as Protest Fails to Deter Van Van's Fans," *Miami Herald*, October 10, 1999.

48   Laguna, *Diversión*, 126.

49   See Laguna, *Diversión*, for an analysis of the role of humor in the diaspora.

50   Mañach, *Indagación de choteo*, 66, 67.

51   *Choteo* has been the object of study in Cuban scholarship for roughly one hundred years and extensive analysis of the debates over its meaning is beyond the scope of this study. For further examination of *choteo*, see Reyes, *Humor and the Eccentric Text*; Pérez Firmat, *Literature and Liminality*; Hidalgo, *Choteo*.

52   Scholars have examined the central role of *choteo* in the works of notable Cu-

ban artists Guillermo Cabrera Infante and Virgilio Piñera, and of diasporic performances by artists like Carmelita Tropicana, Eddie Calderón's impersonations of Fidel Castro in Miami's 1970s television show *¿Qué Pasa, USA?*, and the immensely popular radio show *Aquí Está Álvarez Guedes*, featuring the distinguished comedian Guillermo Álvarez Guedes. See, for example, Aching, *Masking and Power*; Aguilú de Murphy, *Los Textos Dramáticos De Virgilio Piñera*; Laguna, "Aquí está Álvarez Guedes"; Muñoz, *Disidentifications*.

53   Laguna, "Aquí está Álvarez Guedes," 514.

54   Media Ciclo, "Cristinito y El Monólogo De La Cultura Cubana!!!," YouTube video, October 6, 2015, 8:54, https://www.youtube.com/watch?v=4wyie2q22nA&ab_channel=CicloMedia.

55   Gopinath, *Impossible Desires*.

56   Gopinath, *Impossible Desires*, 7.

57   Ciclomedia, "Alexis Valdes- Chistes Cubanos," YouTube video, August 12, 2015, 10:59, https://www.youtube.com/watch?v=nl_1AoLOsoQ&t=49s&ab_channel=alexisvaldesoficial.

58   Hall, "Cultural Identity and Diaspora," 245.

59   For example, see Roigarm, "Hugo Chavez en Esta Noche Tu Night 7 (HighDef)," YouTube video, June 28, 2011, 4:56, https://www.youtube.com/watch?v=JEppAFVBgHM60.

60   Laguna, *Diversión*.

61   For example, see Alexisvaldesoficial, "Alexis Valdes Monico Pino Un Dia Como Hoy 8 25 10," YouTube video, September 1, 2010, 5:28, https://www.youtube.com/watch?v=cLoVyY1MpRA&ab_channel=alexisvaldesoficial.

62   Roigarm, "Osvaldo Doimeadios como mañeña En Esta Noche Tu Night 11 (HighDef)," YouTube video, November 16, 2010, 4:25, https://www.youtube.com/watch?v=ReOS36CqiPA&ab_channel=Roigarm.

63   Laguna, *Diversión*, 139, 140, 141.

64   MegaTv, "Yeyo Vargas y El Nuevo Presidente De La República Dominicana, Danilo Medina," YouTube video, May 22, 2012, 9:17, https://www.youtube.com/watch?v=fUK2HjduJhc.

65   Gustavo Rios, "Jochy Santos, Yeyo y Obama," YouTube video, July 10, 2011, 12:07, https://www.youtube.com/watch?v=3UgQRmkIfnM.

66   This still image of Yeyo is taken from a YouTube video. See LaRisaTerapia, "Monologo con Alexis Valdés y Yeyo Vargas en Esta Noche Tu Night (4-2-12)," YouTube, YouTube video, April 19, 2012, 11:11, https://www.youtube.com/watch?app=desktop&v=AMtNBBDlkvU&t=13s.

67   Arroyo, *Caribe 2.0*, 51.

68   Capó, *Welcome to Fairyland*, 143.

69   Diamond, "Introduction," 1.

70   Lane, *Blackface Cuba*.

71   Lane, *Blackface Cuba*; Leal, *Breve historia del teatro cubano*. For more on the independence struggle in Cuba during that period, see Ferrer, *Cuba insurgente*.

72   While US minstrel troupes traveled to Cuba, teatro bufo was also influ-
      enced by a variety of theater traditions including Spanish and Italian opera,
      and blackface performance in Cuba predates the first minstrel show in the
      1830s. The actor Francisco Covarrubias is the first Cuban actor known to
      blacken his face to impersonate a negrito on stage in 1812. See Lane, *Black-
      face Cuba*, 29; Leal, *Teatro bufo siglo XIX*, 31; Thomas, *Cuban Zarzuela*, 82.
      These theater scholars trace the genealogy of teatro bufo to traditions of
      the Italian and Spanish opera.

73   Lane, *Blackface Cuba*, 3.

74   Lane, *Blackface Cuba*; Moore, *Nationalizing Blackness*.

75   Lane, *Blackface Cuba*, 3.

76   For the evolution of teatro bufo, see Martiatu Terry, *Bufo y nación*, 15, 16;
      Moore, *Nationalizing Blackness*; Leal, *Breve historia del teatro cubano*; Lin-
      ares, *Introducción a Cuba*.

77   For more on teatro bufo during the postindependence and prerevolutionary
      era, see Suárez Durán, "El teatro bufo cubano." See also Arredondo, *La vida
      de un comediante*.

78   Moore, *Nationalizing Blackness*; Leal, *Breve historia del teatro cubano*; Lin-
      ares, *Introducción a Cuba*.

79   Moore, *Nationalizing Blackness*.

80   Benson, *Antiracism in Cuba*; see also Frederik, *Trumpets in the Mountains*.

81   Benson, *Antiracism in Cuba*; De la Fuente, *Nation for All*.

82   De la Fuente, *Nation for All*; Croucher, *Imagining Miami*; López, *Unbecom-
      ing Blackness*.

83   Robaina, *El Negro en Cuba*; Clealand, *Power of Race in Cuba*; Benson, *Anti-
      racism in Cuba*.

84   Helg, "Afro-Cuban Protest."

85   See Casal, *Revolution and Race*; Moore, *Castro, the Blacks, and Africa*; Saw-
      yer, *Racial Politics in Post-Revolutionary Cuba*.

86   Frederik, *Trumpets in the Mountains*, 51.

87   Although the Cuban revolution banned teatro bufo in the 1970s, the Con-
      sejo Nacional de Cultura (CNC) endorsed a play, *The Tragedy of King
      Christophe*, with white actors in blackface in the late 1960s, despite fierce
      opposition from many Afro-Cubans. As Lilian Guerra so eloquently details
      in her study of negrista mobilization in the early years of the Cuban revolu-
      tion, an all-black cast and all-black production team led by Roberto Blanco
      staged the play *María Antonia* in protest of the CNC's endorsement of us-
      ing white actors in blackface in the *Tragedy of King Christophe*—ironically, a
      play that sought to commemorate black revolutionaries' fight for indepen-
      dence in Haiti; see Guerra, *Visions of Power in Cuba*.

88   For the turn to privatization and erosion of inequality, see De la Fuente,
      "Afro-Cuban Cultural Movement," 715; Blue, "Erosion of Racial Equality."

89   In 1997, the bufo play *El Tío Francisco y las Leandras* (Uncle Francisco and

the Leandras) had an extended run in Havana's prestigious Hubert de Blank theater and, in 2004, La Cruzada Teatral performed a bufo play on its trip to the mountains; see Frederik, *Trumpets in the Mountains*, 262.

90 Frederik, *Trumpets in the Mountains*.

91 Moore, *Nationalizing Blackness*, 60.

92 Moore, "Black Music in a Raceless Society," 23.

93 See Clealand, *Power of Race in Cuba*; Moore, "Black Music in a Raceless Society." Hip hop has been a crucial site for black articulations of experiences of racism in Cuba. For more on Cuba's hip hop movement, see Perry, *Negro Soy Yo*; Fernándes, *Cuba Represent!*. On teatro bufo during the Special Period, see Frederik, *Trumpets in the Mountains*.

94 The decline of the socialist state and the turn towards neoliberalism during the Special Period greatly exacerbated racial inequality in Cuba. The reliance on education as a dependable instrument of social and economic mobility was upended and replaced with a collective reliance on remittances from relatives living abroad. Black families own fewer resources and are therefore unable to earn from home-based restaurants, by renting rooms to tourists, or through other lucrative business activities from the self-employed sector in Cuba. See De la Fuente, "New Afro-Cuban Cultural Movement," 715; Blue, "Erosion of Racial Equality."

95 Capó, *Welcome to Fairyland*, 143.

96 Capó, *Welcome to Fairyland*, 144.

97 On theater in Miami, see Manzor, *Marginality beyond Return*. See the Cuban Heritage Collection at the University of Miami for its interview with Néstor Cabell.

98 For more on these satirical newspapers and Añorada Cuba, see the "Cuban Heritage Collection Exile Newspapers" at the Cuban Heritage Collection at the University of Miami.

99 In some versions, the mother offers a melon or a mamey. A *babalao* is a shaman or spiritual leader.

100 Lillian Manzor, "Añorada Cuba," Sites That Speak: Miami through Its Spanish Performing Arts Series, https://scalar.usc.edu/hc/sites-that-speak/aorada-cuba?path=dade-county-auditorium.

101 "Boncó y la ciencia negrológica," AmericaTeve Miami, YouTube video, December 23, 2009, 7:55, https://www.youtube.com/watch?v=Xa-UPDY7PZM&ab_channel=AmericaTeVeMiami.

102 Laguna, *Diversión*, 41, 42.

103 Aja, *Miami's Forgotten Cubans*.

104 Arroyo and Hernández-Reguant, "Brownface of Latinidad in Cuban Miami."

105 This is a still image of Yeyo Vargas and Alexis Valdés from a YouTube video. Roigarm, "Alexis Valdes-Entrevista a Yeyo Vargas (HighDef)," YouTube, YouTube video, July 18, 2010, https://www.youtube.com/watch?v=PCbVdZsvNOA.

106 For the entire conversation, see MegaTv, "Esta Noche Tu Night 05 05 2009 Yeyo Vargas," YouTube, YouTube video, May 5, 2009, 2:37, https://youtube .com/watch?v=jHkgM8B9NFw.

107 MegaTv, "Yeyo Vargas, Asesor del Cumplimiento de Proesas del Presidente Barack Obama," YouTube, YouTube video, November 9, 2012, 9:01, https:// www.youtube.com/watch?v=Bu2Ygdyl9TM.

108 Carlos Marrero, "Yeyo Vargas con el alcalde Raúl Martinez, 'Esta Noche Tu Night' 05.11.2011," YouTube video, May 11, 2011, 10:11, https://www.you tube.com/watch?v=Po5tNcYECSY&ab_channel=CarlosMarrero.

109 Bailey, *Misogynoir Transformed*.

110 In 2015, a popular talk show host, Rodner Figueroa from Univisión, was fired for comparing Michelle Obama to a character from *Planet of the Apes*; see "Univision Fires Rodner Figueroa for Michelle Obama 'Planet of the Apes' Comment," NBC News, March 12, 2015, https://www.nbcnews.com /news/latino/univisions-rodner-figueroa-fired-planet-apes-michelle -obama-comment-n322166.

3. Flipping the Racial Script: Blackface Performance as Resistance in Colombia

1 Liliana Angulo also exhibited a much smaller version of *Mambo negrita* at Museo La Tertulia in Cali in 2011, but I focus on the debut version because it is the biggest iteration of the piece. The images I discuss here consist of 13 photographs, digital print press, 35 × 26 inches each. The three models are Liliana Angulo Cortés, Andrea Angulo Cortés, and María Adelaida Cuero.

2 I am indebted to students, especially Gavin Pak, who took my Winter 2017 course "Introduction to Latin American Theatre and Performance," in which we closely examined this exhibition.

3 Although many black men and women arrived in the Andean highland city with Spaniards in the sixteenth and seventeenth centuries, patterns of migrations to the city in the twentieth and twenty-first centuries have caused black people to perceived as foreigners; Larissa Brewer García, email, January 26, 2024. For more on histories of blackness in Colombia, see Flórez Bolívar, *La vanguardia intellectual*; and Rhenals Doria and Flórez Bolívar, "Escogiendo entre los indeseables."

4 Some examples of artistic works focused on the Afro-Bogotan experience are Wilson Borja's *Color piel/Skin Color* (2015), Mercedes Angola and Maguemati Wagbou's publication *Llegamos a Bogotá 1940/1950/1960* (2015), and their exhibit *Exposición presencia negra en Bogotá*—a photographic and research series that focused on the Afro-Bogotán presence from the 1940s onward. The research activities took place from 2010 to 2013 at la Universidad Nacional de Colombia. The IRA collective has a Facebook page

whose posts typically feature artistic work, roundtables, and events on Afro-Bogotán art. In 2021, Colectivo Aguaturbia organized an artistic event about black art and the experiences of black people living in Bogotá titled *Sobre la historia, el archivo y ninguno de los dos*. They also launched Archivo Imaginación Radical Afro during the COVID-19 pandemic.

5   Ligiéro, "Liliana Angulo."

6   Angulo, "Artist Statement."

7   For an example of her engagement with black female iconography in Colombia's historical archives and the history of slavery, see Liliana Angulo, *Retrato de Lucy Rengifo, nacida en Medellín*, which was part of the series *Presencia negra* (2007). Examples of an engagement with black hair include *Quieto pelo* (2008) and the series *Pelucas porteadoras* (1999–2001). An example of her work commemorating the history of slavery includes *Un caso de reparación—performance en el santuario de San Pedro Claver* (2019), with the dance group Compañía Permanencias in Cartagena. For an extensive examination of Angulo's oeuvre, see Escobar, *Retratos en blanco y afro*. For other treatments of her individual artistic work, see Lane, "Hemispheric America in Deep Time"; Ligiéro, "Liliana Angulo"; Levin, *Performing Ground*; Cartier, "De la taxonomía al estereotipo."

8   Ricardo Arcos-Palma, "Liliana Angulo, del otro lado del espejo," *Escáner Cultural*, April 4, 2007, https://www.revista.escaner.cl/node/78.

9   Hooker, "Indigenous Inclusion/Black Exclusion"; Hale, "Does Multiculturalism Menace?"

10 Paschel, "Beautiful Faces of My Black People"; Wade, *Blackness and Race Mixture*.

11 Appelbaum, *Muddied Waters*.

12 Rosero-Labbé et al., *Debates sobre ciudadanía y políticas raciales*.

13 Paschel, *Becoming Black Political Subjects*, 29. Paschel also notes that while influential thinkers such as Colombian president Laureano Gómez (1950–1953) saw racial mixture as a sign of degeneracy, over time other thinkers such as the Colombian writer Luis López de Mesa concluded that racial miscegenation was in fact the solution to overcoming the country's black and indigenous elements. Despite their differences, both López de Mesa and Gómez believed in the moral, aesthetic, and intellectual superiority of Europeans.

14 Wade, *Blackness and Race Mixture*, 16.

15 Paschel, *Becoming Black Political Subjects*, 40. Flórez Bolívar, "Celebrando y redefiniendo el mestizaje."

16 Paschel, "Beautiful Faces of My Black People"; Wade, *Blackness and Race Mixture*, 16.

17 Wade, *Blackness and Race Mixture*, 17; De Friedemann and Arocha, *De sol a sol*.

18 Sanders, *Contentious Republicans*; Paschel, *Becoming Black Political Subjects*, 42.

19 Paschel, *Becoming Black Political Subjects*, 40.

20 Wade, *Blackness and Race Mixture*; De Friedemann, "Contextos religiosos," 69.

21 For more on the cultural topography of race, see part II of Wade, *Blackness and Race Mixture*, 49; see also Paschel, *Becoming Black Subjects*, 42.

22 Restrepo, "Imágenes del 'negro'"; Paschel, *Becoming Black Subjects*, 42.

23 McKittrick, *Demonic Grounds*, xiv.

24 McKittrick, *Demonic Grounds*, xi.

25 Flórez Bolívar, *La vanguardia intelectual*; Múnera, *Fronteras imaginadas*.

26 Sanders, *Contentious Republicans*, 195.

27 Hooker, "Indigenous Inclusion/Black Exclusion"; Hale, "Does Multiculturalism Menace?"

28 Paschel, "Right to Difference." Paschel explains that in the late 1980s, numerous countries began to institutionalize the formal recognition of cultural difference and human rights. In the same decade, the World Bank started contracting anthropologists to develop indigenous-specific programming through its Latin America and Caribbean Region's Environment Division, partnering with other international institutions to provide aid to Latin American governments to help demarcate collective ethnic territories and invest in social inclusion. These shifts were crucial to the multicultural turn in Colombia. See also Paschel, *Becoming Black Political Subjects*, 85.

29 Paschel, "Right to Difference." The ILO convention recognizes the right of indigenous people to self-determination and to land. Hooker, "Indigenous Inclusion/Black Exclusion"; Hale, "Does Multiculturalism Menace?"

30 Restrepo, "Ethnicization of Blackness in Colombia."

31 The first political reform was Article 55 of the 1991 Constitution and the second was the Law of 70 in 1993. For more, see Wade, "Cultural Politics of Blackness."

32 Ng'weno, *Turf Wars*; Asher, *Black and Green*; Agudelo, *Retos del multiculturalismo en Colombia*; Paschel, "Beautiful Faces of My Black People."

33 Paschel, *Becoming Black Political Subjects*; Hooker, "Indigenous Inclusion/Black Exclusion"; Van Cott, *Friendly Liquidation of the Past*.

34 Van Cott, *Friendly Liquidation of the Past* and "Political Analysis of Legal Pluralism in Bolivia and Colombia."

35 The ANC justified the exclusion of these groups by claiming that an explicit engagement with race would only add to ethnic conflict or division in an already war-torn country. See Paschel, *Becoming Black Political Subjects*; Van Cott, *Friendly Liquidation of the Past*.

36 Paschel, *Becoming Black Political Subjects*.

37 Hooker, "Indigenous Inclusion/Black Exclusion."

38 Paschel, *Becoming Black Political Subjects*, 87.

39 Paschel, *Becoming Black Political Subjects*.

40 The centrality of a neoliberal agenda to the emergence of Latin American multiculturalism is another crucial rationale for the types of racial advances

that the reforms permitted. For example, scholars suggest that the emphasis on the Pacific rural communities was economically advantageous to the state, and that development plans were already underway at the time of the reforms. For more on this, see Hooker, "Indigenous Inclusion/Black Exclusion"; Wade, "Articulations of Eroticism and Race"; Ng'weno, *Turf Wars*.

41 Scholars have rightly argued that the census recentered white and mestizo identities as normative unmarked categories. While the census asked for indigenous and black people to identify, *white* and *mestizo* as categories were notably absent from the form. Subsequently, whiteness remained an unmarked, normative category around which notions of racial difference cohered. Nevertheless, it remains significant because it was the very first time since the colonial era that the nation sought to collect ethno-racial data and to clearly define racial categories. Urban activist groups came to play a more central role in the production of the census. See Paschel, "Beautiful Faces of My Black People."

42 Cunin, *Identidades a flor de piel*; Ng'weno, *Turf Wars*; Hoffmann, *Communautés noires dans le Pacifique colombien*.

43 Mosquera Rosero-Labbé et al., *Afrodescendientes en las Américas*.

44 For information on *Viaje sin mapa*, see Angola and Álvarez Cristancho, *Viaje sin mapa*. For analysis of *Velorios y santos vivos*, see González Ayala, "Black, Afro-Colombian, Raizal and Palenquero Communities." For *¡Mandinga sea!*, see Restrepo and Cristancho, *¡Mandinga sea! África en Antioquía*.

45 Cristancho, "Viaje sin mapa."

46 Angola and Cristancho, *Viaje sin mapa*, 11.

47 Angola and Cristancho, *Viaje sin mapa*, 11. For more information on the Afro-Colombian contribution to music, see Wade, *Música, raza y nación*.

48 Angola, "Invisibilidad y Representación."

49 Liliana Angulo identifies as a cis-woman, and dressing in drag is neither a common feature of her artistic work nor her lived experience. *Negro utópico* is the only artistic piece in which she dresses in drag. I use the gender-neutral pronoun "they" to describe the protagonist of the artwork and not as a reference to the artist's gender identity.

50 Levin, *Performing Ground*, 31.

51 Levin, *Performing Ground*, 58.

52 Brooks, *Bodies in Dissent*, 8.

53 Brooks, *Bodies in Dissent*, 8.

54 Brooks, *Bodies in Dissent*, 8.

55 Post, "Williams, Walker, and Shine," 94.

56 Liliana Angulo has expressed resistance to the term *blackface* because when she first painted herself black, she had no idea what it meant, and she understands the word to refer to a tradition of US blackface minstrelsy. As explained in the introduction, I note her resistance to the word to emphasize that the term *blackface* is a space of tension.

57 Mara Viveros, "Alteridad, género, sexualidad y afectos: Reflexiones a partir

de una experiencia investigativa en Colombia," *Cadernos Pagu* 41 (2013): 49, https://doi.org/10.1590/S0104-83332013000200005.

58 Moten, *In the Break*, 2.

59 Liliana Angulo, Skype conversation, 2017.

60 Giraldo Escobar, *Retratos en blanco y afro*, 108, 109.

61 Lane, "Hemispheric America in Deep Time," 122.

62 Viveros, "La imbricación de los estereotipos racistas," 511.

63 Brooks, *Bodies in Dissent*, 8.

64 Angulo, "Artist Statement."

65 Angulo, "Liliana Angulo," 102.

66 Angulo, "Liliana Angulo," 102.

67 Gontovnik, "Performing Race in the Barranquilla Carnival," 10.

68 Brown, "On Kitsch, Nostalgia, and Nineties Femininity," 43.

69 Bernstein, *Racial Innocence*, 71.

70 Image from Colombian newspaper *La República*. See Ruíz Rico, "Nestlé cambió la imagen del producto "Beso de negra" por mensaje racista," *La República*, June 23, 2020, https://www.larepublica.co/empresas/nestle -cambio-imagen-y-nombre-del-producto-beso-de-negra-3021211.

71 Nestle's Danish version of the chocolate was called Negerkys, which can mean "negro kiss" or "negro bun," but it has been renamed Flodeboller. In Germany, the chocolates were commonly known as Negerkuss or Mohren-kopf (Moor's head), while in the Netherlands they were referred to as Negerzoenen. These products were eventually renamed. For more on these debates, see Sou-Jie Van Brunnersum, "German Baker Selling Black-face Pastries Stirs Racism Debate," *Deutsch Welle*, February 6, 2020, https:// www.dw.com/en/german-bakery-selling-blackface-pastries-stirs-racism -debate/a-52400351; see also "Heads Will Roll: Hemma Ditches 'Moorkop' for 'Chocoladebol,'" Dutchnews, February 6, 2020, https://www.dutchnews .nl/news/2020/02/heads-will-roll-hema-ditches-moorkop-for-chocoladebol/.

72 Hartman, *Scenes of Subjection*, 21.

73 For image, see item for sale on Megaseo's website, "Límpido 1800 + 460 ml regular oferta, https://megaseo170.com/products/limpido-1800-460-ml -regular-oferta.

74 Cárdenas Sánchez, "Blanquita, la cara negra de Límpido," *Conexión Externado*, June 21, 2021, https://conexion.uexternado.edu.co/blanquita -la-cara-negra-de-limpido/.

75 Diana Castrillón, "Clorox y Nestlé cambian imágenes de 'Blanquita' de Límpido y Beso de Negra por considerarlas inapropiadas," CNN Español, June 19, 2020, https://cnnespanol.cnn.com/2020/-6/19/Clorox-y-nestle -cambian-imagenes-de-blanquita-de-limpido-y-beso-de-negra-por -considerarlas-inapropiadas/.

76 Cunin, *Identidades a flor de piel*; Shouse Tourino, "Fed by Any Means Necessary."

77 Lane, *Blackface Cuba*, 20.

78 Shouse Tourino, "Fed by Any Means Necessary," 238; Cunin, *Identidades a flor de piel*, 251; Lago, *La política vista por Nieves*, 202.

79 Image from Nieves-Consuelo Lago, "¡Los caleños somos sol y salsa!," Facebook, August 31, 2016, https://www.facebook.com/NievesCaricatura /photos/pb.100059866372903.-2207520000/1773938289520428/?type=3.

80 Lago, *La política vista por Nieves*, 13.

81 Image of Negrita Pulloy from Angie, "Carnival of Barranquilla," *My beautiful city Barranquilla* (blog), March 21, 2011, https://mybeautifulcity barranquilla.blogspot.com/2011/03/carnival-of-barranquilla.html.

82 Gontovnik, "Performing Race in the Barranquilla Carnival."

83 Gontovnik, "Performing Race in the Barranquilla Carnival."

84 Gontovnik, "Performing Race in the Barranquilla Carnival."

85 Gontovnik, "Performing Race in the Barranquilla Carnival," 3.

86 Gontovnik, "Performing Race in the Barranquilla Carnival," 4.

87 "Las mujeres más poderosas del Valle del Cauca," Revista *¡Hola!* N3614, December 7, 2011.

88 Fanon, *Black Skin, White Masks*.

89 Zea, *Cohabitar: IX bienal de arte de Bogotá*, 7.

90 Angulo, personal communication, Lima, Peru, 2017.

91 Moten, *In the Break*, 1.

92 McMillan, *Embodied Avatars*, 8, 9.

93 Angulo, *Museo de Arte Moderno de Bogotá*, 107.

94 Lugo-Ortiz and Rosenthal, *Slave Portraiture in the Atlantic World*.

95 hooks, *Black Looks*; Mulvey, *Visual Pleasure and Narrative Cinema*.

96 Lott, *Love and Theft*, 145.

97 Chude-Sokei, *Last "Darky,"* 67.

98 Campt, *Black Gaze*, 38, 39.

99 Du Bois, *Souls of Black Folk*.

100 Angulo, personal communication, Lima, Peru, 2017.

101 Lugo-Ortiz and Rosenthal, *Slave Portraiture in the Atlantic World*.

102 Lugo-Ortiz and Rosenthal, *Slave Portraiture in the Atlantic World*, 7.

103 Vázquez, *Listening in Detail*.

4. The Postcolonial Below: Roots Theater and Black Enjoyment in Jamaica

1 Since there are no formal publications of any of the plays I analyze in this chapter at the time of writing, all the performances referenced are my transcriptions of YouTube videos or DVDs released by Stages Production.

2 Unless stated otherwise, all translations of Jamaican creole are mine.

3 BLA Productions, "Di Driva FULL PLAY Shebada and Delcita at It Again,"

YouTube video, April 3, 2022, 2:26:41, https://www.youtube.com/watch?v
=7SS-c3HBsQ4&ab_channel=BLAProductions.

4   Figures 4.1 and 4.2 are screenshots from BLA Productions, "Di Driva FULL
        PLAY Shebada and Delcita at It Again," YouTube video, April 3, 2022,
        2:26:41, https://www.youtube.com/watch?v=7SS-c3HBsQ4&ab_channel
        =BLAProductions.

5   For more on Ralph Holness's role in developing the form, see Hope, "'Pon
        Di Borderline.'" See also Small, "Empowerment through the Theater." In
        my conversations with Bunny Allen, the producer of Stages Production, he
        expressed ambivalence about the name "roots theatre." Allen suggests that
        "roots" is a derogatory word from *tapanaris* (upper-class) people who reject
        it as a bastardized theatrical genre produced by and for the masses. Instead,
        he refers to the genre as "popular theater." There is ongoing discussion
        about the politics of naming the genre among practitioners and producers
        alike. In the absence of any consensus surrounding a new term, I register
        this discomfort to emphasize spaces of ambivalence around the politics of
        naming. I employ the term *roots theater*, however, since it remains the most
        identifiable name for the genre and to invoke the very social prejudices and
        discourses of abjection that this chapter seeks to interrogate. In my opinion,
        the terms *popular theater* and *Jamaican comedy* as proposed alternatives are
        simply too vague or general to name a known local tradition and do not ad-
        equately capture the prejudices that I am seeking to analyze.

6   Bennett and Bennett, *Jamaican Theatre.*

7   Jones, "'Black Below,'" 139.

8   See Puri, *Caribbean Postcolonial*, 2; see also Brathwaite, *Development of Creole
        Society in Jamaica.*

9   Puri, *Caribbean Postcolonial*, 1.

10   Sheller, *Citizenship from Below.*

11   For examples of this, see Anderson, "From Blackface to 'Genuine Negroes.'"
        See also Toll, *Blacking Up.*

12   Studies of Bert Williams, such as Louis Chude-Sokei's, are an exception to
        this in that they focus on the role of the black minstrel in humanizing black
        subjects; Chude-Sokei, *Last "Darky."*

13   Richard Johnson, "Paul O. Beal Remembered," *Jamaican Observer*, Novem-
        ber 24, 2019.

14   The Caribbean Camera Inc, "Jamaican Playwright Paul O. Beale dies at 57,"
        Caribbean Camera Inc, November 28, 2019.

15   An example of public perceptions of awards for roots theater is encapsu-
        lated in the outcry in March 2007, when roots actor Garfield "Bad boy
        Trevor" Reid rejected an acting award for his performances in roots plays.
        The outcry centered around the term *roots* and problems with the language
        the judges used to define the category. They described roots plays as "rudi-
        mentary" with "ludicrous" representations of social character types, which

actors felt framed the category as substandard. For more on this controversy, see Hope, "'Pon Di Borderline.'"

16 Beale, *Delcita Coldwater*, 7–8.

17 Nelson A. King, "Love Saga," *Caribbean Life*, October 10, 2019.

18 Initially, Andrea Wright did not perform in blackface. It is unclear if Paul Beale decided she should use blackface or if this was Wright's decision.

19 Michael Edwards, "Of Black Face and Public Face: Two Actresses in the Jamaican Star System," MNI *Alive*, January 29, 2013.

20 Andrea Wright, WhatsApp, June 21, 2023. Because Wright declined my interview request, questions I have regarding material she used to black up and the decision-making process around her embodiment of the character remain unanswered.

21 Hill, *Jamaican Stage*; Thelwell, *Exporting Jim Crow*; Hoxworth, "Jim Crow Global South."

22 Thelwell, *Exporting Jim Crow*, 190.

23 Tate, *Decolonising Sambo*; Nettleford, *Mirror Mirror*.

24 See Thelwell, *Exporting Jim Crow*; and for the transoceanic dimension in particular, see Hoxworth, "Jim Crow Global South."

25 For other work on blackface performance that centers on the arrival of US minstrel troupes, see Hill, "Plays of the English-Speaking Caribbean." Errol Hill's work, however, also suggests there is a deeper history of blackface performance on stage prior to the arrival of US minstrel troupes. Furthermore, I only found one moment where blackface was deployed on the Jamaican stage after independence, and it took place in the performance *The Crossing* (1978) by the National Dance Theatre Company. The dancer Michael Dunn's use of blackface is extremely brief, appearing in the dance's recounting of the shared black diasporic experience of crossing from Africa to the Americas and life on the plantation before obtaining freedom (Alaine Grant, phone conversation, March 15, 2024; Chris Walker, personal communication, in person, March 2024). This was an exceptional moment and because the deployment of blackface was so brief, in my view, it does not suggest that blackface is part of contemporary standard theatrical practice in Jamaica as was the case during the colonial era. Despite this singular occurrence, I maintain that blackface is a colonial sign.

26 For more on blackface as shine, see Post, "Williams, Walker, and Shine."

27 Hope, *Inna di Dancehall*, 1.

28 Thomas, *Modern Blackness*; Hope, "'Pon Di Borderline.'"

29 Thompson, *Shine*.

30 Barnes, *Cultural Conundrums*, 108.

31 Barnes, *Cultural Conundrums*, 107.

32 Kobena Mercer, quoted in Barnes, *Cultural Conundrums*, 109.

33 Barnes, *Cultural Conundrums*, 110.

34 For more, see Kelley, *Race Rebels*, 169.

35   Thompson, *Shine*.

36   For more on unvisibility, see Thompson, *Shine*, 39, 40.

37   Thompson, *Shine*, 22.

38   Gilroy, "To Be Real."

39   For more on the failure to adequately capture black people on film, see Arthur Jafa, Peter Hessli, and Pearl Bowser's "Notion of Treatment"; see also Yue, *Girl Head*.

40   Hope, "From Browning to Cake Soap."

41   Thomas, "Democratizing Dance"; Thomas, *Modern Blackness*.

42   Nettleford, *Mirror Mirror*.

43   Nettleford, *Caribbean Cultural Identity*, 4.

44   Thomas, *Modern Blackness*, 12.

45   For more on this matter, see Puri, *Caribbean Postcolonial*.

46   Kamugisha, *Beyond Coloniality*.

47   Thomas, "Democratizing Dance," 518.

48   Thomas, *Modern Blackness*.

49   Thomas, *Modern Blackness*, 13.

50   Roper and Wint, "Tambourine Army."

51   Puri, "Beyond Resistance"; Thomas, *Modern Blackness*, 4.

52   Tracy Robinson explains that given the persistent colonial anxieties about "missing men" and hypervisible mothers in black families, "the nationalist project was not only dominated by men, [but] it was also concerned with Caribbean masculinity . . . and became inseparable from the epistemological issue of defining West Indian manhood"; Robinson, "Mass Weddings in Jamaica," 76. She further contends that while poor black women were often targets of uplift campaigns such as mass weddings in the 1940s and 1950s, which sought to encourage legal marriage among poor black women in heterosexual relationships, black women did not generally have the same political space to articulate their own nationalist philosophies. Furthermore, the attention to reforming black families operated in tandem with the development of technologies of sexual regulation that targeted homosexuality. When the Vice President of the People's National Party ordered an inquiry about homosexuality in the police force in 1951, for example, it represented an instance in which the political class rendered queerness incompatible with the nascent national project and cast homophobia as an expression of anticolonial and anti-imperialist ideology; see Chin, "Antihomosexuality and Nationalist Critique."

53   Alexander, *Pedagogies of Crossing*, 26. This recolonization has been ushered in through the rise of local fundamentalist lobby groups in Jamaica who have campaigned against laws prohibiting marital rape and against the repeal of the colonial-era buggery laws. See also Roper and Wint, "Tambourine Army."

54   Francis, "Spirit of Inquiry," 184; see also Hope, *Inna Di Dancehall*.

55   I use the term *social* to qualify whiteness because social whiteness is not a

category involving white skin with European phenotypical features that may refer, for example, to Jamaicans with Syrian, Jewish, or European ancestry. Rather, it is a social category that coalesces around economic privileges, valuation of Eurocentric ideals, and light skin that enables the descendants of the enslaved to ascend into a creole class and distance themselves from the black underclass.

56 Wynter, "Re-enchantment of Humanism," 131.

57 Brown-Glaude, "Don't Hate Me 'Cause I'm Pretty."

58 Mohammed, "But Most of All Mi Love," 24.

59 Carnegie, "How Did There Come to Be?"

60 Hunter, "Buying Racial Capital."

61 BLA Productions, "Di Driva FULL PLAY."

62 Swanston Baker, "Sounding in the Wake." The Jamaican duppy is not quite the trickster figure that Swanston Baker talks about, but it is indeed a symbol of folk knowledge that has been easily dismissed as *obeah*—a European colonial term for any African-derived religious practice.

63 For more information, see "Glimpses of Jamaican Folklore," *Jamaica Observer*, August 6, 2012.

64 Gray, *Radicalism and Social Change in Jamaica*; Stone, *Class, Race, and Political Behavior*.

65 As Deborah Thomas explains, rudie refers to the phenomenon of the "rude boy" and is exemplified by Jimmy Cliff's iconic character in the film *The Harder They Come* (dir. Perry Henzell, Jamaica: International Films Inc., 1972). For more on these counterideological formations, see Thomas, *Modern Blackness*; Meeks, *Narratives of Resistance*.

66 Lacey, *Violence and Politics in Jamaica*; Gray, *Radicalism and Social Change in Jamaica*; Lewis, "Walter Rodney." The Henry Rebellion was an armed rebellion led by Reynold Henry, son of a prominent Rastafarian, who sought to overthrow the colonial government and incoming nationalist Jamaican government and to establish a black government with the goal of repatriation back to Africa. The Henry Rebellion played a crucial role in animating middle-class and creole fears and suspicions of Rastafarianism. The Coral Gardens disturbance was an uprising in which a group of Rastafarians attacked a Shell gas station in Montego Bay in April 1963. In August and September 1965, anti-Chinese disturbances were ignited by a physical fight between a black Jamaican shop worker and Chinese proprietors. The reprisal of the PNP refers to the tensions between different factions of the political movement. Some factions of the movement, such as the Garvey's People's Political Party (PPP), had explicitly racialized visions of liberation that emphasized cultural ties to Africa. Its visions were rejected by other factions of the party, such as the Marxist People's Freedom Party under the leadership of Millard Johnson, who represented the aspirations of the black entrepreneurial middle class.

67 Thomas, *Modern Blackness* and "Democratizing Dance."

68 Brown-Glaude, "Don't Hate Me 'Cause I'm Pretty."

69 Thomas, *Modern Blackness*, 13.

70 Thomas, *Modern Blackness*; Puri, "Beyond Resistance"; Roper and Wint, "Tambourine Army."

71 Hope, *Inna Di Dancehall*; Stanley Niaah, *Dancehall*; Roper and Wint, "Tambourine Army."

72 Bennett, "Jamaican Theatre."

73 Schweitzer, "'Too Much Tragedy in Real Life'"; Hill, "Plays of the English-Speaking Caribbean"; Wilson, *Island Race*.

74 Fowler, "History of Theater in Jamaica"; Bennett, "The Jamaican Theater."

75 Hill, "Plays of the English-Speaking Caribbean"; Schweitzer, "'Too Much Tragedy in Real Life.'"

76 The Roman Vicariate's production of the pageant *Jamaica Triumphant*, written by the American Jesuit Daniel Lord in 1937, was the first attempt to stage a national theater, as it recounted a national history from the Arawaks, the Spanish conquest, British colonial rule, African enslavement, and the post-emancipation period. In keeping with a creole vision, the play "mingled European elements . . . with Jamaican rhythms" and its protagonist, Jamaica, was portrayed as a light-skinned brown woman—the exemplar of Jamaican creole multiracial nationalism—who embraced Columbus as a welcomed son. Mining folk blackness, versions of the pageant included a performance of John Canoe to showcase one of the cultural practices of the black majority; see Brooks-Delphin, "*Jamaica Triumphant*," 471, 478. Jamaican theater scholars have long hailed the importance of *Jamaica Triumphant* in the formation of a national theater both for its inclusion of wide sectors of the population in its casting and in overseeing sections of the script. Similarly, NDTC's valorization of black cultural forms and their centrality to the formation of a national and indigenous theater and arts are undeniable. Deborah Thomas has noted, however, that NDTC, too, has, at times, espoused a creole image of the nation in some of their productions, which has emphasized and celebrated the possibilities of different racial elements working together; Thomas, "Democratizing Dance," 51.

77 Tea Parties were informal, community gatherings or concerts in which people performed poetry or songs. During the performances, audience members had bidding contests that determined whether individual performers would remain, leave, or return to the stage; see Nettleford, *Caribbean Cultural Identity*.

78 Hall, "What Is This 'Black,'" 25.

79 Other key moments in the fight to establish a Caribbean theater include Errol Hill's founding of the Federal Theatre Company, Wycliff Bennett's founding of the Jamaica Drama League, and the insistence on local and Caribbean scripts and programs at the University of the West Indies by Derek

Walcott, Ada Thompson, Noel Vaz, and so many others. See Small, "Empowerment through the Theatre."

80 Anancy is a trickster figure of Jamaican folklore with connections to West African culture.

81 Roots theater was created after the golden age of Jamaican local theater, which occasioned the rise and influence of key writers and actors J. M Cupidon, Una Marson, Roger Mais, Charles Hyatt, Easton Lee, Ancille Gloudon, and others from the 1930s to the 1970s. This period is important because it led to the development of small-theater business and the establishment of the Barn—a small theater built in 1965—which served as a home to the work of major directors such as Trevor Rhone, Louis Mariott, and others. The work of these esteemed Caribbean directors and writers in small-theater business created opportunities for the rise of comedic stalwarts and actors Oliver Samuels, Fae Ellington, Voiler "Maffie" Johnson, Leonie Forbes, Barbara McCalla, and later Glenn "Titus" Campbell and others. See Small, "Empowerment through the Theatre."

82 Scott, *Refashioning Futures*, 193.

83 McMahon, *Black Circuit*; see also Lauterbach, *Chitlin' Circuit*.

84 For examples of this, see Cooke, "Roots Theatre Declared 'Dead'—Now under the 'Mainstream Theatre' Umbrella," *Jamaica Gleaner*, April 5, 2009.

85 See Hall, "What Is This 'Black,'" 24.

86 Hall, "What Is This 'Black,'" 32.

87 BLA Productions, "Di Driva FULL PLAY."

88 BLA Productions, "Di Driva FULL PLAY."

89 IG2MC, "The Xtortionistz Jamaican play," April 13, 2022, YouTube video, 1:57:13, https://www.youtube.com/watch?v=idsn9En80CQ&t=460s&ab_channel=IG2MC.

90 Adrian Washington, "Money Worries," April 13, 2022, YouTube video2:12:26, https://www.youtube.com/watch?v=cKnQyoYXe50&t=34s&ab_channel=AdrianWashington.

91 Washington, "Money Worries."

92 Jamaican Plays, "Andrea Wright's Miss Elsayda," April 14, 2022, YouTube video, 0:32, https://www.youtube.com/watch?v=eGA4aymPBNA&ab_channel=JamaicanPlays.

93 BLA Productions, "Di Driva FULL PLAY."

94 The common entrance exam was formerly a national examination that children took for high school entry.

95 Hall, "What Is This 'Black,'" 26.

96 Jones, "Black Below."

97 Muñoz, *Disidentifications*.

98 Alvarado, *Abject Performances*, 7.

99 Shimakawa, *National Abjection*, 2.

100 Shimakawa, *National Abjection*, 3; Kristeva, *Powers of Horror*, 2.

101 Alvarado, *Abject Performances*, 7; Shimakawa, *National Abjection*, 3; Kristeva, *Powers of Horror*, 4; Scott, *Extravagant Abjection*, 15.

102 Alvarado, *Abject Performances*, 4, 10.

103 Hennefeld and Sammond, *Abjection Incorporated*, 9.

104 Hennefeld and Sammond, *Abjection Incorporated*, 9.

105 Hennefeld and Sammond, *Abjection Incorporated*, 9.

106 Brock, *Distributed Blackness*, 130; Stallings, "Hip Hop," 136.

107 McMahon, *Black Circuit*, 3.

108 McMahon, *Black Circuit*, 168.

Conclusion: Hemispheric Blackface and Its Afterlives

1 Although they focus heavily on blackface at the carnival in Trinidad, see Hill, *Calypso Calaloo*; and Liverpool, *Rituals of Power and Rebellion*.

2 Canada has a long history of blackface minstrelsy. See Le Camp, "Racial Considerations of Minstrel Shows." Philip S. S. Howard offers a good reading of blackface performance and its relationship to the nationalist fiction of postracialism in Canada in his article "On the Back of Blackness." Racial caricature in Mexico has been at the heart of hemispheric disputes about blackface performance. When the Mexican government's postage stamp commemorating the cartoon character Memín Pinguín—a boy with simian features—circulated across the United States, it sparked outrage. Since then, scholars have critically engaged how sympathizers wielded a nationalist defense to ward off interrogation of the antiblackness on display in the cartoon. See Sue and Golash-Boza, "It Was Only a Joke"; and Dorr, "Putting a Stamp on Racism." For other work on racial impersonation in Mexico, see González, *Afro-Mexico*.

3 For blackface performance in Panama, see Zien, *Sovereign Acts*. Charles Hale has also theorized blackface performance in Guatemala in what he calls "a racial eruption"; see Hale, "Racial Eruptions." At the time of writing, I am unaware of extensive work on blackface performance in Central America more broadly. This would be a welcome addition to the field.

4 For examples of scholarship tracing the influence of US blackface minstrelsy in the Dominican Republic and Argentina, see Derby, *Dictator's Seduction*; and Karush, "Blackness in Argentina."

5 Lane, *Blackface Cuba*; Leal, *Teatro Bufo Siglo XIX*.

6 There has been some attempt to wrestle with blacking up in places like Argentina and Brazil. But there remains very little work, especially in English, on other traditions in the Americas. For Argentina, Adamovsky, "Los negros, la primera comparsa." For Brazil, see Conner, "Brazilian Blackface."

7 Conquergood, "Performance Studies," 145.

Abercrombie, Thomas. "La fiesta del carnaval postcolonial en Oruru: clase, etnicidad y nacionalismo en la danza folklórica." *Revista andina* 10, no. 2 (1992): 279–352.

Aching, Gerard. *Masking and Power: Carnival and Popular Culture in the Caribbean.* Minneapolis: University of Minnesota Press, 2002.

Adamovsky, Ezequiel. "Los negros, la primera comparsa de blancos personificando negros del carnaval Porteño (1865–1870)." *Cuadernos de antropología social,* no. 54 (September 24, 2021): 7–27.

Agudelo, Carlos Efrén. *Multiculturalismo en Colombia: Política, inclusión y exclusión de poblaciones negras.* Medellín: Carreta Editores; Institut de recherche pour le développement, Universidad Nacional de Colombia; Instituto Colombiano de Antropología e Historia, 2005.

Agudelo, Carlos. *Retos del multiculturalismo en Colombia: Política y poblaciones negras.* Medellín: La Carreta, 2005.

Aguilú de Murphy, Raquel. *Los textos dramáticos de Virgilio Piñera y el teatro del absurdo.* Madrid: Editorial Pliegos, 1989.

Aja, Alan A. *Miami's Forgotten Cubans: Race, Racialization, and the Miami Afro-Cuban Experience.* New York: Palgrave Macmillan, 2016.

Alarco, Rosa. *Los negritos de Huánuco.* Lima: Pontificia Universidad Católica Del Perú and Museo de Arte Popular, 1975.

Alberto, Paulina, and Jesse Hoffnung Garskof. "'Racial Democracy' and Racial Inclusion: Hemispheric Histories." In De la Fuente and Andrews, *Afro-Latin American Studies,* 264–316.

Alexander, M. Jacqui. *Pedagogies of Crossing: Meditations on Feminism, Sexual Politics, Memory, and the Sacred.* Durham, NC: Duke University Press, 2006.

Alvarado, Leticia. *Abject Performances: Aesthetic Strategies in Latino Cultural Production.* Durham, NC: Duke University Press, 2018.

Anderson, Lisa. "From Blackface to 'Genuine Negroes': Nineteenth-Century Minstrelsy and the Icon of the Negro." *Theatre Research International* 21, no. 1 (1996): 17–23.

Andrews, George Reid. *Afro-Latin America: Black Lives, 1600–2000.* Cambridge, MA: Harvard University Press, 2016.

Andrews, George Reid. "Remembering Africa, Inventing Uruguay: Sociedades de Negros in the Montevideo Carnival, 1865–1930." *Hispanic American Historical Review* 87, no. 4 (November 1, 2007): 693–726.

Angola, Mercedes. "Invisibilidad y representación: El viaje a través de las imágenes." In Angola and Cristancho, *Viaje sin mapa*, 4–9.

Angola, Mercedes, and Raúl Álvarez Cristancho, eds. *Viaje sin mapa: Representaciones afro en el arte contemporáneo colombiano*. Bogotá: Banco de La República, 2006.

Angulo, Liliana. "Artist Statement." *emisférica* 5, no. 2 (December 2008). https://archive.hemispheric.org/eng/publications/emisferica/5.2/artistpresentation/angulo/statement.html.

Angulo, Liliana. "Liliana Angulo." In Zea, *Cohabitar: IX Bienal De Arte De Bogotá*, 102–3.

Appelbaum, Nancy P. *Muddied Waters*. Durham, NC: Duke University Press, 2003.

Appelbaum, Nancy P., Anne S. Macpherson, and Karin Alejandra Rosemblatt, eds. *Race and Nation in Modern Latin America*. Chapel Hill: University of North Carolina Press, 2003.

Arredondo, Enrique. *La vida de un comediante*. Havana: Editorial Letras Cubanas, 1981.

Arroyo, Jossianna. *Caribes 2.0: New Media, Globalization, and the Afterlives of Disaster*. New Brunswick, NJ: Rutgers University Press, 2023.

Asher, Kiran. *Black and Green: Afro-Colombians, Development, and Nature in the Pacific Lowlands*. Durham, NC: Duke University Press, 2009.

Bailey, Moya. *Misogynoir Transformed: Black Women's Digital Resistance*. New York: New York University Press, 2021.

Bakhtin, Mikhail. *Rabelais and His World*. Translated by Hélène Iswolsky. Bloomington: Indiana University Press, 1984.

Barnes, Natasha. *Cultural Conundrums: Gender, Race, Nation and the Making of Caribbean Cultural Politics*. Ann Arbor: University of Michigan Press, 2006.

Beale, Paul O. *Delcita Coldwater: Mi Waan Leave Mama House*. CreateSpace, 2018.

Becerra, Miguel. "Stereotypes of Afro-Peruvians through the Media: The Case of the Peruvian Blackface." In *Converging Identities: Blackness in the Modern African Diaspora*, edited by Julius Adekunle and Hettie V. Williams, 285–97. Durham, NC: Carolina Academic Press, 2013.

Benitez-Rojo, Antonio. *The Repeating Island: The Caribbean and the Postmodern Perspective*. Translated by James E. Maraniss. Durham, NC: Duke University Press, 1997.

Bennett, Wycliffe. "The Jamaican Theatre: A Preliminary Overview." *Jamaica Journal* 8, nos. 2–3 (1974): 3–9.

Bennett, Wycliffe, and Hazel Bennett. *The Jamaican Theatre: Highlights of the Performing Arts in the Twentieth Century*. Mona, Jamaica: University of the West Indies Press, 2011.

Benson, Devyn Spence. *Antiracism in Cuba: The Unfinished Revolution*. Chapel Hill: University of North Carolina Press, 2016.

Benzanquen de Araújo, Ricardo. *Guerra y paz: Casa-Grande and Senzala e a obra de Gilberto Freyre nos anos 30*. Sao Paulo: Editora 34, 1994.

Bergson, Henri. *Laughter: An Essay on the Meaning of the Comic*. Translated by Cloudesley Brereton and Fred Rothwell. Mansfield Centre, CT: Martino Fine Books, 2014.

Berlant, Lauren, and Sianne Ngai. "Comedy Has Issues." *Critical Inquiry* 43, no. 2 (January 2017): 233–49.

Bernstein, Robin. *Racial Innocence: Performing American Childhood from Slavery to Civil Rights*. New York: New York University Press, 2011.

Bigenho, Michelle. "El baile de los negritos y la danza de las tijeras: Un manejo de contradicciones." In *Música, danzas y máscaras en los Andes*, edited by Raul Romero, 219–52. Lima: Pontificia Universidad Católica Del Perú, 1988.

Blue, Sarah. "The Erosion of Racial Equality in the Context of Cuba's Dual Economy." *Latin American Politics and Society* 49, no. 3 (2007): 35–68.

Boskin, Joseph. *Sambo: The Rise and Demise of an American Jester*. New York: Oxford University Press, 1988.

Bowser, Frederick P. *The African Slave in Colonial Peru, 1524–1650*. Stanford, CA: Stanford University Press, 1974.

Brathwaite, Kamau. *The Development of Creole Society in Jamaica, 1770–1820*. Oxford: Clarendon Press, 1971.

Brewer-García, Larissa. "Imagined Transformations: Color, Beauty, and Black Christian Conversion in Seventeenth-Century Spanish America." In *Envisioning Others: Race, Color, and the Visual in Iberia and Latin America*, edited by Pamela A. Patton, 111–41. Leiden: Brill, 2016.

Brock, Andre. *Distributed Blackness*. New York: New York University Press, 2020.

Brooks, Daphne A. *Bodies in Dissent: Spectacular Performances of Race and Freedom, 1850–1910*. Durham, NC: Duke University Press, 2006.

Brooks-Delphin, Roy. "*Jamaica Triumphant* (1937): Daniel Lord, Pageantry, and the Foundations of Jamaican National Theatre." In *Crossings and Dwellings: Restored Jesuits, Women Religious, American Experience*, edited by Stephen R. Schloesser and Kyle B. Roberts, 454–95. Leiden: Brill, 2017.

Brown, Anna, and Mark Hugo López. "Mapping the Latino Population, By State, County and City." Pew Research Center, August 29, 2013. https://www.pewresearch.org/race-and-ethnicity/2013/08/29/mapping-the-latino-population-by-state-county-and-city/.

Brown, Stephanie. "On Kitsch, Nostalgia, and Nineties Femininity." *Studies in Popular Culture* 22, no. 4 (2000): 39–54.

Brown-Glaude, Winnifred. "Don't Hate Me 'Cause I'm Pretty: Race, Gender, and the Bleached Body in Jamaica." *Social and Economic Studies* 62, no. 1 (2013): 53–78.

Bunge, Carlos Octavio. *Nuestra América: Ensayo de psicología social*. Buenos Aires: Casa Vaccaro Chiampi, Irlemar, 1918.

Campt, Tina M. *A Black Gaze: Artists Changing How We See*. Cambridge, MA: MIT Press, 2021.

Cánepa Koch, Gisela, ed. *Identidades representadas: Performance, experiencia y memo-*

ria en los Andes. Lima: Pontificia Universidad Católica del Perú and Fondo Editorial, 2001.

Cánepa Koch, Gisela. *Máscara, transformación e identidad en los Andes: La fiesta de la Virgen Del Carmen Paucartambo-Cuzco.* Lima: Pontificia Universidad Católica del Perú and Fondo Editorial, 1998.

Capó, Julio, Jr. *Welcome to Fairyland: Queer Miami before 1940.* Chapel Hill: University of North Carolina Press, 2017.

Carbonell, Walterio. *Crítica cómo surgió la cultural nacional.* Havana: Ediciones Yaka, 1961.

Carnegie, Charles. "How Did There Come to Be a 'New Kingston'?" *Small Axe* 54 (2017): 138–51.

Carpio, Glenda. *Laughing Fit to Kill: Black Humor in the Fictions of Slavery.* Oxford: Oxford University Press, 2008.

Carr, Morwenna. "Material/Blackness: Race and Its Material Reconstructions on the Seventeenth-Century English Stage." *Early Theatre* 20, no. 1 (2017): 77–96.

Cartier Barrera, Nicole. "De la taxonomía al estereotipo: Reinterpretaciones de las estéticas del cuerpo 'de color' desde el arte contemporáneo en América." MA thesis, Universidad de los Andes, 2018.

Casal, Lourdes. *Revolution and Race: Blacks in Contemporary Cuba.* Washington, DC: Wilson Center, 1979.

Cassanello, Robert, and Daniel S. Murphee. "The Epic of Greater Florida: Florida's Global Past." *Florida Historical Quarterly* 84, no. 1 (2005), https://stars .library.ucf.edu/fhq/vol84/iss1/3.

Chin, Matthew. "Antihomosexuality and Nationalist Critique in Late Colonial Jamaica." *Small Axe* 63 (2020): 81–96.

Chude-Sokei, Louis. *The Last "Darky": Bert Williams, Black-on-Black Minstrelsy, and the African Diaspora.* Durham, NC: Duke University Press, 2005.

Chude-Sokei, Louis. "Uncanny History of Minstrels and Machines, 1835–1923." In Johnson, *Burnt Cork,* 104–32.

Clealand, Danielle Pilar. *The Power of Race in Cuba: Racial Ideology and Black Consciousness during the Revolution.* Oxford: Oxford University Press, 2017.

Cobb, Jelani. *The Substance of Hope: Barack Obama and the Paradox of Progress.* New York: Walker, 2010.

Cockrell, Dale. *Demons of Disorder: Early Blackface Minstrels and Their World.* Cambridge: Cambridge University Press, 1997.

Cole, Catherine. "American Ghetto Parties and Ghanaian Concert Parties: A Transnational Perspective on Blackface." In Johnson, *Burnt Cork,* 223–58.

Cole, Catherine M., and Tracy C. Davis. "Routes of Blackface." *TDR: The Drama Review* 57, no. 2 (2013): 7–12.

Conner, Ronald C. "Brazilian Blackface: Maracatu Cearense and the Politics of Participation." MA thesis, University of California, Riverside, 2009.

Conquergood, Dwight. "Performance Studies: Interventions and Radical Research." *TDR: The Drama Review* 46, no. 2 (2002): 145–56.

Cordis, Shanya. "Forging Relational Difference: Racial Gendered Violence and Dispossession in Guyana." *Small Axe* 60 (2019): 18–33.

Crabtree, John. "Indigenous Empowerment in Evo Morales's Bolivia." *Current History* 116, no. 787 (2017): 55–60.

Cristancho, Raúl. "Viaje sin mapa." In *Viaje sin mapa: Representaciones afro en el arte contemporáneo Colombiano*, 10–17. Bogotá: Biblioteca Luis-Angel Arango, 2006. Exhibition catalog.

Crosson, Brent. "Race, Nation, and Diaspora in the Southern Caribbean: Unsettling the Ethnic Conflict Mode." *Journal of Latin American and Cultural Anthropology* 27, no. 3 (2022): 408–29.

Croucher, Sheila L. *Imagining Miami: Ethnic Politics in a Postmodern World*. Charlottesville: University Press of Virginia, 1997.

Cuche, Denys. *Poder blanco y resistencia negra en el Perú: Un estudio de la condición social del negro en el Perú después de la abolición de la esclavitud*. Lima: Instituto Nacional de Cultura, 1975.

Cunin, Elisabeth. *Identidades a flor de piel: Lo "negro" entre apariencias y pertenencias— categorías raciales y mestizaje en Cartagena (Colombia)*. Bogotá: Instituto Colombiano de Antropología e Historia; Universidad de los Andes; Instituto Francés de Estudios Andinos; Observatorio del Caribe Colombiano, 2003.

De Friedemann, Nina S. "Contextos religiosos en un área negra de Barbacoas (Nariño). *Revista Colombiana de Folclor* 4, no. 10 (1966): 63–83.

De Friedemann, Nina S., and Jaime Arocha. *De sol a sol: Génesis, transformación y presencia de los negros en Colombia*. Bogotá: Planeta, 1986.

De la Cadena, Marisol. "Are Mestizos Hybrids? The Conceptual Politics of Andean Identities." *Journal of Latin American Studies* 37, no. 2 (2005): 259–84.

De la Cadena, Marisol. "Silent Racism and Intellectual Superiority in Peru." *Bulletin of Latin American Research* 17, no. 2 (1998): 143–64.

De la Fuente, Alejandro. *A Nation for All: Race, Inequality, and Politics in Twentieth-Century Cuba*. Chapel Hill: University of North Carolina Press, 2001.

De la Fuente, Alejandro. "The New Afro-Cuban Cultural Movement and the Debate on Race in Contemporary Cuba." *Journal of Latin American Studies* 40, no. 4 (2008): 697–720.

De la Fuente, Alejandro, and George Reid Andrews, eds. *Afro-Latin American Studies: An Introduction*. Cambridge: Cambridge University Press, 2018.

De la Fuente, Alejandro, and George Reid Andrews. "The Making of a Field: Afro-Latin American Studies." In De la Fuente and Andrews, *Afro-Latin American Studies*, 1–24.

Derby, Lauren. *The Dictator's Seduction: Politics and the Popular Imagination in the Era of Trujillo*. Durham, NC: Duke University Press, 2009.

Diamond, Elin. "Introduction." In *Performance and Cultural Politics*, edited by Elin Diamond, 1–12. New York: Routledge, 1996.

Dorr, Kirstie. "'Putting a Stamp on Racism.'" *Aztlán: A Journal of Chicano Studies* 39, no. 1 (2014): 13–39.

Duany, Jorge. *Blurred Borders: Transnational Migration between the Hispanic Caribbean and the United States*. Chapel Hill: University of North Carolina Press, 2011.

Du Bois, W. E. B. *The Souls of Black Folk*. CreateSpace Independent Publishing Platform, 2018.

Dunn, Marvin. *Black Miami in the Twentieth Century*. Gainesville: University Press of Florida, 2016.

Eckstein, Susan Eva. *The Immigrant Divide: How Cuban Americans Changed the US and Their Homeland*. New York: Routledge, 2009.

Fanon, Frantz. *Black Skin, White Masks*. New York: Grove Atlantic, 2008.

Feldman, Heidi. *Black Rhythms of Peru: Reviving African Musical Heritage in the Black Pacific*. Middletown, CT: Wesleyan University Press, 2006.

Feldman, Heidi. "Strategies of the Black Pacific: Music and Diasporic Identity in Peru." In *Comparative Perspectives on Afro-Latin America*, edited by Kwame Dixon and John Burdick, 42–71. Gainesville: University Press of Florida, 2012.

Fernándes, Sujatha. *Cuba Represent! Cuban Arts, State Power, and the Making of New Revolutionary Cultures*. Durham, NC: Duke University Press, 2006.

Fernández de la Reguera Tayá, Tánit. *Cuba y Cataluña en la segunda mitad del Siglo XIX: Teatro popular e identidades (proto) nacionales*. Madrid: Editorial Pliegos, 2020.

Ferrer, Ada. *Cuba insurgente: Raza, nación y revolución: 1868–1898*. Havana: Editorial de Ciencias Sociales, 2011.

Figueras, Francisco. *Cuba y su evolución colonial*. Havana: Isla, 1959.

Flórez Bolívar, Francisco Javier. "Celebrando y redefiniendo el mestizaje: Raza y nación durante la República Liberal, Colombia 1930–1947." *Memorias*, no. 30 (May 15, 2019): 93–116.

Flórez Bolívar, Francisco Javier. *La Vanguardia intelectual y política de la nación*. Bogotá: Crítica Colombia, 2023.

Fowler, Henry. "A History of Theatre in Jamaica." *Jamaica Journal* 2, no. 1 (1968): 53–59.

Francis, Donette. "A Spirit of Inquiry: Convening Jamaica as Method." *Small Axe* 63 (2020): 181–86.

Francis, Donette, and Allison Harris. "Introduction: Looking for Black Miami." *Anthurium* 16, no. 1 (2020): 1–17.

Frederik, Laurie A. *Trumpets in the Mountains: Theater and the Politics of National Culture in Cuba*. Durham, NC: Duke University Press, 2012.

Freyre, Gilberto. *The Masters and the Slaves: A Study in the Development of Brazilian Civilization*. Translated by Samuel Putnam. New York: Knopf, 1956.

Frisancho, Ignacio Pineda. *Negros en el altiplano puneño*. Puno: Editorial S. Frisancho Pineda, 1983.

García Canclini, Néstor. *Transforming Modernity: Popular Culture in Mexico*. Translated by Lidia Lozano. Austin: University of Texas Press, 1993.

Geler, Lea. *Andares negros, caminos blancos: Afroporteños, estado y nación—Argentina a fines del Siglo XIX*. Rosario, Argentina: Prohistoria Ediciones and TEIAA (Taller de Estudios e investigaciones Andino-Amazónicas), 2010.

Gilroy, Paul. "'To Be Real': The Dissident Forms of Black Expressive Culture." In *Let's Get It On: The Politics of Black Performance*, edited by Catherine Ugwu, 12–33. Seattle: Bay Press, 1995.

Giraldo Escobar, Sol Astrid. *Retratos en blanco y afro: Liliana Angulo*. Bogotá: Ministerio de Cultura, 2013.

Golash-Boza, Tanya Maria. "Does Whitening Happen? Distinguishing between Race and Color Labels in an African-Descended Community in Peru." *Social Problems* 57, no. 1 (2010): 138–56.

Golash-Boza, Tanya Maria. *Yo Soy Negro: Blackness in Peru*. Gainesville: University Press of Florida, 2011.

Goldstein, Donna M. *Laughter out of Place: Race, Class, Violence, and Sexuality in a Rio Shantytown*. Berkeley: University of California Press, 2003.

Gómez, Napoleón, and Rubén Pinto López. *Caporales 100% boliviano: Origen e historia de los caporales*. Self-published, 2019.

Gómez-Barris, Macarena. *Beyond the Pink Tide: Art and Political Undercurrents in the Americas*. Berkeley: University of California Press, 2018.

Gontovnik, Monica. "Performing Race in the Barranquilla Carnival: The Case of the Negritas Puloy de Montecristo." *Social Identities* 25, no. 5 (2018): 662–78.

González, Anita. *Afro-Mexico: Dancing between Myth and Reality*. Austin: University of Texas Press, 2021.

González, Sofía Ayala. "Black, Afro-Colombian, Raizal and Palenquero Communities at the National Museum of Colombia: A Reflexive Ethnography of (in)Visibility, Documentation, and Participatory Collaboration." PhD diss., University of Manchester, 2016.

Gopinath, Gayatri. *Impossible Desires: Queer Diasporas and South Asian Public Cultures*. Durham, NC: Duke University Press, 2005.

Gosin, Monika. *The Racial Politics of Division: Interethnic Struggles for Legitimacy in Multicultural Miami*. Ithaca, NY: Cornell University Press, 2019.

Gray, Obika. *Radicalism and Social Change in Jamaica, 1960–1972*. Knoxville: University of Tennessee Press, 1991.

Greene, Shane. "Entre lo Indio, lo Negro, y lo Incaico: The Spatial Hierarchies of Difference in Multicultural Peru." *Journal of Latin American and Caribbean Anthropology* 12, no. 2 (2007): 441–74.

Greene, Shane. "Todos Somos Iguales, Todos Somos Incas: Dilemmas of Afro-Peruvian Citizenship and Inca Whiteness in Peru." In *Comparative Per-*

spectives on *Afro-Latin America*, edited by Kwame Dixon and John Burdick, 282–304. Gainesville: University Press of Florida, 2012.

Guerra, Lillian. *Visions of Power in Cuba: Revolution, Redemption, and Resistance, 1959–1971*. Chapel Hill: University of North Carolina Press, 2012.

Guss, David M. *The Festive State: Race, Ethnicity, and Nationalism as Cultural Performance*. Berkeley: University of California Press, 2000.

Hale, Charles. "Does Multiculturalism Menace? Governance, Cultural Rights and the Politics of Identity in Guatemala." *Journal of Latin American Studies* 34, no. 2 (2002): 485–524.

Hale, Charles R. *Más que un indio = More Than an Indian: Racial Ambivalence and Neoliberal Multiculturalism in Guatemala*. Santa Fe, NM: School of American Research Press, 2006.

Hale, Charles. "Racial Eruptions: The Awkward Place of Blackness in Indian-Centered Spaces of Mestizaje." Paper presented at the conference Race and Politics in Central America, University of Texas at Austin, February 24–25, 2006.

Hall, Stuart. "Cultural Identity and Diaspora." In *Theorizing Diaspora: A Reader*, edited by Jana Evans Braziel and Anita Mannur, 233–46. Malden, MA: Blackwell, 2003.

Hall, Stuart. "Cultural Studies and Its Theoretical Legacies." In *Stuart Hall: Critical Dialogues in Cultural Studies*, edited by David Morley and Kuan-Hsing Chen, 262–75. London: Routledge, 1996.

Hall, Stuart. "What Is This 'Black' in Black Popular Culture?" In *Black Popular Culture (Discussions in Contemporary Culture)*, edited by Gina Dent, 21–33. Seattle, WA: Bay Press, 1998.

Hartman, Saidiya V. *Scenes of Subjection: Terror, Slavery, and Self-Making in Nineteenth-Century America*. Oxford: Oxford University Press, 1997.

Hay, Michelle. *I've Been Black in Two Countries: Black Cuban Views on Race in the U.S.* El Paso, TX: LFB Scholarly LLC, 2009.

Helg, Aline. "Afro-Cuban Protest: The Partido Independiente de Color 1908–1912." *Cuban Studies* 21 (1991): 101–21.

Henken, Ted. "Balseros, Boteros, and el Bombo: Post-1994 Cuban Immigration to the United States and the Persistence of Special Treatment." *Latino Studies* 3, no. 3 (2005): 393–416.

Hennefeld, Maggie, and Nicholas Sammond. *Abjection Incorporated: Mediating the Politics of Pleasure and Violence*. Durham, NC: Duke University Press, 2020.

Hernández, Tanya Katerí. *Racial Innocence: Unmasking Latino Anti-Black Bias and the Struggle for Equality*. Boston: Beacon Press, 2022.

Hernández, Tanya Katerí. *Racial Subordination in Latin America: The Role of the State, Customary Law, and the New Civil Rights Response*. Cambridge: Cambridge University Press, 2013.

Hernández Regaunt, Ariana, and Jossianna Arroyo. "The Brownface of Latinidad in Cuban Miami." *Cuban Counterpoints: Public Scholarship about a Changing*

Cuba, July 13, 2015. https://cubacounterpoints.com/archives/1600
.html.

Hidalgo, Narciso J. *Choteo: Irreverencia y humor en la cultura cubana*. Bogotá: Siglo del
Hombre Editores, 2012.

Hill, Donald R. *Calypso Calaloo: Early Carnival Music in Trinidad*. Gainesville: University Press of Florida, 1993.

Hill, Errol. *The Jamaican Stage, 1655–1900: Profile of a Colonial Theatre*. Amherst: University of Massachusetts Press, 1992.

Hill, Errol. "Plays of the English-Speaking Caribbean, Part 1 (a Bibliography and
Check List)." *Bulletin of Black Theatre* 1, no. 3 (1972): 11–15.

Hintzen, Percy C. "Creoleness and Nationalism in Guyanese Anticolonialism and
Postcolonial Formation." *Small Axe* 15 (2004): 106–22.

Hobsbawm, Eric. "Introduction: Inventing Traditions." In *The Invention of Tradition*,
edited by Eric Hobsbawm and Terence Ranger, 1–14. Cambridge: Cambridge University Press, 1983.

Hoffmann, Odile. *Communautés noires dans le Pacifique colombien: Innovations et dynamiques ethniques*. Karthala: IRD, 2004.

Hooker, Juliet. "Indigenous Inclusion/Black Exclusion: Race, Ethnicity, and Multicultural Citizenship in Latin America." *Journal of Latin American Studies* 37,
no. 2 (2005): 285–310.

hooks, bell. *Black Looks: Race and Representation*. London: Routledge, 2015.

Hope, Donna P. "From Browning to Cake Soap: Popular Debates on Skin Bleaching in The Jamaican Dancehall." *Journal of Pan-African Study* 4, no. 4 (2011): 165–94.

Hope, Donna P. *Inna Di Dancehall: Popular Culture and the Politics of Identity in Jamaica*. Mona, Jamaica: University of the West Indies Press, 2006.

Hope, Donna P. "'Pon Di Borderline': Exploring Constructions of Jamaican Masculinity in Dancehall and Roots Theatre." *Journal of West Indian Literature* 21,
nos. 1–2 (2012): 105–28.

Howard, Philip S. S. "On the Back of Blackness: Contemporary Canadian Blackface and the Consumptive Production of Post-Racialist, White Canadian
Subjects." *Social Identities* 24, no. 1 (January 23, 2017): 87–103.

Hoxworth, Kellen. "The Jim Crow Global South." *Theatre Journal* 72, no. 4 (2020): 443–67.

Hoxworth, Kellen. *Transoceanic Blackface: Empire, Race, Performance*. Evanston, IL: Northwestern University Press, 2024.

Hunter, Margaret. "Buying Racial Capital, Skin-Bleaching and Cosmetic Surgery in
a Globalized World." *Journal of Pan-African Studies* 4, no. 4 (2011): 142–64.

Hutchison, Elizabeth Q., Thomas Miller Klubock, Nara B. Milanich, and Peter
Winn, eds. *The Chile Reader: History, Culture, Politics*. Durham, NC: Duke
University Press, 2014.

Ingenieros, José. "Las razas inferiores." In *Obras completas* 5:161–72. Buenos Aires:
Ediciones L. J. Rosso, 1919.

Jackson, Shona N. *Creole Indigeneity: Between Myth and Nation in the Caribbean*. Minneapolis: University of Minnesota Press, 2012.

Jafa, Arthur, Peter Hessli, and Pearl Bowser. "The Notion of Treatment: Black Aesthetics and Film, Based on an Interview with Peter Hessli and Additional Discussions with Pearl Bowser." In *Oscar Micheaux and His Circle: African-American Filmmaking and Race Cinema of the Silent Era*, edited by Pearl Bowser, Jane Gaines, and Charles Musser, 11–18. Bloomington: Indiana University Press, 2016.

Johnson, Stephen Burge, ed. *Burnt Cork: Traditions and Legacies of Blackface Minstrelsy*. Amherst: University of Massachusetts Press, 2012.

Johnson, Stephen Burge. "Introduction: The Persistence of Blackface and the Minstrel Tradition." In Johnson, *Burnt Cork*, 1–17.

Jones, Douglas. "'The Black Below': Black Minstrelsy, Satire, and the Threat of Vernacularity." *Theatre Journal* 73, no. 2 (2021): 129–46.

Jones, Nicholas R. *Staging Habla de Negros: Radical Performances of the African Diaspora in Early Modern Spain*. University Park, PA: Penn State University Press, 2021.

Júnior, João Feres, Verônica Toste Daflon, and Luiz Augusto Campos. "Lula's Approach to Affirmative Action and Race." *NACLA Report on the Americas* 44, no. 2 (March 2011): 34–37.

Kamugisha, Aaron. *Beyond Coloniality: Citizenship and Freedom in the Caribbean Intellectual Tradition*. Bloomington: Indiana University Press, 2019.

Kaplan, Paul H. D. *The Rise of the Black Magus in Western Art*. Ann Arbor: UMI Research Press, 1985.

Karush, M. B. "Blackness in Argentina: Jazz, Tango and Race before Peron." *Past and Present* 216, no. 1 (2012): 215–45.

Katzew, Ilona. *Casta Painting: Images of Race in Eighteenth-Century Mexico*. New Haven, CT: Yale University Press, 2004.

Kelley, Robin D. G. *Race Rebels: Culture, Politics, and the Black Working Class*. New York: Free Press, 1994.

Kristeva, Julia. *Powers of Horror: An Essay on Abjection*. Translated by Leon S. Roudiez. New York: Columbia University Press, 1982.

Kutzinski, Vera M. *Sugar's Secrets: Race and the Erotics of Cuban Nationalism*. Charlottesville: University Press of Virginia, 1993.

Lacey, Terry. *Violence and Politics in Jamaica, 1960–70: Internal Security in a Developing Country*. Manchester: Manchester University Press, 1977.

Lago, Consuelo. *La política vista por Nieves*. Bogotá: Editorial Villegas, 2006.

Laguna, Albert. "Aquí Está Álvarez Guedes: Cuban Choteo and the Politics of Play." *Latino Studies* 8, no. 4 (2010): 509–31.

Laguna, Albert. "Before the Thaw: The Transnational Routes of Cuban Popular Culture." *Latin American Research Review* 54, no. 1 (2019): 151–64.

Laguna, Albert. *Diversión: Play and Popular Culture in Cuban America*. New York: New York University Press, 2017.

Lane, Jill. *Blackface Cuba, 1840–1895*. Philadelphia: University of Pennsylvania Press, 2005.

Lane, Jill. "Hemispheric America in Deep Time." *Theatre Research International* 35, no. 2 (2010): 111–25.

Lane, Jill. "Problems of Framing: National or Colonial Approaches to Blackface Performance." In *Colonial-Era Caribbean Theatre*, edited by Julia Prest, 111–34. Liverpool: Liverpool University Press, 2023.

Lane, Jill, and Marcial Godoy-Anativia. "Dossier: Impostura Racial/Racial Impersonation." *emisférica* 5, no. 2 (December 2008). https://hemispheric institute.org/en/emisferica-5-2-race-and-its-others/5-2-dossier /introductory-comments.html.

Lauterbach, Preston. *The Chitlin' Circuit and the Road to Rock 'N' Roll*. New York: Norton, 2011.

Leal, Rine. *Breve historia del teatro cubano*. Havana: Editorial Letras Cubanas, 1980.

Leal, Rine. *La selva oscura: De los bufos a la neocolonial*. Vol. 1, *Historia del teatro cubano desde sus orígenes hasta 1868*. Havana: Editorial Arte y Literatura, 1975.

Leal, Rine. *La selva oscura: De los bufos a la neocolonial*. Vol. 2, *Historia del teatro cubano de 1868 a 1902*. Havana: Editorial Arte y Literatura, 1982.

Leal, Rine. *Teatro bufo siglo XIX: antología*. Havana: Editorial Arte y Literatura, 1975.

Le Camp, Lorraine. "Racial Considerations of Minstrel Shows and Related Images in Canada." PhD diss., University of Toronto, 2005.

Ledgister, F. S. J. *Only West Indians: Creole Nationalism in the British West Indies*. Trenton, NJ: Africa World Press, 2010.

Leonardo-Loayza, Richard. "Doblemente subalternizada: Corporalización, racialización y afrodescendencia en 'Muchachita negra' (1945), de Blanca Varela." *Revista de Crítica Literaria Latinoamericana* 46, no. 92 (2020): 369–86.

Levin, Laura. *Performing Ground: Space, Camouflage, and the Art of Blending In*. New York: Palgrave Macmillan, 2014.

Lewis, Rupert. "Walter Rodney: 1968 Revisited." *Social and Economic Studies* 43, no. 3 (1994): 7–56.

Lhamon, W. T. *Jump Jim Crow: Lost Plays, Lyrics, and Street Prose of the First Atlantic Popular Culture*. Cambridge, MA: Harvard University Press, 2022.

Ligiéro, Zeca. "Liliana Angulo: An Afro-Colombian Performance." *emisférica* 5, no. 2 (December 2008). https://archive.hemispheric.org/eng/publications /emisferica/5.2/artistpresentation/angulo/essay.html.

Linares, María Teresa. *Introducción a Cuba: La música popular*. Havana: Instituto del Libro; Editorial Ciencias Sociales, 1970.

Liverpool, Hollis. *Rituals of Power and Rebellion: The Carnival Tradition in Trinidad and Tobago, 1763–1962*. Trinidad and Tobago: Frontline Distribution, 2001.

López, Antonio M. *Unbecoming Blackness: The Diaspora Cultures of Afro-Cuban America*. New York: New York University Press, 2012.

Lott, Eric. *Love and Theft: Blackface Minstrelsy and the American Working Class*. Oxford: Oxford University Press, 2013.

Lowe, Lisa. *The Intimacies of Four Continents*. Durham, NC: Duke University Press, 2015.

Lugo-Ortiz, Agnes I., and Angela Rosenthal. *Slave Portraiture in the Atlantic World*. Cambridge: Cambridge University Press, 2013.

Lusane, Clarence. *The Black History of the White House*. San Francisco: City Lights Books, 2011.

Maidana-Rodríguez, Freddy. *La danza de los caporales: Construyendo identidad*. La Paz: Fundación Cultural Del Banco, 2011.

Mañach, Jorge. *Indagación del choteo*. Miami: Ediciones Universal, 1991.

Manning, Marable. "The Fire This Time: The Miami Rebellion, May 1980." *Black Scholar* 11, no. 6 (1980): 2–18.

Manzor, Lillian. *Marginality beyond Return: US Cuban Performances in the 1980s and 1990s*. London: Routledge, 2023.

Martí, José. *Nuestra América*. Havana: Casa de las Américas, 1991.

Martiatu Terry, Inés. *Bufo y nación: Interpelaciones desde el presente*. Havana: Letras Cubanas, 2008.

Martínez Melanchi, Nereida Apaza Mamani, Sharon Pérez, Alice Samson, and Laura Osorio Sunnucks. "Artist Perspectives on the Politics of Andean Negrería Dances." *Revista: Harvard Review of Latin America* (July 27, 2021). https://revista.drclas.harvard.edu/artist-perspectives-on-the-politics-of-andean-negreria-dances/.

McKittrick, Katherine. *Demonic Grounds: Black Women and the Cartographies of Struggle*. Minneapolis: University of Minnesota Press, 2006.

McMahon, Rashida Z. Shaw. *The Black Circuit: Race, Performance, and Spectatorship in Black Popular Theatre*. New York: Routledge, 2020.

McMillan, Uri. *Embodied Avatars: Genealogies of Black Feminist Art and Performance*. New York: New York University Press, 2015.

Meeks, Brian. *Narratives of Resistance: Jamaica, Trinidad, the Caribbean*. Mona, Jamaica: University of the West Indies Press, 2000.

Mendoza-Walker, Zoila. "Contesting Identities through Dance: Mestizo Performance in the Southern Andes of Peru." *Repercussions* 3, no. 2 (Fall 1994): 50–80.

Mohammed, Patricia. "'But Most of All Mi Love Me Browning': The Emergence in Eighteenth and Nineteenth-Century Jamaica of the Mulatto Woman as the Desired." *Feminist Review* 65, no. 1 (2000): 22–48.

Mohl, Raymond. "Whitening Miami: Race, Housing, and Government Policy in Twentieth- Century Dade County." *Florida Historical Quarterly* 79, no. 3 (2001): 319–45.

Moore, Carlos. *Castro, the Blacks, and Africa*. Berkeley: University of California, 1988.

Moore, Robin. "Black Music in a Raceless Society: Afro-Cuban Folklore and Socialism." *Cuban Studies* 37, no. 1 (2006): 1–32.

Moore, Robin. *Nationalizing Blackness: Afrocubanismo and Artistic Revolution in Havana, 1920–1940*. Pittsburgh: University of Pittsburgh Press, 1997.

Mosquera Rosero-Labbé, Claudia, Agustín Laó-Montes, and César Rodríguez Garavito, eds. *Debates sobre ciudadanía y políticas raciales en las Américas negras*. Bogotá: Universidad Nacional de Colombia, Universidad del Valle, 2010.

Mosquera Rosero-Labbé, Claudia, Mauricio Pardo, and Odile Hoffmann, eds. *Afrodescendientes en las Américas: Trayectorias sociales e identitarias: 150 años de la abolición de la esclavitud en Colombia*. Bogotá: Universidad Nacional de Colombia, Instituto Colombiano de Antropología e Historia ICANH; Institut de recherche pour le développement IRD; ILSA, Instituto Latinoamericano de Servicios Legales Alternativos, 2002.

Moten, Fred. *In the Break: The Aesthetics of Black Radical Tradition*. Minneapolis: University of Minnesota Press, 2003.

Mulvey, Laura. *Visual Pleasure and Narrative Cinema*. Oxford: Oxford University Press, 1999.

Múnera, Alfonso. *Fronteras imaginadas: la construcción de las razas y de la geografía en el siglo XIX colombiano*. Bogotá: Crítica Colombia, 2020.

Muñoz, José Esteban. *Disidentifications: Queers of Color and Performance of Politics*. Minneapolis: University of Minnesota Press, 1999.

Nascimento, Abdias do. *O Negro revoltado*. Rio de Janeiro: Edições GRD, 1968.

Nascimento, Abdias do, and Elisa Larkin Nascimento. "Apresentação." In *Quilombo: Vida, problemas e aspirações do negro* 34 (2003), 7–10.

Ndiaye, Noémie. *Scripts of Blackness: Early Modern Performance Culture and the Making of Race*. Philadelphia: University of Pennsylvania Press, 2022.

Nettleford, Rex M. *Caribbean Cultural Identity: The Case of Jamaica*. Kingston, Jamaica: Ian Randle, Global, 2003.

Nettleford, Rex M. *Mirror Mirror: Identity, Race, and Protest in Jamaica*. Kingston: LMH Publishing, 2006.

Ng'weno, Bettina. *Turf Wars: Territory and Citizenship in the Contemporary State*. Stanford, CA: Stanford University Press, 2007.

Nijman, Jan. *Miami: Mistress of the Americas*. Philadelphia: University of Pennsylvania Press, 2011.

Nowatzki, Robert. *Representing African Americans in Transatlantic Abolitionism and Blackface Minstrelsy*. Baton Rouge: Louisiana State University Press, 2010.

Nyongó, Tavia. *The Amalgamation Waltz: Race, Performance, and the Ruses of Memory*. Minneapolis: University of Minnesota Press, 2009.

Obama, Barack. *The Audacity of Hope: Thoughts on Reclaiming the American Dream*. Edinburgh: Canongate, 2008.

Obama, Barack. *Dreams from My Father: A Story of Race and Inheritance*. New York: Times Books, 1995.

Ortiz, Fernando. "José Antonio Saco y sus ideas." *Revista Bimestre Cubana* 3 (1929): 360–409.

Ortíz, Fernando. *Martí y las razas*. Havana: Comisión Nacional Organizadora de los Actos y Ediciones del Centenario y del Monumento de Martí, 1953.

Ortiz, Renato. *Cultura brasileira e identidade nacional*. São Paulo: Brasiliense, 1985.

Paschel, Tianna. "'The Beautiful Faces of My Black People': Race, Ethnicity and the Politics of Colombia's 2005 Census." *Ethnic and Racial Studies* 36, no. 10 (2013): 1544–63.

Paschel, Tianna. *Becoming Black Political Subjects: Movements and Ethno-Racial Rights in Colombia and Brazil*. Princeton, NJ: Princeton University Press, 2016.

Paschel, Tianna. "Rethinking Black Mobilization in Latin America." In De la Fuente and Andrews, *Afro-Latin American Studies*, 222–63.

Paschel, Tianna. "The Right to Difference: Explaining Colombia's Shift from Color Blindness to the Law of Black Communities." *American Journal of Sociology* 116, no. 3 (2010): 729–69.

Pérez Firmat, Gustavo. *Literature and Liminality: Festive Readings in the Hispanic Tradition*. Durham, NC: Duke University Press, 1986.

Perry, Marc D. *Negro Soy Yo: Hip Hop and Raced Citizenship in Neoliberal Cuba*. Durham, NC: Duke University Press, 2016.

Pierre, Gemima. "Growing Up Haitian in Black Miami: A Narrative in Three Acts." *Anthurium* 16, no. 1 (2020). https://doi.org/10.33596/anth.376.

Poole, Deborah A. "Accommodation and Resistance in Andean Ritual Dance." *TDR: The Drama Review* 34, no. 2 (1990): 98–126.

Portes, Alejandro, and Aaron Puhrmann. "A Bifurcated Enclave: The Peculiar Evolution of the Cuban Immigrant Population in the Last Decades." *Un pueblo disperso: Dimensiones sociales y culturales de la diáspora cubana*, edited by Jorge Duany, 122–49. Valencia, Spain: Aduana Vieja, 2013.

Portes, Alejandro, and Alex Stepick. *City on the Edge: The Transformation of Miami*. Berkeley: University of California Press, 1993.

Post, Tina. "Williams, Walker, and Shine: Blackbody Blackface, or the Importance of Being Surface." *TDR: The Drama Review* 59, no. 4 (2015): 83–100.

Pratt, Mary Louise. "Arts of the Contact Zone." *Profession* (1991): 33–40.

Puri, Shalini. "Beyond Resistance: Notes toward a New Caribbean Cultural Studies." *Small Axe* 14 (2003): 23–38.

Puri, Shalini. *The Caribbean Postcolonial: Social Equality, Post-Nationalism, and Cultural Hybridity*. New York: Palgrave Macmillan, 2004.

Rahier, Jean Muteba. *Blackness in the Andes: Ethnographic Vignettes of Cultural Politics in the Time of Multiculturalism*. New York: Palgrave Macmillan, 2014.

Rahier, Jean Muteba. "The Multicultural Turn, the New Latin American Constitutionalism, and Black Social Movements in the Andean Sub-Region." In *The Andean World*, edited by Linda J. Seligmann and Kathleen S. Fine-Dare, 389–402. Abingdon, UK: Routledge, 2018.

Rahier, Jean Muteba, and M. D. Prosper. "Afrodescendants, the Multicultural Turn and the 'New' Latin American Constitutions and Other Special Legislations: Particularities of the Andean Region." In Rahier, *Blackness in the Andes*, 89–103.

Rama, Angel. *The Lettered City*. Translated by John Chasteen. Durham, NC: Duke University Press, 1996.

Restrepo, Eduardo. "Ethnicization of Blackness in Colombia: Toward De-racializing Theoretical and Political Imagination." *Cultural Studies* 18, no. 5 (2004): 698–753.

Restrepo, Eduardo. "Imágenes del 'negro' y nociones de raza en Colombia a principios del siglo XX." *Revista de Estudios Sociales* 27 (2008): 46–61.

Restrepo, Luz Adriana Maya, and Raúl Cristancho. *¡Mandinga sea! África en Antioquía*. Bogotá: Universidad de los Andes, 2015.

Reyes, Israel. *Humor and the Eccentric Text in Puerto Rican Literature*. Gainesville: University Press of Florida, 2005.

Rhenals Doria, Ana Milena, and Francisco Javier Flórez Bolívar. "Escogiendo entre los extranjeros 'Indeseables': Afro-Antillanos, Sirio-Libaneses, raza e inmigración en Colombia, 1880–1937." *Anuario colombiano de historia social y de la cultura* 40, no. 1 (2013): 243–71.

Ribeiro, Darcy. *O povo Brasileiro: A formação e o sentido do Brasil*. Sao Paolo: Companhia Das Letras, 1995.

Rivero, Yeidy. *Tuning Out Blackness: Race and Nation in the History of Puerto Rican Television*. Durham, NC: Duke University Press, 2005.

Roach, Joseph R. *Cities of the Dead: Circum-Atlantic Performance*. New York: Columbia University Press, 1996.

Robaina, Tomás. *El negro en Cuba, 1902–1957: Apuntes para la historia de la lucha contra la discriminación racial*. Havana: Editorial de Ciencias Sociales, 1994.

Robinson, Tracy. "Mass Weddings in Jamaica and the Production of Academic Folk Knowledge." *Small Axe* 63 (2020): 65–80.

Rockefeller, Stuart Alexander. "'There Is a Culture Here': Spectacle and the Inculcation of Folklore in Highland Bolivia." *Journal of Latin American Anthropology* 3, no.2 (1998): 118–49.

Romero, Sílvio. *Estudos sobre a poesia popular do Brasil*. Petrópolis, Brazil: Editora Vozes, 1977.

Roper, Danielle. "Blackface at the Andean Fiesta: Performing Blackness in the Danza de Caporales." *Latin American Research Review* 54, no. 2 (June 25, 2019): 381–97.

Roper, Danielle, and Tracy-Ann Wint. "The Tambourine Army: Sonic Disruptions and the Politics of Respectability." *Small Axe* 62 (2020): 35–52.

Rosenblat, Ángel. *La población indígena de américa: Desde 1492 hasta la actualidad*. Buenos Aires: Institución Cultural Española, 1945.

Rubenstein, Anne. *Bad Language, Naked Ladies, and Other Threats to the Nation: A Political History of Comic Books in Mexico*. Durham, NC: Duke University Press, 1998.

Saco, Josí Antonio. *Colecciones de papeles científicos, históricos y políticos sobre la isla de Cuba*. Vol. 2. Paris: Imprenta de D'Aubusson y Kugelmann, 1858.

Saco, Josí Antonio. *Colecciones de papeles científicos, históricos y políticos sobre la isla de Cuba*. Vol. 3. Paris: Imprenta de D'Aubusson y Kugelmann, 1858.

Salas-Carreño, Guillermo. *Representación de la esclavitud en danzas peruanas*. Lima: Biblioteca Nacional de Peru; Pontificia Universidad Nacional, 1998.

Sánchez, Walter C. "Identidades sonoras de los afrodescendientes de Bolivia." *Revista Argentina de Musicología* 9 (2008): 63–99.

Sánchez-Patsy, Mauricio. "País de caporales: Los imaginarios del poder y la danza de los caporales en Bolivia." PhD diss., Universidad Nacional de Cuyo, 2006.

Sanders, James E. *Contentious Republicans: Popular Politics, Race, and Class in Nineteenth-Century Colombia*. Durham, NC: Duke University Press, 2004.

Sawyer, Mark W. *Racial Politics in Post-Revolutionary Cuba*. Cambridge: Cambridge University Press, 2006.

Schechner, Richard. *Between Theater and Anthropology*. Philadelphia: University of Pennsylvania Press, 1985.

Schweitzer, Marlis. "'Too Much Tragedy in Real Life': Theatre in Post-Emancipation Jamaica." *Nineteenth-Century Theatre and Film* 44, no. 1 (2017): 8–27.

Scott, Darieck. *Extravagant Abjection: Blackness, Power, and Sexuality in the African American Literary Imagination*. New York: New York University Press, 2010.

Scott, David. *Refashioning Futures: Criticism after Postcoloniality*. Princeton, NJ: Princeton University Press, 1999.

Sharpe, Christina. *In the Wake: On Blackness and Being*. Durham, NC: Duke University Press, 2016.

Shell-Weiss, Melanie. *Coming to Miami: A Social History*. Gainesville: University Press of Florida, 2009.

Sheller, Mimi. *Citizenship from Below: Erotic Agency and Caribbean Freedom*. Durham, NC: Duke University Press, 2012.

Shimakawa, Karen. *National Abjection: The Asian American Body Onstage*. Durham, NC: Duke University Press, 2002.

Shouse Tourino, Corey. "Fed by Any Means Necessary: Omnivorous Negritude and the Transnational Semiotics of Afro-Colombian Blackness in the Work of Liliana Angulo." *Human Rights and Latin American Cultural Studies* 4, no. 1 (2009): 228–46.

Sigl, Eveline, and David Mendoza Salazar. *No se baila así no más*. Vol. 1. La Paz, Bolivia: published by the authors, 2012.

Small, Jean. "Empowerment through the Theatre." *Caribbean Quarterly* 47, no. 1 (2001): 30–41.

Smith, Christopher J. *The Creolization of American Culture: William Sidney Mount and the Roots of Blackface Minstrelsy*. Urbana: University of Illinois Press, 2017.

Sommer, Doris. *Foundational Fictions: The National Romances of Latin America.* Berkeley: University of California Press, 2007.

Stallings, L. H. "Hip Hop and the Black Ratchet Imagination." *Palimpsest* 2, no. 2 (2013): 135–39.

Stam, Robert. *Subversive Pleasures: Bakhtin, Cultural Criticism, and Film.* Baltimore: Johns Hopkins University Press, 1992.

Stanley Niaah, Sonjah. *Dancehall: From Slave Ship to Ghetto.* Ottawa: University of Ottawa Press, 2010.

Stepan, Nancy. *The Hour of Eugenics: Race, Gender, and Nation in Latin America.* Ithaca, NY: Cornell University Press, 1991.

Stevens, Andrea Ria. "Black: Mastering Masques of Blackness." In *Inventions of the Skin: The Painted Body in Early English Drama, 1400–1642,* 87–120. Edinburgh: Edinburgh University Press, 2022.

Stone, Carl. *Class, Race, and Political Behavior in Urban Jamaica.* Mona, Jamaica: University of the West Indies Press, 1973.

Suárez Durán, Esther. "El teatro bufo cubano, la vastedad de su universo." *Bufo y nación: Interpelaciones desde el presente,* edited by Inés María Martiatu, 239–37. Havana: Letras Cubanas, 2008.

Sue, Christina A., and Tanya Golash-Boza. "'It Was Only a Joke': How Racial Humour Fuels Colour-Blind Ideologies in Mexico and Peru." *Ethnic and Racial Studies* 36, no. 10 (October 2013): 1582–98.

Sue, Christina A., and Tanya Golash-Boza. "More Than 'a Hidden Race': The Complexities of Blackness in Mexico and Peru." *Latin American and Caribbean Ethnic Studies* 8, no. 1 (2013): 76–82.

Swanston Baker, Jessica. "Sounding in the Wake: Thinking with Jumbies in the Caribbean Archipelago." Paper presented at Sounding the Spectral: A Symposium, at the University of Chicago, May 13, 2023.

Tate, Shirley Anne. *Decolonising Sambo: Transculturation, Fungibility and Black and People of Colour Futurity.* Bingley, UK: Emerald Publishing, 2020.

Taylor, Diana. *The Archive and the Repertoire: Performing Cultural Memory in the Americas.* Durham, NC: Duke University Press, 2003.

Telles, Edward Eric. *Pigmentocracies: Ethnicity, Race, and Color in Latin America.* Chapel Hill: University of North Carolina Press, 2014.

Templeman, Robert. "We Are People of the Yungas, We Are the Saya Race." In *Blackness in Latin America and the Caribbean: Social Dynamics and Cultural Transformations,* edited by Arlene Torres and Norman E. Whitten, 426–44. Bloomington: Indiana University Press, 1998.

Tesler, Michael, and David O. Sears. *Obama's Race: The 2008 Election and the Dream of a Post-Racial America.* Chicago: University of Chicago Press, 2010.

Thame, Maziki. "Racial Hierarchy and the Elevation of Brownness in Creole Nationalism." *Small Axe* 54 (2017): 111–23.

Thelwell, Chinua. *Exporting Jim Crow: Blackface Minstrelsy in South Africa and Beyond.* Amherst: University of Massachusetts Press, 2020.

Thomas, Deborah. "Democratizing Dance: Institutional Transformation and Hegemonic Reordering in Postcolonial Jamaica." *Cultural Anthropology* 17, no.
4 (2002): 512–50.

Thomas, Deborah. *Modern Blackness: Nationalism, Globalization, and the Politics of
Culture in Jamaica*. Durham, NC: Duke University Press, 2004.

Thomas, Evan. *"A Long Time Coming": The Inspiring, Combative 2008 Campaign and
the Historic Election of Barack Obama*. New York: PublicAffairs, 2009.

Thomas, Susan. *Cuban Zarzuela: Performing Race and Gender on Havana's Lyric Stage*.
Urbana: University of Illinois Press, 2009.

Thompson, Krista. *Shine: The Visual Economy of Light in African Diasporic Aesthetic
Practice*. Durham, NC: Duke University Press, 2015.

Toll, Robert C. *Blacking Up: The Minstrel Show in Nineteenth-Century America*. Oxford: Oxford University Press, 1974.

Tompkins, William David. "The Musical Traditions of the Blacks of Coastal Peru."
PhD diss., University of California Los Angeles, 1981.

Trouillot, Michel-Rolph. *Silencing the Past: Power and the Production of History*. Boston: Beacon Press, 1995.

Van Cott, Donna Lee. *The Friendly Liquidation of the Past: The Politics of Diversity in
Latin America*. Pittsburgh: University of Pittsburgh Press, 2000.

Van Cott, Donna Lee. "A Political Analysis of Legal Pluralism in Bolivia and Colombia." *Journal of Latin American Studies* 32, no. 1 (2000): 207–34.

Vasconcelos, José. *The Cosmic Race: A Bilingual Edition*. Translated by Didier Tisdel
Jaén. Baltimore: Johns Hopkins University Press, 1997.

Vazquez, Alexandra T. *Listening in Detail: Performances of Cuban Music*. Durham,
NC: Duke University Press, 2013.

Viveros, Mara. "Alteridad, género, sexualidad y afectos: Reflexiones a partir de una
experiencia investigativa en Colombia." *Cadernos Pagu* 41, 2013, https://
www.scielo.br/j/cpa/a/tnsC3DfpXwRqhCXDpFspgpJ/.

Viveros, Mara. "La imbricación de los estereotipos racistas y sexistas: El caso de
Quibdó." In *150 años de la abolición de la esclavización en Colombia: Desde la
marginalidad a la construcción de la nación*, 508–29. Bogotá: Aguilar, 2013.

Wade, Peter. "Articulations of Eroticism and Race: Domestic Service in Latin
America." *Feminist Theory* 14, no. 2 (2013): 187–202.

Wade, Peter. *Blackness and Race Mixture: The Dynamics of Racial Identity in Colombia*.
Johns Hopkins Studies in Atlantic History and Culture. Baltimore: Johns
Hopkins University Press, 1993.

Wade, Peter. "The Cultural Politics of Blackness in Colombia." *American Ethnologist*
22, no. 2 (May 1995): 341–57.

Wade, Peter. *Música, raza y nación: Música tropical en Colombia*. N.p.: Vicepresiden-
cia de La República, 2002.

Walker, Charles F. *The Tupac Amaru Rebellion*. Cambridge, MA: Harvard University
Press, 2014.

Weheliye, Alexander G. *Habeas Viscus: Racializing Assemblages, Biopolitics, and Black Feminist Theories of the Human*. Durham, NC: Duke University Press, 2014.

Weismantel, Mary, and Stephen F. Eisenman. "Race in the Andes: Global Movements and Popular Ontologies." *Bulletin of Latin American Research* 17, no. 2 (1998): 121–42.

Welcome, Leniqueca A. "To Be Black Is To . . . : The Production of Blackness in and beyond Trinidad." *Small Axe* 68 (2022): 108–18.

Whitten, Norman E., Jr., and Arlene Torres, eds. *Blackness in Latin America and the Caribbean: Social Dynamics and Cultural Transformations*. Bloomington: Indiana University Press, 1998.

Williams, Eric. *The Historical Background of Race Relations in the Caribbean*. Port-of-Spain: Trinidad College Press, 1955.

Wilson, Kathleen. *The Island Race: Englishness, Empire, and Gender in the Eighteenth Century*. London: Routledge, 2003.

Wirtz, Kristina. *Performing Afro-Cuba: Image, Voice, Spectacle in the Making of Race and History*. Chicago: University of Chicago Press, 2014.

Wittmann, Matthew W. "Empire of Culture: U.S. Entertainers and the Making of the Pacific Circuit, 1850–1890." Ph.D diss., University of Michigan, 2010.

Wright, Winthrop R. *Café con leche: Race, Class, and National Image in Venezuela*. Austin: University of Texas Press, 1990.

Wynter, Sylvia. "The Re-enchantment of Humanism." *Small Axe* 8 (2000): 119–207.

Yang, Caroline H. *The Peculiar Afterlife of Slavery: The Chinese Worker and the Minstrel Form*. Stanford, CA: Stanford University Press, 2020.

Yúdice, George. *The Expediency of Culture: Uses of Culture in the Global Era*. Durham, NC: Duke University Press, 2004.

Yue, Genevieve. *Girl Head: Feminism and Film Materiality*. New York: Fordham University Press, 2021.

Zea, Gloria, ed. *Cohabitar: IX Bienal De Arte De Bogotá*. Bogotá: Instituto Distrital de Cultura y Turismo, 2006.

Zien, Katherine A. *Sovereign Acts: Performing Race, Space, and Belonging in Panama and the Canal Zone*. New Brunswick, NJ: Rutgers University Press, 2017.

Martí, José, 11–12, 69, 84, 184n31

masculinity, 77, 153; black, 115; Caribbean, 207n52; Dominican, 80; female, 52, 55–56; queer, 115

Medina, Danilo, 75, 79–80

MegaTv, 61, 73, 192n1. See also *Esta Noche Tu Night*

mestizaje, 2, 11, 13, 15, 22, 67, 96, 143, 154, 176; blackface and, 83; in Colombia, 103, 105–7, 124–25; in Cuba, 103; cultural, 35–36; in Miami, 89, 103; nationalist fictions of, 12, 21, 23; in Peru, 32, 34–35, 37, 103, 124, 174; racial fictions of, 42; racial scripts of, 18, 20, 32–33, 37, 58, 84, 96, 103, 125, 172, 174–75

mestizo autóctono, 11–123, 184n31

Miami, 15, 19, 63–69, 121, 167, 174, 194n19, 194n23; abjection in, 67, 90; antiblackness in, 23, 66; blackface in, 1–5, 8, 10, 68, 82–83, 87; blackness in, 194n19; Cuban artists in, 195n47; Cuban diaspora in, 22, 62, 65–66, 69, 75, 82, 85–86, 88–90, 95–96, 177, 193nn13–14, 193–94n15; Cuban exiles in, 60, 84; English-only campaigns in, 194n21; Haitian experience in, 194n28; immigrants in, 64, 67–68, 75; mestizaje in, 89, 103; nationalist fictions and, 15; Nicaraguans in, 194n27; Obama and, 70–71, 93–94, 177; police brutality in, 194n20; racial conjuring and, 24; racial politics of, 60; racial scripts in, 22; theater in, 198n97; whiteness in, 16, 23, 66–67. See also *Esta Noche Tu Night*; Marrero, Carlos; MegaTv; *paquete semanal*; Valdés, Alexis

migrants, 65; Andean, 27; Cuban, 68

minstrel performances, 83, 87, 192n80, 192n80

minstrelsy: blackface, 4, 6, 144, 171–72, 177, 183n21, 202n56, 211n2, 211n4; US, 176, 181n7, 182n11; watermelon imagery, 191n79

misogynoir, 94–95

mockery, 72, 74–76, 94–95, 127

modernity, 77, 104, 162; Western, 6, 57, 182n10

Morales, Evo, 70, 181n5

multiculturalism, 2, 11, 15, 17–18, 23–24, 103, 134, 174, 189n43; celebrations of, 110, 126, 171; in Colombia, 125; Latin American, 201n40; mestizo and, 12; regional turn to, 39

multicultural turn, 18–19; in Colombia, 103, 107–9, 126, 201–2n28; in Latin America, 32

musicality, 7, 95; black, 3, 82; blackness and, 132

national fictions, repeating 11, 13, 15–19, 23–25, 63–64, 89, 144, 171–73, 176, 178; of mestizaje, 12; Obama and, 70; of racial democracy, 4, 10, 12

national identity, 2, 16, 38, 69, 93; blackface and, 6, 83, 144; in Colombia, 105, 121; Cuban, 12, 22, 72, 83, 87, 142; folkloric performances and, 187n13; in Jamaica, 143, 152, 158; mestizo and, 105; negrito and, 84, 86; in Peru, 32; racial mixture and, 11, 67

nationalism, 153; black, 156; brown, 185n48; Cuban, 86; European, 152; Latin American, 12; liberal, 13; postracial, 22. *See also* creole nationalism

negrería, 27; dances, 40, 42–43; pantheon, 39–40

negrita, 23, 88, 97, 104, 110, 114, 117–19, 121–22, 125–27, 132–34, 144; as archetype, 129, 133, 178; as figuration of blackness, 174; *puloy*, 123–24; Tundique and, 47

negrito, 6, 22, 55, 62–63, 82–89, 121, 197n72; Danza de Caporales and, 49; mestizaje and, 96; in Peru, 39–41, 186n5; queer masculinity and, 115; Tundique and, 43, 45, 48. See also *teatro bufo*

Nettleford, Rex, 152, 158

New Song Movement, 47, 190n64

Nicaraguans, 67, 177, 194n27

racial conjuring, 2–5, 7–10, 17, 19, 24, 60, 64, 96, 143, 167, 172, 174–75, 177–78; African diasporic communities and, 144, 175; in Angulo's work, 103–4, 116, 125, 127–28, 132; in Cuba, 84; *Esta Noche Tu Night* and, 87; in Jamaica, 23; politics of, 25; racial enjoyment and, 171; Sambos Illimani and, 33–34, 39; in Wright's work, 148–49, 151

racial democracy, 10–13, 176, 184n35; myths of, 2, 6, 11–12, 15–16, 18–19, 24, 67, 172, 181n4; nationalist fictions of, 2, 4, 10, 173

racial difference, 6, 11, 14, 93, 96, 202n41; in Colombia, 103, 106; creole nationalist erasure of, 155; Danza de Caporales and, 49; ethno-racial difference, 17; recognition of, 18; sexual encounter with, 119; Three Kings and, 43

racial distancing, 91, 93

racial distortion, 7–8

racial enjoyment, 4–5, 9, 19–21, 24–25, 58, 104, 179; abject pleasures and, 23; in Angulo's work, 128; antiblackness and, 95, 96; black enjoyment and, 167, 169; carnival and, 33; economies of, 142–44, 171–76, 178; laughter and, 170; resistance and, 23, 102–3, 135; subjection and, 21–23, 34, 55, 64, 71, 96, 134, 174; subjugation and, 32, 57; *Tres viudas* and, 2, 17

racial equality, 2, 85–86, 172–73, 181n5

racial erasure, 12, 51

racial exclusion, 2, 11, 96, 105, 124, 173

racial fantasies, 2, 7–8, 20, 22, 33, 42–43, 45, 121; blackness and, 52, 63, 89, 125; black womanhood and, 117; slavery and, 57

racial fluidity, 9, 16, 67

racial formation, 3, 10, 19, 38, 41, 60, 70; in the Americas, 64; in Colombia, 106; in the twenty-first century, 6, 174

racial geographies, 10, 15

racial harmony, 14–15, 21, 85, 124, 135, 143, 153–54, 156

racial hierarchies, 13, 16–17, 20–21, 96, 175; blackface and, 6; in Colombia, 103, 106, 124; in Cuba, 84, 89; Cuban diaspora and, 78, 82; creole nationalism and, 152; heteropatriarchal recolonization and, 153; in Jamaica, 161; in Miami, 15, 63–65, 67, 82

racial ideology, 9, 38, 155

racial innocence, 17, 117

racialization, 131–32; future of, 91; instruments of, 103; processes of, 42, 90, 95, 113; violence of, 113

racial memories, 41, 43, 45, 53

racial miscegenation, 11–13, 105, 185nn36–38, 200n13

racial mixture, 2, 11–13, 17, 28, 67, 105, 144, 184n24; degeneracy and, 185n38, 200n13; zambo and, 26

racial play, 4, 34, 41, 92, 135, 149, 151

racial power, 9, 19, 24, 32, 34, 40–41, 52, 57; in Angulo's work, 104, 115, 125; anti-blackness and, 17, 71; black enjoyment and, 167; blackface and, 6, 173; class and, 163; hierarchies of, 175; in Miami, 65–66; queer desire and, 56; racial conjuring and, 104; racial enjoyment and, 20

racial scripts, 2–3, 13, 17, 21–24, 34, 39; in Angulo's work, 104; of black disappearance, 21, 33, 38, 174; of black invisibility, 33, 42, 57; of black servitude, 125; of black women, 21, 23, 116, 134; of creole nationalism, 144, 151–53, 155–57; in *Di Driva*, 154; of mestizaje, 18, 20, 32–33, 37, 58, 84, 96, 103, 125, 172, 174–75; of nationalist fictions, 19, 124; of postcolonial nation-state, 142; racial hierarchies and, 82

racial signification, 9, 114

racial silence, 4, 10, 16, 37, 68, 103–4, 134, 175–76

racial stratification, 10–11, 65, 148, 158

racial uplift, 149, 170

racism, 3, 13, 35–36, 39, 102, 106–7; anti-black, 24–25, 48, 66; in Colombia, 108,

trickster figures, 144, 167, 208n62, 210n80

Trinidad and Tobago, 14, 185n50

Trump, Donald, 3, 78; administration of, 177

Tundique, 8, 22, 27, 33, 42–49, 52, 53, 190n60. *See also* Danza de Caporales

Urus de Gran Poder, 48, 50, 191n75

Valdés, Alexis, 59–62, 71–74, 76–80, 90–95, 102, 198n105. See also *Esta Noche Tu Night*

Vasconcelos, José, 12–13

Velasco, Martha, 1–4, 10, 19–21, 24

Viaje sin mapa: Representaciones Afro en el arte contemporáneo colombiano (exhibition), 108–10, 126, 202n44

Viveros, Mara, 113, 115

Wade, Peter, 106, 200n21, 202n47

West Indies, 4, 14, 16; British, 158

white Cubans, 2, 15, 65–67, 193–94n15, 194n26

whiteness, 13–17, 28, 91, 104–5, 150, 155, 185n37, 202n41; colonial, 158; creole, 16, 186n57; in Cuba, 23; Cuban, 15, 62, 64–69, 72, 76, 88, 95, 177; hemispheric creole, 67, 174; impersonation and, 41; in Miami, 23; social, 154, 207–8n55; transnational, 71

white supremacy, 20, 67, 143, 148, 176

Williams, Bert, 87, 205n12

Williams, Eric, 13–14, 69

Wright, Andrea, 8, 136, 146–51, 206n18, 206n20

zambo/sambo figure, 22, 26–28, 30, 49, 54, 56, 63, 89

www.ingramcontent.com/pod-product-compliance
Lightning Source LLC
Chambersburg PA
CBHW071737270326
41928CB00013B/2705